THE ILLUSTRATED HISTORY

VANS, TRUCKS & PSVs

CW00519449

THE ILLUSTRATED HISTORY OF

VANS, TRUCKS & PSVs

MICHAEL ALLEN & LES GEARY

Foulis

Haynes

A **FOULIS** Motoring book

First published 1988
© Michael Allen & Les Geary 1988
All rights reserved. No part of this book
may be reproduced or transmitted in any
form or by any means, electronic or
mechanical, including photocopying,
recording or by any information storage
or retrieval system, without permission of
the publisher.

Published by:
Haynes Publishing Group
Sparkford, Nr. Yeovil, Somerset
BA22 7JJ, England

Haynes Publications Inc.
861 Lawrence Drive, Newbury Park,
California 91320 USA

**British Library Cataloguing in
Publication Data**

Allen, Michael, *1939 Mar. 11-*
Ford vans, trucks & buses :
an illustrated history.
1. Ford trucks—History 2. Ford vans—
History 3. Ford buses—History
I. Title II. Geary, L.
629.2'24 TL230.5.F6
ISBN 0-85429-632-8

Library of Congress catalog card number 87-82837

Editor: Robert Iles
Page layout: Tim Rose
Printed in England by: J.H. Haynes & Co. Ltd.

Contents

Dedication

I would like to dedicate this book to the truck engineers who worked with me with enthusiasm to put Ford of Britain on top of the commercial vehicle field. From the beginning Ford of Britain's commercial ranges were manufacturered and built from Ford of Detroit's designs.

It was not until the end of the Second World War when a small section of engineers designed, developed and tested the first all British Ford commercial vehicle range: the Thames Trader. Many mistakes were made and problems overcome to make the truck range a high production seller.

The team's enthusiasm went higher, working long hours, gaining experience and contributing everything they knew into the design of Britain's best selling truck range, the Ford 'D' series. A complete world beater.

It was type approved in the European and Scandinavian countries: France, Germany where with modifications became known as the 'N' series, Belgium, Denmark, Italy, Switzerland, Netherlands, Portugal, Sweden, Finland and Norway with documentation and visits to the overseas Ford plants and agents by three experienced principal engineers with remarkable success.

The book shows the progress made over the years, commencing with the model 'T' and 'TT' commercials, through each successive range to the new Transit and the Ford Cargo.

It can be said without any doubt that Ford of Britain attained more in fifteen years with respect to commercial vehicles than any other commerical vehicle manufacturer in the U.K. had accomplished in fifty years, a life time.

Thanks fellows, a job well done.

Les. Geary.
Ex-Senior Engineering Manager,
Medium and Heavy Trucks,
Ford of Britain.

Acknowledgements

The authors wish to gratefully acknowledge the assistance given in the preparation of this book by Ford Motor Company Corporate History Manager; David Burgess-Wise; Steve Clark and Sheila Knapman, of Ford Photographic Services, the Imperial War Museum; and County Tractors Ltd. for their permission to use photographs of the County Commercial six-wheel conversions. For other information and the loan of material, thanks are also due to the following: Dacre Harvey; Alex Manch; Steve Scott; and Steve Waldenberg.

1 The beginnings in Britain

The origins of the Ford Motor Company in Britain can be traced back to 1896 when, in answer to an advertisement in the *Birmingham Post* for someone willing to do "hard and useful work", a young man named Percival Perry journeyed to London in order to meet the advertiser, one Harry Lawson.

Lawson, who later that year would be largely responsible for the abolition of the legal requirements for motor vehicles to be preceded by a man on foot, was attempting to establish a motor industry in Britain by importing and acquiring the production rights of leading continental makes. The association with Lawson, from which Perry learned much, was unfortunately to be cut short when an uncle's urgent request saw Perry return to work in the family printing business. It would not be until 1904 that Perry would again become involved in the motor trade.

In June the previous year (1903), in what was his third attempt at the motor manufacturing business, Henry Ford, and several partners, had got the Ford Motor Company into being and within weeks were advertising the Fordmobile Model A. Two Model A Fords arrived in Britain by early 1904, imported, it is believed in some quarters, by Percival Perry, although information surrounding these is scant. Certainly, Perry was at a meeting held in Britain at about that time, and from which resulted the London based Central Motor Car Company with sole rights to sell Ford products in Britain for the following five years.

Although, after a rather shaky start, a useful number of Fords would be sold in Britain – 600 Model Ns, for example, in 1906 – those years were to be fraught with difficulties; Ford's insistence on payment for vehicles upon loading in New York being a problem which often stretched the London company's financial resources. Loans from Perry's father-in-law, and later, a capital injection from two new partners kept the operation going. However, when the five year sales agreement period was over, Henry Ford stepped in, reorganising the company into the London branch of the Ford Motor Company on a similar basis to his branch outlets across the United States. This was to prove only a short term arrangement, as the realization of the manufacturing possibilities in Britain resulted in the formation of the subsidiary Ford Motor Company (England) Ltd. in 1910, with Percival Perry at its head.

The new company's early activities naturally consisted simply of sales, these being made through their 55, Shaftsbury Avenue, London premises, but by late 1911 a manufacturing base had been established in Manchester's western outskirts at Trafford Park. From here were to emerge the recently established Model T Fords, assembled from imported parts being shipped direct from America to the Salford Docks which formed the terminus of the Manchester Ship Canal.

The Model T's unbeatable price ensured its widespread acceptance in Britain; here, just as in its native America, it quickly pushed the Ford Motor Company ahead of all rivals. Conceived as a passenger car, but consisting of a standardized separate chassis frame upon which a variety of bodywork could be fitted, the Model T lent itself easily to the role of small commercial vehicle. The parent company first offered a van-bodied derivitive themselves for 1911, and during 1912 a Model T Delivery Van was catalogued in Britain. To the local tradesman using a horse-drawn vehicle for his deliveries etc., the new Ford was a most attractive proposition doing away with as it did with the feeding, stabling, cleaning etc., in addition of course to its primary function of speeding up the deliveries out of all proportion. A maximum payload of 750 lbs (340 kilos) plus driver seemed rather modest for a relatively lightweight vehicle powered by a 2.9 litre engine, but was insisted upon by Ford bearing in mind that this had been designed as a passenger carrying chassis only. Nevertheless, a chassis with just the normal engine cover and bulkhead etc. (to be known simply as a chassis front end) was also made available for sale, thus allowing an operator to choose from a variety of British made commercial type bodies from outside sources; these included light pick-up rear ends in addition to van variants. One of these, the Dixie Convertible, consisted of a rear chassis modification which then allowed a quick changeover facility between any one of a range of seven body types (hence convertible), these being a van, wagonette, ambulance, hearse, lorry, pig/sheep dray, and a hay wagon.

Much greater rear overhang than on the Ford-built and some other van/pick-up type bodies was a feature of the Dixie Convertible arrangements; and because of this, which could lead to excessive loading of the rear axle, Ford did not wholly approve of the Dixie. The anxiety here was not so much in respect of increased weight affecting the rear axle from a mechanical point of view, but that the excessively tail heavy weight distribution possible with this layout could seriously affect the steering characteristics of the Model T.

Coming into existence in 1914, the British & American Import Co., trading simply under the name BAICO, concentrated their efforts on the development of commercial vehicle adaptations of the Model T Ford, including an ingenious lengthened wheelbase design which completely overcame the objections to the Dixie, and allowed a maximum 20 cwt payload. This was achieved by clamping the original rear axle to the chassis frame, replacing the rear wheels at this point with sprockets from which chains carried the drive to a new dead axle mounted further aft on a chassis frame extension. Built in BAICO's own workshops, their complete variety of bodywork for both the normal wheelbase Ford and their own converted chassis received the full approval of the Ford Motor Company; in fact only being available to the customer through the Ford retail dealer network.

In addition to the provision of alternative bodywork, British suppliers had quickly become involved also with the original Ford product, furnishing bodywork and other components manufactured locally exactly to Ford drawings and therefore dovetailing into the production of the regular Ford line up. Local content was to prove particularly useful during the First World War, as Henry Ford adopted his pacifist stance in the early stages (later to be reversed completely) and was not happy about Fords with American sourced parts being involved in European hostilities.

Although finding use by the military as a scout car, machine gun carrier, and supply truck with pick-up type rear bodywork, it was as an ambulance that the Model T would act out its principle role in the conflict. With its high ground-clearance and virtually unbreakable chassis/running gear combination, the Model T was an excellent off-road vehicle capable of getting in almost anywhere where the wounded lay, its sterling activities in this role of mercy quickly earning it the affectionate nickname of "The Jumping Bedstead". Ambulance bodywork came from many sources in the early days of the war, before Trafford Park went into production with its own purpose-built variant in 1915. Constructed of wood and canvas, these were capable of carrying four sitting patients, or alternatively two stretcher cases. Due to the previously mentioned adverse effects possible with unequal weight distribution, the extended ambulance body still remained rather shorter than the long-handled stretchers; four holes drilled in the tailboard, and covered with canvas bags with which to obviate draughts, neatly overcame the problem. Ambulances such as these were leaving Trafford Park at the rate of more than a 100 per day before the war was finished.

By that time, an altogether more significant Ford commercial vehicle – the Model TT One Ton Truck – had made its appearance in America, and was to go into production at Trafford Park the following year. The contemporary motoring press considered that there was a mystery surrounding the Ford one-tonner, reporting that it believed that for some time before Trafford Park announced the model, the British Government had been importing the truck for their own use. Just what this use was, however, was not made clear.

As we have seen, it was the short wheelbase and chassis limitations rather than running gear or engine/transmission considerations which had resulted in the relatively modest maximum payloads quoted for the commercial adaptations of the Model T car so far. Rectifying this now, the Model TT consisted of a substantially strengthened chassis of appreciably greater wheelbase. At the front, this housed the familiar Ford running gear and engine/gearbox unit, whilst at the rear featuring a new overhead-worm-driven rear axle assembly. The rear suspension was still by courtesy of a single transverse leaf spring, but another change at this end of the vehicle could be seen in the adoption of solid rear tyres for the artillery type wooden spoked wheels. Deeper, pneumatic tyres on smaller diameter rims were introduced sometime later in production.

The one ton capacity was still well within the capabilities of the big four-cylinder engine and its associated two-speed epicyclic gearbox, although the all-up weights now possible could perhaps be regarded as on the heavy side when related to the truck's braking system which was remaining as on the car and consisting of a transmission brake and rear wheel drums only. Nevertheless, this long-wheelbase model offered a far greater scope for the commercial vehicle operator than had the previous car-derived variants. Here, very definitely, was a "real" lorry from Ford, which would give them a firm foothold in this sector upon which they would build considerably over successive generations.

Available initially only as a chassis front end, the TT was soon to be seen in a variety of interesting configurations; petrol tankers for British Petroleum, and Pratts Spirits; char-a-bancs (motor coaches), furniture vans etc., and trucks with both sided and open platform bodies quickly became available from outside sources. One such specialist offering was the attractive dual purpose lorry/bus body built for the Ford chassis by Messrs. Gray, Podmore and Company, of Anderson's Garage, Manchester. Of steel panelled construction the wide, open Gray Podmore body featured three rows of twin seats either side of a narrow central gangway, with accommodation for two additional passengers alongside the driver up front. Easily removable, the seats were attached to a wide flat floor giving excellent carrying capacity in the truck configuration; a nearside front door gave passenger access, whilst a detachable tailgate facilitated cargo loading. A folding hood for the protection of passengers or freight if necessary was another useful feature.

The new long wheelbase Ford chassis had, of course, rendered the earlier BAICO one-ton conversion rather superfluous; but, there were plenty of operators always looking for greater capacity still, and it was to their needs now that the enterprising Fulham Road company turned its attention to further developments.

The "Extendatonna" was soon to become a popular example of BAICO's expertise. This consisted of a considerably longer, and suitably strengthened Model TT chassis which retained the conventional drive by courtesy of an appropriately stretched torque tube arrangement to the regular Ford axle relocated further aft. The Ford transverse leaf spring however was replaced by a pair of longitudinally mounted semi-elliptics; these modifications gave a 30 cwt capacity. With similar chassis modifications to the Extendatonna, but using chain drive arrangements as on the earlier conversions, was a two ton model with a four-speed transmission and a specially strengthened rear axle. The ultimate though was the "Supertonna" with a $2^1/2$ ton capability and available in several wheelbase lengths with torque tube drive. A conventional three-speed gearbox behind the Ford epicyclic two-speeder was standard equipment on the Supertonna as were also improved braking arrangements, although still confined to the rear wheels only.

Always attractively priced, at £160 for the Extendatonna and £230 for the Supertonna in the mid 1920s, the BAICO-Ford chassis sold well alongside the regular bargain-basement Ford one ton chassis at just £110. The standard Ford-bodied open One Ton Truck was £170, with £190 being asked for the fully enclosed One Ton Van.

As with the Model T cars, the TT specification remained fundamentally unchanged until the eventual production demise in Britain of the entire Ford Model T car and commercial vehicle range in August 1927.

Below: Ford works at Trafford Park, Manchester, around 1911. Model 'T' chassis being tested prior to the mounting of bodies.

Opposite page top: Trafford Park Works around 1911. Model 'T' engines and transmissions on dynamometer engine test beds.

Opposite page bottom: One of the earliest Ford commercial vehicles, a 1913 Trafford Park built Model 'T' used by a well-known bakery for bread deliveries.

Left: Red Cross Ambulance on Ford Model 'T' 1914 chassis for the home front. A wooden plank built body with canopy over the driver was the only weather protection. Several were built and sent overseas in addition to those used at home.

Below: Early Model 'T' van used by a local Lancashire baker and confectioner in Oldham for baker's deliveries. Note spare tyre and wheel rim assembly. These were pushed onto the wheels and secured by bolted-on clamps; around 1919.

Right: Early Model 'T' van probably around 1913 with opening windscreen, electric headlamps and paraffin oil sidelamps. Note: tyres fitted on well-base wheel rims and the wooden constructed van body.

Below: An early Model 'T' pick-up with opening windscreen, taking part in a Ford rally.

Opposite page top: A model 'TT' one ton flat platform truck body with detachable tailboard, and hanger rail. Note: larger rear single tyre equipment with bolted-on tyre and rim assembly, electric headlamps and paraffin oil sidelamps.

Opposite page bottom: A 1923 Model 'T' van still in regular service in 1963 with Cheswick and Wright of Blackpool, exhaust silencer suppliers to Ford of Britain. This won first prize in a concours d'elegance for commercial vehicles at Brighton. On the Friday previous to the Brighton Run the van had delivered a consignment of exhaust silencers to the Ford Works at Dagenham.

Above right: A Royal Mail van body on Model 'T' chassis. Side curtain, spotlight, toolbox, larger single rear tyre equipment, with bolted-on tyre and rim assemblies for both front and rear wheels were features of this vehicle. The driver's view was very limited due to wide van body.

Middle: 1924 Ford Model 'T' van for delivery of sausages and pies for Brazil's, Amersham, Bucks. John Brazil test drives the van in later years when entered in the Historic Commercial Vehicle Club run from Clapham to Brighton. Half of their fleet of 257 vehicles were Fords.

Right: A standard right-hand drive model 'TT' one ton van 1923. Half doors were fitted with canvas curtains and opening windscreen. Note absence of sidelamps. A front view showing single transverse semi-elliptic leaf suspension for the front.

[blank box]

One ton Model 'TT' Truck – 1921. Left-hand drive model. Featured are electric headlamps, paraffin oil sidelamps, half doors, side curtains for weather protection, Epicyclic transmission and overhead worm drive rear axle for drive line, with torque tube enclosed propeller shaft.

Below: Model 'TT' one ton truck with drop sides and tailboard. This fine photograph clearly showing suspension, bolt-on tyre and rim assemblies and body mounting.

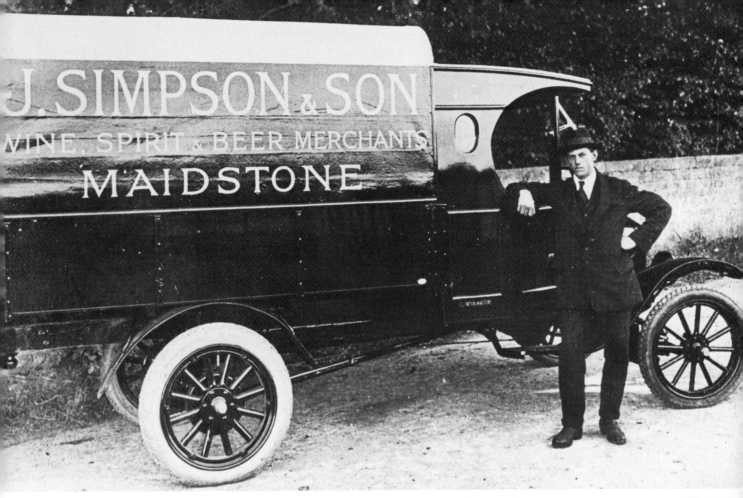

Above: Model 'TT' one ton high sided truck body, drop sides and tailboard with full canvas tilt, special build cab for J. Simpson and Sons, Maidstone, Kent, in 1926.

1914-18 Great War. This Model 'T' Scout Car is bogged down in sand in the desert war zone, Middle East. Assistance is from the people of the desert.

Right: A local railway shuttle service train, 1920. This unusual vehicle consists of two power cars, one either end, based on two Model 'T' chassis, and one centre coach all fitted with railway flanged wheels, and can provide a shuttle service either way without turning round.

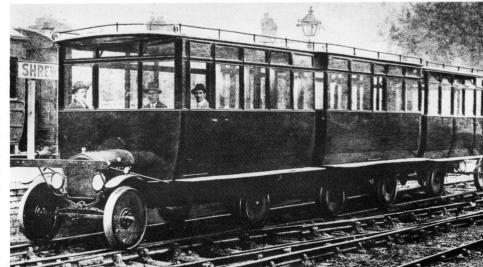

An advertisement showing how fragile goods can be transported by the Ford Model 'TT' one ton truck chassis with special bodies.

Below: An advertisement on Ford Delivery Model 'T' vans.

2 Beyond 'Tin Lizzie'

Reluctant to accept that his beloved "Tin Lizzie" could not survive into eternity, Henry Ford had continued Model T production despite constant pressure from his associates, and his own son, Edsel Ford. Finally, after indulging in what he once said was "the hardest work of all" – thinking – Henry decided that a successor to his Model T must indeed be built, and to this end he terminated production in May 1927 and turned over his vast resources to the design and development of a new generation Ford.

Britain, Europe, and of course America, had to wait patiently for Henry's latest creation with which he was to start the "alphabet" series all over again. It was not until December 2nd, 1927, that the new Model A was unveiled, and such was the build up of public curiosity by then that during the first two days an estimated ten million Americans queued up to see it at Ford agencies nationwide. The British announcement and presentation was made at London's Holland Park Hall, and included the two commercial vehicle derivatives which completed the model range.

The Model A light commercial was a 10 cwt van based on the $103^1/2$ inch wheelbase car chassis and front end with an integral van body, whilst the other commerical variant was the Model AA truck chassis with a wheelbase of $131^1/2$ inches. A large capacity, 150 cubic feet van body was also available in Model AA configuration. The power unit was a new in-line four-cylinder sidevalve of 3.2 litres, rated at 24 hp for taxation purposes and developing 40 bhp at 2200 rpm. A narrow-bored version, of 2.1 litres and 14.9 hp rating, therefore attracting a lower annual road tax imposition, was available for the car and 10 cwt commercial models. This engine developed 28 bhp, and the vehicles so equipped were designated Model AF. Initially, the engines were supplied to Britain by Ford's Irish plant, Henry Ford & Son, Cork, prior to being adopted for production in England.

A conventional clutch and three-speed crash change (non synchromesh) gearbox was also new, and with the option of an additional epicyclic secondary gear for the 30 cwt models giving six forward speeds and two reverse. Completing the driveline came a torque tube enclosed propeller shaft to a three quarter floating spiral bevel final drive assembly on the Model A, and to an overhead worm gear driven axle on the 30 cwt AA.

The suspension arrangements for the 10 cwt van was as on the passenger car, consisting of a single transversely mounted semi-elliptic leaf spring at both front and rear as in previous Ford practice. However, whilst continuing this theme at the front, the 30 cwt chassis broke away from this tradition at the rear with the fitment now of two longitudinal semi-elliptic cantilever springs. Each of these was mounted at its centre to a pivot bracket on the chassis frame sidemember, with the spring's front eye being attached to a shackle bracketed to the frame. The rear eye was attached to a bracket on the rear axle casing, with the bracket being allowed to rotate and therefore cater for the lengthening and shortening of the springs which took place when in use due to flexing. Four-wheel brakes throughout the range were a very welcome improvement over the preceding Ford, and in all the Model A series looked set to re-establish Ford's fortunes which had waned somewhat during the Model T's later days.

Nevertheless, during 1929 changes were made which broadened the new Ford's appeal further still. Disc wheels replaced the wire-spoked type on the 30 cwt models early in 1929, and allowed the fitting of dual rear equipment if desired, whilst later that year a 2 ton capacity

Model AA made its appearance. This newcomer was available in both short (131^1/$_2$ inch) and long (157 inch) wheelbases and was powered by the existing 24 hp engine, but featured a completely new four-speed crash change gearbox. The torque tube drive was now to a three-quarter floating spiral bevel axle as on the smaller models, and dual rear tyre equipment was standard. The suspension remained the same as on the 30 cwt chassis, which itself was inheriting the new four-speed gearbox and spiral bevel rear end to replace the former three-speed and dual gear option, and the overhead worm drive axle.

In order to ensure that its English subsidiary was fully conversant with just what could be accommodated on the Ford chassis, Detroit issued a 48-page booklet to be distributed amongst dealers here. Titled *Commercial Bodywork on the Ford Chassis,* this gave information under separate chapter headings, these being: "The Utility of the Ford Commercial Vehicle"; "Maintaining an Efficient Delivery Service"; "Special Purpose Van Bodies"; "Running Costs on Van Deliveries"; "Truck Bodies"; "Fleet Management"; "Tipping Trucks and Municipal Vehicles"; "Outstanding Features of the Ford Commercial Chassis"; "Transport of Bulky Goods"; "Bodies for Bulky Goods"; "Farmer and the Ford"; "Cattle and Produce Bodies"; "Ease and Comfort in Running"; "Ambulance Bodies"; "Bodywork that Builds Business"; "Travelling Shop and other Novel Bodies"; also included were full specifications, with the slogan "To Accommodate Bodies for Every Conceivable Purpose". The Booklet illustrated some 68 uses of the Ford van and truck chassis, with a variety of 26 alternative bodies.

The price asked for the Model AA chassis equipped with some of these Ford-approved bodies make interesting reading today, examples being:

Horse box on the 2 ton 157 inch wheelbase	£382
Petrol tanker on the 2 ton 157 inch wheelbase	£369
Refuse collector on the 30 cwt 131^1/$_2$ inch wheelbase	£294
Steel-bodied end tipper with hand operated front ram on the 30 cwt 131^1/$_2$ inch wheelbase	£224
Steel-bodied end tipper with hand operated front ram on the 2 ton 131^1/$_2$ inch wheelbase	£320

The Model A 10 cwt van, fully equipped with an electric starter, petrol gauge, and a spare wheel was just £185. These prices did not include delivery charges, but £50 down would secure any Ford car or commercial vehicle complete with delivery charges, road tax, and insurance included, under a hire purchase agreement.

It was indeed fortunate that the company now had such a versatile range of commercial vehicle chassis on offer, and these proved to be Ford's mainstay in Britain during a time when the popularity of their passenger car range was at an all time low. This was because in 24 hp configuration the Model A car was subjected to penal road taxation, whilst with the lower taxed 14.9 hp engine it had insufficient performance for this class of car. The £1 per one horsepower road tax imposed during 1921 had latterly affected Model T car sales in Britain, and had angered Henry Ford who considered that this imposition was directed primarily at his products. Nevertheless, looking considerably further ahead, Ford had purchased several hundred acres of Essex marshland upon which he planned to eventually build his "Detroit of Europe" alongside the River Thames at Dagenham. After crossing the Atlantic himself on a fact-finding mission to Europe in 1928 Ford decided upon a reconstituted Ford of Britain to be based at Dagenham. Perry, by this time Sir Percival Perry, and who had left the company some time earlier, was re-engaged to head the new Ford of Britain and oversee the construction of the Dagenham plant.

Chosen almost wholly because of its deep water frontage and ready access for ocean going vessels, the marshy nature of the Essex site presented a serious difficulty to the architects and construction engineers. This problem was however overcome by supporting the huge complex on some 22,000 concrete piles, sunk to a depth of 75 feet into the soft ground. Going into vehicle production on October 1st, 1931, the Dagenham complex included the new premises of the Kelsey Hayes Wheel Company, and Briggs Motor Bodies who, as Ford's principle supplier in the United States were now to be responsible for virtually all of Ford of Britain's standard range of car and commercial vehicle bodies.

The first vehicle to leave the Dagenham assembly line on October 1st was a Model AA sided truck, short wheelbase model with single rear tyre equipment, and destined, somewhat ironically as production had ceased at Trafford Park a week or so earlier, for Manchester's Ford dealers, Messrs Quicks of Manchester Ltd. During its first few months of operation, Dagenham was to rely very heavily indeed on the success of the Model A vans and various AA trucks as passenger car production slumped to almost nil before the desperately needed 8 hp Ford, Model Y, made its appearance in August 1932.

By that time, Detroit had released the Model B car and its commercial vehicle counterpart Model BB, with the necessary information being despatched to Ford of Britain enabling them to tool up for production of this updated range. Uprated to 12 cwt capacity and 86 cubic feet load space on its increased wheelbase of 106 inches, the Model B van featured synchromesh between the upper two ratios of its three-speed gearbox and usefully improved brake horsepower outputs from both its 14.9 hp and 24 hp engines; these now developed 42 bhp at 3000 rpm and 52 bhp at 2600 rpm, respectively. Completing the van's power train was the torque tube drive and three quarter floating spiral bevel rear axle unit.

The 30 cwt truck chassis retained the $131\frac{1}{2}$ inch wheelbase, with the latest 2 ton once again being available on both $131\frac{1}{2}$ inch and 157 inch wheelbase lengths. The trucks featured a new four-speed gearbox, although still devoid of synchromesh, with the familiar torque tube drive now to a new fully floating spiral bevel rear axle assembly.

The suspension arrangements of the single transverse semi-elliptic leaf spring at either end of the vehicle remained as before on the Model B vans; whereas, having gone through one radical change with the Model AA, the rear suspension was now subjected to a further revision on the BB trucks. The longitudinal semi-elliptic leaf springs were now shackled at both eye ends to brackets on the chassis frame rather than being of the previous cantilever type. Disc wheels with single rear tyre equipment on the 12 and 30 cwt models, and dual rear equipment for the 2 tonners were the standard fitment.

Just prior to the announcement of the BB, at the request of its Sales Department, Dagenham had introduced a 1 ton truck and van based on the AA short wheelbase chassis with which to tempt those operators who were not in the 30 cwt market but required something rather more capable than the 10 cwt offering. This model was retained alongside the new BB range, powered by the 24 hp engine but mated to the three-speed gearbox as on the lighter models, with ex-works prices of £180 and £205 for the truck and van, respectively.

In addition to the regular truck bodywork on the BB long wheelbase chassis were a 2 ton box van of 207 cubic feet capacity and a 189 cubic feet Luton van, whilst on the short wheelbase 2 tonner a three way tipper with hand operated tipping ram could also be specified. A 20-seat omnibus/coach body, designed by a reputable outside coachbuilding concern was also approved for mounting on the 2 ton long wheelbase chassis, with the complete vehicle being available for £520, plus a delivery charge.

Finally, there were six-wheel conversions on both the long and short wheelbase chassis, designed by County Commercial Cars Ltd., of Fleet, in Hampshire, and who had latterly offered a six-wheel conversion on the Model AA. Two versions of this extended theme were available, one of which, known as the Surrey, being the single-drive model which retained the normal Ford axle in the foremost position with an additional dead axle to the rear completing the six wheel set up. The other, the double-drive Sussex, featured a two spiral bevel crownwheel and pinions assembly in the foremost axle which continued the drive via its second pinion to a standard Ford axle in the rear, thus providing drive to all four wheels of the new rear end arrangements. Marketed in Britain by Ford, who approved the conversion but nevertheless would not stand any warranty claims on failure, the single-drive and double-drive models were priced at £120 and £125, respectively, over the figure for the appropriate 2 ton chassis.

The Model BB was a better engineered truck chassis than its predecessor, the AA, which had featured a constant inward taper from the rear crossmember to the front without a break. In contrast, the new chassis frame was of parallel design from the rear crossmember to the crossmember immediately aft of the gearbox, from where it then tapered inwards to the front. This design gave a far better chance of maintaining correct alignment of the frame with the rear springs and axle, and the success of the BB chassis was such that it was destined to become the basis of future Ford commercials for many years.

Henry Ford's legendary V8-cylinder engine had made its debut early in 1932, and whilst having been conceived as a high-performance passenger car unit, it nevertheless quickly found its way into the Ford commercial vehicle range. Of 90 degree V formation, the 30 hp rated 3.6 litre sidevalve engine developed 75 bhp at 3300 rpm, and was to gain an excellent reputation in respect of its vibrationless running and the formidable performance which it provided. Detroit offered the new engine to Dagenham right away as an optional power plant for the BB 20-seater passenger coach chassis, an application where its smooth and quiet running qualities would be most appreciated.

Before the V8 could be manufactured at Dagenham a new engine assembly line with its associated sub assembly facilities, and new machine tooling etc., had to be installed. Additionally, with the V8 being revolutionary in that its cylinder block was being cast in one piece for the first time on a production V configuration engine, new production techniques had to be learned from Detroit. Continued development of the V8 was taking place in Detroit to overcome teething troubles experienced on some early examples, and Dagenham spent a considerable time on development and prolonged engine testing to ensure uniformity of power outputs before the V8 was released as the regular engine throughout the BB range in Britain for 1935, with the 24 hp four-cylinder unit being relegated to optional equipment status.

Ever anxious to widen their market, Ford were again issuing literature to dealers with recommendations on approved special bodies and the appropriate truck chassis for various sections of the community. One such special body was a farming multi-purpose utility truck designed to carry livestock, seeds, fertilizer, implements, and building and fencing materials. The body sides and tailboard were easily removed altogether if required, and the outfit came complete with a loading ramp. Meeting so many of the farmer's requirements, this was an attractive proposition at £249 when mounted on the 2 ton long wheelbase chassis.

As municipal operations are so often of a very specialised nature, body and equipment specialists were asked to co-operate in providing a suitable range. An ambulance chassis was devised, based upon the 30 cwt BB. Running on low pressure tyres with single rear equipment, this was powered by the new V8 engine, and featured bodywork providing ten different interior layouts to meet varying health authority requirements. This model was in addition to the existing Ford ambulance on the old 1 ton Model AA chassis equipped with an air bed for critical patients, red cross lamp, an alarm gong plus other accessories, and which was still available at a price of £404. A further specialised model, based on the 2 ton short wheelbase chassis windshield, was a fire engine equipped with a transmission power take off driving a self-priming turbine type pump capable of delivering 250 gallons of water per minute. Completing the fire fighting specification were extension ladders, and crew accommodation for an officer, driver and six firemen.

With the V8, which by this time had been developed to produce 81.5 bhp at 3700 rpm, now being in production at Dagenham, Ford of Britain undertook an all out drive to supply commercial vehicles to a much wider sector of the popular market. New V8 powered forward control models based on the normal control BB range were introduced, and designated BBE. These were a 2 ton, 340 cubic feet van, and a 2 ton truck chassis, both on a wheelbase of

118 inches. In addition to the forward control layout, the BBE also differed from the BB in that the familiar Ford single transverse front spring had now given way to a pair of longitudinal semi-elliptics, shackled at their front eye. These two models entered production on December 14th, 1934, and were joined during 1935 by a third BBE model, this being a County Commercial Surrey single-drive six wheeler with single rear tyre equipment, and a very useful 6 ton payload rating.

An updated normal control range appeared, powered by the 30 hp V8 and designated Model 51. Two wheelbase lengths, 131^1/2 inches and 157 inches were available, providing loading lengths of 106 inches and 136^1/2 inches, respectively. Both 2 and 3 ton capacity versions were being offered on both wheelbase lengths. A 2 ton tipper, with hand operated ram, and a 3 ton model with underfloor hydraulic tipping ram and steel body with underframe could be specified for the short wheelbase chassis. Completing this range came the County Commercial six wheelers in both single and double-drive configuration, and on both wheelbase lengths. The Models BBE and 51 continued as the mainstays of the commercial vehicle range for 1936.

The ageing 14.9 hp Model AF 10 cwt van and its 12 cwt stablemate, the Model BF, were finally discontinued in October 1935 after a combined production total of 18,586 vehicles. Replacing these came a new van of 15 cwt payload, with a 120 cubic feet capacity and on a 112 inch wheelbase chassis. This was designated Model 50F, and featured a narrow-bored version of the V8 engine which, rated at only 22 hp for taxation purposes, developed 60 bhp at 3500 rpm. Curiously, the Model 50F was extremely short-lived, being deleted at the end of the year after only 230 examples had been built.

Also announced in October 1935, although not actually reaching production until June the following year was the Model 61, a new forward control 25 cwt truck/van chassis on a 106 inch wheelbase. This could be equipped with a 100 inch length float (open body) or a 230 cubic feet van body. The power unit was again the small-bore V8, transmitting the power via a three-speed non-synchromesh gearbox and torque tube drive to a fully floating spiral bevel rear axle. Another 15 cwt van now appeared, the Model 67, on a 112 inch wheelbase chassis and with American inspired styling. For this model power was provided by the 3.6 litre V8, with the drive line consisting of the three-speed gearbox with synchromesh between second and top gear, torque tube enclosed propeller shaft and a three-quarter floating final drive. The suspension arrangements were by the traditional Ford single transverse leaf springs front and rear, thus completing a technical specification which very closely matched that of the large V8-powered passenger saloons.

A 5 cwt van, based on the successful Model Y 8 hp car had been in production since late in 1932, and had firmly established Ford in the light commercial market. An interesting variation of this model had appeared in 1935 as a result of the County Commercial company believing there was a ready market for both a compact three-wheeler van, and a three-wheeled articulated tractor unit which would compete in the market being catered for by the Karrier and Scammell ''Mechanical Horse'' models. In line with County Commercial's policy of naming its Ford derivitives the van was to be named Devon, whilst the tractor unit would be known by the somewhat less appealing, but quite appropriate name of Tug.

The major objective behind the design of the three-wheeled model was to achieve a highly manoeuvrable vehicle with a turning circle small enough to permit a turn around almost within its own length. This would allow much easier parking and manoeuvrability in confined spaces where difficulties could be encountered with the conventional four-wheeled model, thus easing delivery problems in narrow service roads etc.

The Devon was a van of 12/15 cwt payload and 120 cubic feet capacity on an extended chassis frame with a 126^3/4 inch wheelbase. The front end bodywork and engine compartment was that of the Model Y car, including the front doors behind which a panel was inserted to form a driver's cab. The van body was attached at its front to the cab to produce a neatly finished off conversion. Suspension for the single front wheel consisted of a coil spring mounted on rubber bushes, whilst at the rear the arrangement was the transverse leaf spring exactly as on the car; a turning circle of only 20 feet was the very useful outcome. With the same suspension arrangements, but of much shorter wheelbase, the Tug chassis terminated just aft of the two door cabin which itself was virtually as that of the Devon. Two variations of the Tug were considered, a simple tractor for hauling either two- or four-wheeled drawbar trailers, and capable of handling a 3 ton gross load, with an articulated unit for semi-trailers having a gross combination weight of 4 tons.

Absolute performance in terms of speed and acceleration was not a very serious consideration, and the Model Y car's 933 cc 8 hp engine was chosen for both the Devon and the 3 ton tractor model, whilst the articulated 4 ton Tug was to be powered by the 1172 cc 10 hp engine from the Model C passenger car. As some concession to the all up weights they were expected to handle, both tractor units were to be equipped with a four-speed crash change gearbox, whereas the Model Y three-speed synchromesh transmission was considered adequate for the not-so-heavily-loaded Devon van; the Y type three quarter floating spiral bevel final drive would be used throughout.

In the event, a single model Tug which could handle both drawbar and articulated trailers was produced, and surprisingly, powered only by the 933 cc engine, although the four-speed gearbox did remain. Dagenham produced and marketed the Tug themselves, leaving County Commercial to build and market the Devon van and a further, pick-up truck variant. The idea was good, but seems to have been insufficiently developed and promoted as these three-wheeler Fords failed to make a significant impact. Whereas Scammell alone sold 20,000 of their Mechanical Horse, Ford only managed to produce 111 Tugs between September 1935 and the July of 1937, soon after which the model was phased out. Exactly how many Devons were completed by County Commercials is not clear, but it would appear that the number was very small.

Whereas previously Ford of Britain had considered the smaller commercial vehicles as Fords, and only used the "Fordson" title on those of 2 tons capacity and above, Dagenham had now decided that all its commercial vehicles would be under the Fordson banner. Additionally, for 1937 the commercial vehicle coding was to commence with the number 7 to denote the year, with the curious exception of the Model 61 which was to retain this identity despite slight revisions in its specification.

The range this year consisted of: Model 73 and Model 77, two 15 cwt vans; Model 79, 2 ton and 3 ton short and long wheelbase normal control range; Model 61, 25 cwt short wheelbase forward control truck and van; Model 7V, an entirely new 2 ton and 3 ton short and long wheelbase forward control range to replace the Model BBE.

The Model 77 15 cwt van was to be the same specification as the previous 3.6 litre V8 Model 67, but with re-styled radiator grille and bonnet, whilst the Model 73 was as the Model 77 but with the small-bore V8 engine. The Model 79 was a continuation of the Model 51, but with the wheelbase increased from $131^1/2$ inches to 134 inches on the short wheelbase version. The long wheelbase alternative remained at 157 inches. Both the 2 and 3 ton short wheelbase models provided a 109 inch float length, whereas the long wheelbase models accommodated a $136^1/2$ inch float on the 2 ton chassis, and a 150 inch float on the 3 tonner due to the latter featuring a chassis frame longer by 12 inches than on the lighter model. The 3.6 litre 30 hp V8 remained as the standard power unit, but with the elderly four-cylinder 24 hp engine still available as an option. The Model 61 was now classified as a 25/35 cwt vehicle, although remaining unchanged apart from the adoption of the synchromesh three-speed gearbox in place of the earlier crash change three-speeder.

The new forward control Model 7V range featured a box-shaped cab with a sun roof above the passenger seat, and a rather large internal engine cowling which almost completely separated the driver from his mate. The power unit was the 30 hp V8, driving through the familiar heavy-vehicle transmission arrangements consisting of a four-speed crash change gearbox and torque tube drive to the fully floating spiral bevel rear axle assembly. The chassis frame followed the same pattern as the BB, and as before there were two wheelbase lengths, these being 118 inches and 143^1/$_2$ inches, with float lengths of 136^1/$_2$ inches and 172 inches, respectively. Both 2 and 3 ton payload truck models were available in each wheelbase length, and there was a short wheelbase 2 ton van of 340 cubic feet capacity. Additionally, were the Surrey and Sussex single and double-drive six-wheelers. Available in chassis cab configuration only, for the mounting of bodywork to choice, these were based on both the long and short wheelbase 3 ton 7V chassis, with rear bogie centres of 41^1/$_4$ inches and an 8 ton maximum payload rating.

The 7V range continued without change for 1938, by which time the Ford catalogues were promoting the commercial vehicles under both "Fordson" and "Thames" titles. A new addition to the ranks this year, appearing in March, was the E83W 10 cwt semi-forward control van. This utilised the mechanical elements from the 10 hp passenger car, with the power train consisting of the famous 1172 cc "Ten" engine, three-speed synchromesh gearbox, and torque tube drive to the spiral bevel rear axle of the three quarter floating type. These were offset to the nearside (left) of the vehicle, thus allowing the driving controls to be alongside the engine and therefore lengthening the useful load area within the modest overall length dictated by the 90 inch wheelbase chassis, actual load length was 80 inches, contributing to a total 110 cubic feet capacity. The running gear was also as on the car, with the transverse leaf spring layout at each end, and lever-arm type shock absorbers. The chassis, however, was exclusive to the new van, and also featured its own rather snub-nosed purpose-built bodywork of composite wood and metal construction developed by Briggs Motor Bodies.

£168 would buy the basic E83W van, but additionally, chassis cab and chassis front end were also available for light pick-up truck and other applications, and so popular were these over the ensuing years it seemed that somewhere almost every trade or activity imaginable utilised an E83W Ford in one form or another.

Meanwhile, the Model 61 25/35 cwt had lost its small-bore 22 hp V8 engine, and been re-released with the old four-cylinder 24 hp unit as the Model E88W. This re-designation also brought the model into line with the latest coding system, translating in this instance as follows: E – England; 8 – 1938; 8 – 24 hp 4 cyl; W – Forward control. The tooling and equipment for small-bore V8 production was now shipped to Ford France, some 17,696 22 hp V8s having been produced in Britain between 1935 and the end of 1937. Many of these units remained in stock, and this 22 hp engine was to continue as an option within the 15 cwt van range whilst also powering the Model 62 passenger car through 1938/9. The 15 cwt normal control van range now consisted of the Model 81C with the 30 hp V8 engine; Model 82C, 22 hp V8; and the 24 hp four-cylinder Model 88C. These American type vans featured a restyled frontal treatment in keeping with the normal control truck range which displayed a new grille and rather more bulbous bonnet than the previous year's Model 79. This truck range was now designated 81T in 2 ton short wheelbase form, on which chassis a tipper with hand-operated tipping gear was being offered, and 817T in 3 ton long wheelbase configuration. The code number 7 inserted in the designation here being the last digit in the wheelbase measurement, thus indicating that the 817T was the 157 inch wheelbase model. When fitted with the optional 24 hp four-cylinder engine these models became the E88T and E887T. Demand for these American type normal control models was not high, with production of the 3 ton long wheelbase, for example, being only 1702 vehicles between February 1938 and March 1939.

Much more popular was the forward control 7V, and Dagenham usefully extended the scope of this range for 1939 with the addition of both 4 and 5 ton variants. Each of these were available in both short and long wheelbase configuration, whilst the 2 and 3 ton models were now confined to the short wheelbase chassis, as indeed were the new 4 and 5 ton tippers. The latter models were both of 4 cubic yard capacity and available with either fixed or drop-sided bodywork. With this wider payload range now available on the four-wheeled vehicles, County Commercial now concentrated their six-wheel conversions on the 5 ton chassis with slightly heavier equipment.

The normal control range did remain during 1939, with further slight styling revisions to the grille and bonnet resulting in the designation now being 91T and 917T. The 15 cwt van was similarly treated, and advertised again with all the engine options including the 3.6 litre V8 which by this time had undergone further development work enabling it to produce 85 bhp at 3500 rpm.

The outbreak of the Second World War stopped what would have been a complete breakaway from traditional practices, as new American forward control models were to go into production. As on the British forward control models, these also abandoned the transverse front spring in favour of a pair of longitudinal semi-elliptics; but what was much more interesting now was the open propeller shaft and single-shackled rear springs at last replacing the torque tube enclosed propeller shaft and its associated rear axle radius rods. In the event, these 4 and 6 ton payload models, designated 01W and 018W in their normal and long wheelbase configurations, respectively, did see very limited production at Dagenham during the 1940/41 winter when 9 examples of the 01W and 77 of the 018W were built, presumably for specialized home front duties.

The hostilities declared in Europe had also halted an ambitious Ford of Britain plan which was to have brought about the complete separation of the car and commercial vehicle operations. This would have involved the passenger car division remaining at Dagenham, whilst the new truck operation was to be housed in new premises recently acquired at Trafford Park, Manchester, close to the scene of the earlier Ford plant.

Advertisements during the third quarter of 1939, both in local northern, and national newspapers, announced Ford's requirements for experienced commercial vehicle design and engineering staff. The applicants were interviewed at Dagenham, but with the outbreak of war the venture was called off. However, those candidates who had been successful were still invited to join the company in Essex in order to fill the anticipated need for additional design/engineering staff to help with the forthcoming war effort, and several took up these appointments. Some preliminary work on a new civilian truck range of all British design had already taken place, and the newly recruited staff continued this work until the scheme was abandoned in mid 1940 as the company became wholly involved in government contract work.

Model 'AA' 30 cwt. Normal control timber truck body. Powered by 24 h.p. four cylinder in-line petrol engine. Transverse front leaf spring and cantilever semi-elliptic leaf springs for the rear. 1928.

Model 'AA' 2 ton Long wheelbase, normal control, petrol distribution truck. 24 hp, four-cylinder in-line petrol engine, transverse front leaf spring, cantilever semi-elliptic leaf springs for the rear. 1929.

Model 'AA' 30 cwt. Normal control, drop sided and tailboard truck body. 24 hp., four-cylinder in-line petrol engine, transverse front leaf spring, cantilever rear semi-elliptic leaf spring. Note attachment of cantilever spring to chassis frame, wire spoke wheels, single rear tyre equipment. 1928.

Below: Model 'AA' 30 cwt. Short wheelbase, normal control, flat platform body, operating on farm work. 1928.

Opposite page top: Model 'A' 10 cwt van, normal control, fitted with the later design of van body, transverse front and rear leaf springs, wire spoked wheels, single rear tyre equipment. Powered by 14.9 hp., four-cylinder in-line petrol engine.

Opposite page bottom: Model 'A' 10 cwt van, normal control, sliding side door windows. Powered by 14.9 hp., four-cylinder in-line petrol engine. Transverse leaf springs for front and rear suspension. Wire spoke wheels.

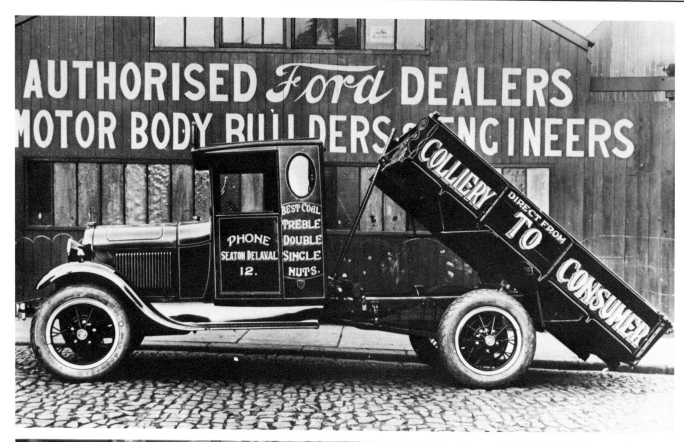

Above: Model 'AA' 30 cwt, short wheelbase, hand-operated tipper body with screw type ram. 24 hp., four-cylinder in-line petrol engine, transverse front leaf spring and cantilever semi-elliptic rear springs. The hand operated screw type tipping gear is clearly shown. 1928.

Left: The last commercial vehicle to leave the assembly line at Trafford Park plant Manchester before the company was transferred to Dagenham. A model 'A' 10 cwt van, normal control, 14.9 hp., four-cylinder in-line petrol engine, three-speed crash change transmission, wire spoke wheels, front & rear transverse springs. October 1931.

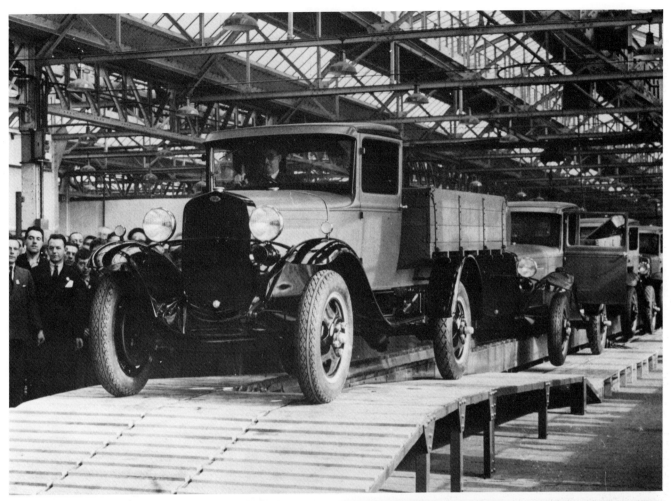

Above: The first commercial vehicle coming off the new assembly line at Dagenham just after the transfer of business from Trafford Park, Manchester. Model 'AA' 30 cwt with dropped side and tailboard truck body. Driven off the assembly line by Rowland Smith (later knighted for his war efforts), then General Manager. 1931.

Right: Model 'AA' 1 ton chassis with ambulance body. 131.5 inch wheelbase. Based on the 30 cwt chassis it was introduced by Dagenham during the time the model 'BB' was starting production and continued as part of the commercial vehicle range. 1932.

Previous page, small inset: Model 'AA' 1 ton chassis with ambulance body. 131.5 inch wheelbase introduced at about the same time as the Model 'BB'.

Previous page, inset: Farmers' utility wagon mounted on Model 'BB' 2-ton chassis. All cratches are detachable, and sides are also hinged for easy loading. Sides and tailboard can be lowered. Dual rear tyre equipment and discs wheels. 24 hp., four cylinder in-line petrol engine and four-speed crash change transmission.

Previous page: Model 'BB' 2 ton chassis with open fire engine body and equipment. Short wheelbase. Dual rear tyre equipment. Transverse front spring and semi-elliptic longitudinal leaf rear springs. Towing trailer with petrol motor operated pump.

Below: Catalogue photograph of model 'BBE' forward control 2-ton truck with semi-elliptic longitudinal front and rear springs. This is the first model away from the transverse front spring. Powered by the famous Ford V8 30 hp. petrol engine, four-speed crash change transmission. Note the shackles for the front springs are located at the front of the chassis. 1936.

Above: Model 'BBE' forward control County Commercial Cars Ltd., six-wheeler conversion. The 'Surrey' single rear axle drive shown with single rear tyre equipment. Powered by the Ford V8 petrol engine. 1936.

Below: Model 'BBE' 2 ton van. forward control model. Powered by the Ford V8 petrol engine. Semi-elliptic longitudinal front and rear springs. This was the first and only model chassis, prewar, to have the modern type of suspension. 1936.

Opposite page top: Model 'BB' 2 ton Luton van on 2 ton long wheelbase chassis cab. Dual rear tyre equipment. Normal control. 1934.

Opposite page middle: Model 'BB' 2 ton chassis front end (less windshield pillars). Long wheelbase. Fordson 157.0 inch wheelbase. 1934.

Opposite page bottom: Model 'BB' chassis cab with County Commercial Cars Ltd., six-wheeler conversion. These conversions were available in both long and short wheelbases. Torque tube enclosed propeller shaft included the short shaft between the rear axles. 1934.

Below: Model 'BB' special ambulance chassis to which special attention was paid to the suspension. To ensure a smooth ride and silent, effortless performance the Ford V8 petrol engine was fitted. There were no less than ten different layouts of the interior. 1935.

Bottom: Model 'B' 12 cwt van. Powered by the 14.9 hp four-cylinder in-line petrol engine. 106.0 inch wheelbase. Transverse leaf springs front and rear. Single rear tyre equipment and wire spoke wheels.

Left: Model 'B' 30 cwt van. Powered by the 24 hp four-cylinder in-line petrol engine. 131.5 inch wheelbase. Transverse front spring, cantilever semi-elliptics longitudinal rear springs. Single rear tyre equipment and disc wheels.

Below: Catalogue photograph of Model '51' County Commercial Cars Ltd., six-wheeler conversion. Double drive 'Sussex' with dual rear type equipment, powered by Ford V8 petrol engine. Small photograph shows the double drive rear axles. Drop sided and tailboard truck body. Long wheelbase shown, short wheelbase available. 1936.

Above: Model '51' Normal control tipper with underfloor telescopic hydraulic tipping ram. Short wheelbase. Powered by the Ford V8 petrol engine. Transverse front spring and semi-elliptic longitudinal leaf springs for the rear. 1936.

Below: County Commercial three-wheeled van, the 'Devon' 12/15 cwt. Based upon the 8 hp., 5 cwt light van chassis, using the model 'Y' front end and engine, but with 4-speed transmission 1936.

Above: Ford built three-wheeled articulated and tractor unit for use with towed and semi-trailers. Designed by County Commercial Cars Ltd. Built to compete with other mechanical horses for the British railway companies. 1936. Using the 8 hp., petrol engine, four-speed transmission. Styling of the front end as the model 'Y' passenger car and the 'Devon' 12/15 cwt van.

Below: Another view of the three-wheeled articulated tractor unit called the 'Tug'.

Above: Model '61' 25 cwt truck and van model versions. Using the light V8 petrol engine of 22 hp. Front transverse spring and semi-elliptic longitudinal rear leaf springs. 1936. Later in 1938 the 24 hp., four-cylinder in-line petrol engine was fitted changing the model designation to E88W.

Below: Model '51' 2 ton truck short wheelbase. Drop sided and tailboard truck float body. Transverse front suspension and longitudinal semi-elliptic leaf rear suspension. 1936.

Below: County Commercial Cars Ltd., six-wheeler conversion double drive bogie. Used on model '51' 1936.

Above: Model 67, box type van body on 112.0 inch wheelbase 15 cwt payload. Powered by the Ford V8 petrol engine. Used by the railway agents of the Great Western Railway, Thos. Bantock & Co., of Wolverhampton. 1936.

Right: Model E83W 10 cwt chassis with estate wagon body, using the 10 hp. four-cylinder in-line petrol engine as used on the model 'C' 10 hp. passenger car. Three-speed synchromesh, on second and third gears, transmission. Transverse leaf springs for both front and rear. 1938.

Above: Model E83W 10 cwt with hand-operated tipper refuse collector. Many special bodies were fitted to this popular chassis. 1938.

Below: Model E83W. Standard 10 cwt van. Same mechanical equipment as the chassis version. Thousands of these vans and chassis were built from 1938 to post war years.

Above: Model E83W light 10 cwt truck with drop sides and tailboard. Single rear tyre equipment. 1939. War time model.

Left: Rear view of the model E83W 10 cwt van. As with the other commercial vehicles became known as the Fordson 10 cwt van. 1939.

Above: Model E83W standard van. Specification as previously described. 1938.

Below: Model 7V. 1937, long wheelbase refuse collector body. Forward control. Powered by the Ford V8 petrol engine with the 24 hp., four cylinder in-line petrol engine as optional. Four-speed crash change transmission. Dual rear tyre equipment. 4 ton capacity.

Ford

Right: Rear of model 7V standard 7 cubic yard refuse collector body. 3 ton short wheelbase. Dual rear tyre equipment. Fordson range 1938.

7 CU.YD. STANDARD REFUSE LOADER

Thames

MOUNTED ON

3 TON. 118"W.B. CHASSIS.

CHASSIS £403 EX-WORKS. DAGENHAM. BODY £229-5-0 EX-WORKS. LICHFIELD.

Below: Model 7V. Short wheelbase 4 ton chassis with special body; 500 gallon gulley and cesspit emptier. 1938.

500 GALLONS CAPACITY COMBINED GULLEY AND CESSPIT EMPTIER

Model 7V. Short wheelbase cesspit and gulley emptier, showing the inspection and discharge door.

Model 7V. Long wheelbase truck with drop sides and tailboard. 4 ton with V8 petrol engine and four-speed crash change transmission, spiral bevel fully floating rear axle. 1939 when the front grille changed to flat type.

Below: Model 7V Forward Control 'Thames' articulated tractor unit 118.0 inch wheelbase. Articulated combination with drop frame machinery carrier semi-trailer. Powered by the Ford V8 petrol engine. 1939.

Model 7V Forward control, horse box body, with the new type radiator grille and chrome plated 'Fordson' badge. Long wheelbase chassis 5 ton.

7V Model, forward control, refuse collector. 4 ton chassis cab version. 1939.

Three models as part of an airport service fleet. Model '48' passenger car chassis with an ambulance body, Model '48' passenger car chassis with a light fire tender body, and a model 'Y' 5 cwt van.

3 Ford in World War 2

At the commencement of the war in Europe in September 1939, Ford of Britain were almost without any vehicle production; it was just as though the Government had forgotten the existence of the company and its enormous facilities.

With the car and commercial vehicle assembly lines quickly being cleared, and unsold vehicles being placed in store pending the outcome of any government decisions, the company waited patiently for instructions. Eventually, almost in despair, an approach was made to the newly appointed Minister of Supply whose recently formed department was to co-ordinate and regulate the supplies, both military and civilian, necessary during wartime conditions.

Having pointed out that their unrivalled mass production facilities could be of tremendous assistance to the war effort by providing the armed forces with much of the equipment they urgently needed, not least of which was transportation, the company received instructions to prepare for the production of a service vehicle range. These were to consist of 15 cwt, 1 ton, 30 cwt, and 3 ton capacity chassis both with and without bodywork. (Due to the off-road nature of much service vehicle use, the designated load capacity of army lorries was usually half that permissible for civilian operation: i.e., a 30 cwt for the services would be a 3 ton vehicle in civilian use).

Not having supplied the military between the wars, Ford were in no position to provide tailor-made service vehicles such as were being supplied by AEC or Leyland, and bearing in mind the urgency of the situation now the decision was taken to appropriately modify the existing Ford range. This would also help considerably in keeping costs down, with engines, drivelines, braking systems etc., able to be produced on existing tooling. For model identification purposes the company's existing designation system would also be used, with the letters W O T being chosen for the service vehicles: W = War Office; O = model introduction year – 1940; and T = truck. The various models within the series would be identified in numerical order: W.O.T.1, W.O.T.2, etc..

Ministry of Supply contracts were for individual models as and when required by the forces, and not for a group of models, with each quantity of a particular vehicle ordered being covered by a separate contract. The first such contract was for a quantity of W.O.T.1, 3 ton general purpose carriers, with a normal control layout within an enclosed cab, and equipped with a 4.4 metre (174 in.) float. As the forward control 7V range was still in limited production for home front needs, from this range was selected a long wheelbase chassis front end with the County Commercial "Sussex" double-drive six-wheeler extension. The power was provided by the 30 hp V8 sidevalve petrol engine. The 7V drawn from stock was taken to the company's experimental workshop where its front end, steering gear, control pedals, and all wheels and hubs were removed. The conversion to normal control commenced, with redesigned steering linkages and relocated pedals etc. being fitted. The existing wheelbase remained unchanged, as it was quite suitable for the float length required. New hubs were necessary to accommodate wheels equipped with either 9.00 x 16 or 10.50 x 16 low-pressure tyres.

A very simply constructed normal control cab and front end was designed by Briggs Motor Bodies. This did not require any complicated tooling, being designed specifically with easy repairs by army engineers in mind either behind the lines or on the field of battle itself. A wooden float with drop sides and demountable tilt completed the job. With production commencing late in September 1939, this contract was completed by the October of 1941.

This was not the only model on the assembly lines during this time, for whilst the Ministry issued separate contracts for each vehicle order the production rates overlapped; by early 1940 W.O.T.1, 2, and 3s were in production at Dagenham. (As Ford of Britain had agreed to put the magnificent Rolls-Royce Merlin V12-cylinder aero engine into quantity production, the Trafford Park premises acquired for the new Commercial Vehicle Division venture was assigned to this task. Applied to the Rolls-Royce engine, Ford's mass production wizardry resulted in the reduction of both man-hours and cost per unit by a staggering 70 per cent, without any sacrifice in quality – every one of the 34,000 plus Ford-built Merlins passed the RAF's acceptance trials.

The Rolls-Royce project was masterminded by Ford's then managing director, Rowland Smith, who subsequently received a knighthood in recognition of the enormous success of this venture).

The second service vehicle contract, for production to begin in November 1939 was for a number of the W.O.T.3, four-wheel 1 ton open lorries. Again with normal control, these were to feature a closed cab and a 2.77 metre float. The Model 7V forward control long wheelbase chassis front end provided the basis for this, being modified along the same lines as the W.O.T.1 except that this contract called for existing wheel and tyre sizes, but with single rear equipment. The November production date was met, with this contract being completed during February 1940. As it had by now been decided to distinguish the variations on a particular theme by adding a suffix letter, this batch were designated W.O.T.3A.

The first contract for what would eventually be produced in the greatest numbers, the W.O.T.2 15 cwt infantry truck, called for production to commence in December 1939. This was for a normal control vehicle with an open cab and a 1.97 metre float; 9.00 x 16 cross country tyres on military type split roadwheels with single rear equipment were specified. The most appropriate civilian example was the Model 61, a forward control 25/35 cwt van and truck chassis on a 106 inch wheelbase, and which was still in limited production at that time. For this conversion the chassis was stripped bare, including the removal of the small-bore 22 hp V8 engine and three-speed gearbox. The 30 hp V8 and four-speed transmission was then installed, thus making a common engine/gearbox combination throughout the whole of the Ford services truck range. With the controls once again relocated, a very simple front end and cab was mounted. Requiring the absolute minimum of tooling, and again emphasing ease of repair, this so-called cab in fact consisted of a metal bulkhead, steel frame with wooden flooring and a canvas canopy. Small individual windscreens were provided for the driver and passenger. Also with provision for a canvas top, the wooden float was equipped with a tailgate and top-half drop sides. This initial contract for the W.O.T.2 was completed in July 1940.

Another service vehicle based upon a civilian model in production at this time was a short wheelbase personnel carrier, designated W.O.C.1. Based on the American Ford 15 cwt van chassis, this was a normal control model which even retained the streamlined car-like bonnet and front wings of the civilian van, but did utilise the stark open cab as on the W.O.T.2. This model was equipped with a specially designed steel float on which was a dual purpose canvas tilt which could be removed for use as a tent.

Ford were now in full production, with certain civilian models still being turned out alongside the War Office designs. Also based on the 15 cwt van chassis were ambulances and vans designated RO1T; of wood and steel composite construction, the ambulance body could accommodate four stretcher cases. A small number of searchlight lorries based on the E917T six-wheeler chassis cab were being turned out for home front use, as were barrage balloon winch models utilising this chassis, too. Deliveries of these were completed by the middle of

1941; but destined to remain in production throughout the war, for civilian uses, was the standard 7V range. Many of these, particularly the tippers, would be active on the home front in demolition and rebuilding work, whilst amongst other uses to which the versatile 7V would be put was that of a fire engine.

Meanwhile, overlapping contracts for the W.O.T.1, 2, and 3 ranges continued to be issued. Amongst the W.O.T.1s supplied were versions able to accommodate a variety of bodywork and special equipment, with 1000 gallon tankers, crash tenders, barrage balloon winches, searchlight lorries and ambulances all being built on this chassis. A hip ring providing access through the cab roof for an observer, or armed guard for crew protection was a feature of some W.O.T.1s. A heavier-duty derivitive, equipped with an auxiliary gearbox, servo-assisted brakes, and additional helper rear springs was designated W.O.T.1A.

The versatile W.O.T.2. eventually appeared in variants from W.O.T.2A to 2H, and was produced in far greater numbers than the other rather more specialized War Office models. The open cab design and seating arrangements of this vehicle resulted in some servicemen experiencing driving difficulties, and from model 2C onwards came longer footpedals in answer to this problem. All-weather versions of this cab, sporting lower half steel doors, side curtains, and full windscreens with wiper equipment were to be found on later W.O.T.2 variants.

As a general purpose truck, the W.O.T.2 was uprated to a 30 cwt capacity vehicle with the introduction of W.O.T.3B. Improved road springs and different tyres were responsible for this change which also applied to the subsequent 3C, 3D, and 3E versions. A number of W.O.T.3s with twin fuel tanks and additional rear helper springs were supplied to the Indian Army as 2/2^1/$_2$ tonners.

Whilst all of these trucks had called for considerable revision to the basic Ford specification, they could nevertheless be regarded as straightforward adaptations of existing lines; whereas, an additional contract issued during 1940 called for something far more radical. This was for a four-wheel-drive chassis, with forward control and available in both short and long wheelbase configuration with capacities of 30 cwt and 3 tons, respectively.

Vehicles such as these were completely new to Ford who had never attempted four-wheel-drive. Nevertheless, design studies indicated that many existing components could be utilised yet again, with the finished article containing much in the way of standard Ford assemblies. The V8 engine, four-speed gearbox and regular Ford torque tube drive arrangements to the rear wheels were retained, whilst a new two-speed transfer gearbox transmitted the power to the front axle via a new, open propeller shaft. Both axles employed the normal Ford spiral-bevel final-drive assemblies. Lower overall gearing was a feature of the long wheelbase (143^1/$_2$ in.) W.O.T.6 model capable of a 3 ton load, which also employed heavier rate springs and shock absorbers than the lighter capacity W.O.T.8 model. The forward control cab used many panels common to the W.O.T.3, and overall, bearing in mind the relative complexity of this type of vehicle, the completely successful utilisation of so many standard Ford parts represented a notable achievement indeed on behalf of Ford. Deliveries of the W.O.T.8 commenced in June 1941, with the W.O.T.6 coming into production during January the following year. A later version, the W.O.T.6 A3, had a cab which could be split along the waistline and so reduce the height of the vehicle for air transportation.

The four-wheel-drive models completed Ford's W.O.T. series, the missing numbers 4, 5 and 7, having been applied to designs mooted but which in the event were never ordered into production.

As part of the Canadian war effort, large numbers of Fords, known as the Canadian Boxed Vehicles, were being shipped to Britain for assembly at Dagenham and other depots. Many of these were assembled just as soon as they left the ships at Ford's private dock, with some use being made of the packing cases to build temporary sheds. Canadian models received were: Model EC098U, a 3 ton dump truck; EC098T, 3 ton chassis cab with truck, workshop, wrecker,

or stores truck bodies mounted; EC096T, long wheelbase chassis cab; EC011DF, light-duties 8 cwt chassis cab, semi-forward control. Four-wheel-drive models were the EC011Q, a short wheelbase field artillery tractor with semi-forward control, and the EC018Q semi-forward control chassis cab able to accommodate similar bodies as the EC098T.

The 'E' prefix denoted the English assembly of these models, which included slight changes made to suit the British military.

Following the fall of France, all vehicles en route from the United States to Europe were diverted to Britain. Naturally enough, Ford of Britain took over the Ford Detroit stock, whilst those from General Motors and others were dealt with by their own British subsidiaries or dealerships. All of this stock, which came in between August 1940 and July 1941, was converted to the Ministry of Supply's requirements by the fitting of appropriate W.O.T. type bodies, and therefore also acquired the 'E' prefix to their original designation. These were normal control vehicles once again retaining the civilian front end designs, and consisted of the EO1Y and EO1T 15 cwt short wheelbase light van and truck chassis, and the 30 cwt E018T general service truck.

In addition to powering all these military applications, Ford's legendary 30 hp sidevalve V8 engine served as the heart of many other machines, not all of which were wheeled vehicles; large numbers of winches, generators, and motor launches relied on Ford V8 power. One other vehicle using the Ford V8 was the Carden Loyd bren gun carrier which had actually been designed around the Ford engine and transmission. Other parts being supplied by Ford for this vehicle were the chassis, and the all important metal tracks which endowed the carrier with its "go anywhere" capabilities.

With the Dagenham factory working to capacity, additional facilities were necessary to meet the demand for the carrier's tracks, and so an empty factory in Leamington Spa was acquired in October 1940. Here, within six months, a new highly mechanised foundry was in operation. The traditional malleable iron tracks used by the bren gun carriers, and light tanks for which Ford were also providing supplies, were proving to be short-lived under intensive wartime use, but Ford tackled this by substituting their own special crankshaft steel for these vital components and so eliminated a potentially very serious problem. Ford's foundry techniques were widely regarded as second-to-none, and for their contribution to the war effort the foundry superintendent, Mr V. Harnet, was awarded the B.E.M., with Ford Metallurgist Mr P.A. Waters receiving the M.B.E..

As they were supplying so many vital parts, it was only logical that Ford should join the manufacturing group involved in the final assembly of complete carriers, and in September 1941 the company received an order for 4,500 of these vehicles. Although containing much Ford hardware, the bren gun carriers did of course differ considerably from normal Ford products, and so demanded somewhat different mass production facilities. Nevertheless, the production engineers soon had a suitable layout designed. This consisted of a main assembly line for the carrier, with other sub-assembly lines for major components. By February 1942 this was installed and operational, and capable of a production rate which made the Ministry's request for 25 carriers per week seem derisory; 100 per week was more in line with Ford's thinking. After much insistence by Ford, the latter figure was eventually accepted by the Ministry, and fortunately so, as the need for these carriers expanded rapidly as the war progressed.

Three variations of the carrier were produced by Ford, these being: A.O.P. (armoured observation post) No. 1 Mk111/W; Universal Carrier No. 1 Mk111/W; and the Anti-Tank six pounder gun carrier Mk1. In all, 13,942 carriers were built by Ford, with the largest output being achieved between January 7th and 15th, 1944, in which week 200 were produced.

Being fighting vehicles, the carriers inevitably saw much action on virtually every front where the British forces were employed, and right there alongside them in many theatres, taking severe punishment in their stride, were the W.O.T. series trucks. For the D-day landings, it was necessary to waterproof the vehicles of the invasion force, and weeks of experimenting with a variety of materials resulted in a red, putty like substance named Trinadite. This was spread over the electrical equipment, and was also used to seal doors, windows, etc.. Snorkel tubes were attached and then similarly sealed to the carburettor intakes and the exhaust pipes. The treatment was proved a success as the invasion vehicles waded ashore on the Normandy beaches.

Whilst all this was going on, other Ford products were equally hard at work on the less publicised home front. As has already been mentioned, the 7V range which had provided the basis for the W.O.T. models continued in production throughout the war, and alongside this the versatile 10 hp E83W chassis found employment in a number of important roles. Whilst serving as an ambulance, small fire tender with the Auxiliary Fire Service, and general purpose small utility vehicle, it was as a mobile canteen that the E83W was perhaps most remembered.

Paid for personally by Henry Ford and his son, Edsel, the Ford Emergency Food Vans consisted of E83W chassis fitted with special bodywork in which food could be cooked and dispensed by servers standing upright. Operated by the Y.M.C.A., the Salvation Army, the Church Army, and the Society of Friends, 450 of these mobile canteens were stationed throughout the country always ready to serve food to the victims of the air raids. Additionally, the vans, which were maintained free of charge by local Ford dealerships, regularly carried food to schools, farms, small workshops, the docks areas, and remote barrage balloon sites and anti-aircraft posts. By the end of the war, no less than 81,649,741 meals had been transported and served from these vans.

At home and abroad, on land, sea, and even in the air, the Ford contribution to the war effort had been considerable indeed with both workforce and the management receiving, and thoroughly deserving, the highest praise. The tremendous efforts by all concerned had, however, altered attitudes irrevocably, and late in 1945 the company suffered a strike by its workforce who sensed there may be a return to prewar conditions which, to many, were now regarded as unacceptable. As a result, many past procedures and orders were scrapped as the company adopted a new attitude towards the future; a future in which, unlike in the past when Dagenham was largely employed in building Detroit designed vehicles, Ford of Britain would now be given a loose rein.

Model 7V 1939. Civilian truck for duty on the Home Front. Drop sided truck body with full height headboard and full canvas tilt. 30 hp. V8 engine. Masked head/side lamps, a war time regulation for night operation during black-out periods. Note:- Larger hood over the nearside headlamp to screen headlamp beam directed onto the side of the road. Many such 7V models assisted in civilian and military transport during the Second World War.

Model R01T Ambulance 1939. Specially built ambulance body on Dearborn's 01T truck range. Steel and wood composite body. 4 stretcher carriers designed for alternative upholstered bench seats for sitting patients. Left-hand drive. Chassis and front end Ex-U.S.A. 30 hp. V8 petrol engine. 134.0 inch wheelbase. Note:- Masked headlamps and large hood over nearside lamp.

Below: American Ford model 01W, on home-front service with London Transport. Masked headlamp and white painted bumper and mudguard edges to comply with black-out regulations. The first Ford with the open propeller shaft, small numbers of these were built at Dagenham in the early part of the war.

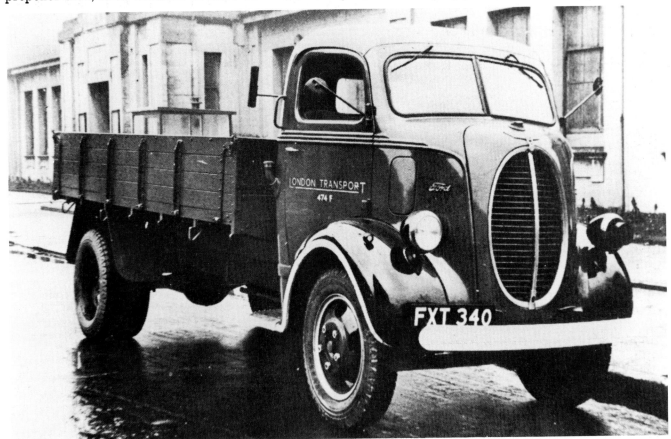

Model W.O.C.1., Infantry truck and personnel carrier based on Dearborn's Model 01C. Chassis front end Ex-U.S.A., Steel open type cab. Canvas canopy. Steel float drop sides and tailboard with full canvas tilt. 112.0 inch wheelbase. One masked headlamp only used. Convoy disc on offside front wing fender.

Below: Canadian boxed vehicle assembled by Fords at Dagenham and other assembly depots. Model EC011Q. F.A. Tractor, four-wheel drive with power winch, steel closed cab. Accommodation for crew of six. Built in Canada, designed by Ford of Britain at Dagenham. 101.0 inch wheelbase. 32 hp. V8 side-valve petrol engine.

W.O.T.1., Six-wheeler 3 ton general service truck. This vehicle was commissioned for civilian duty by the Post Office Telephone Engineering Department. It is fitted with a workshop body, servo assisted braking system and single rear tyre equipment. 143.5 inch wheelbase plus 42.44 inch bogie centres.

Sketch of W.O.T.1., Six-wheeler general service 3 ton truck, with sand tyres all round and single rear equipment, drop sides and tailboard wooden float with full height headboard and lashed down full canvas tilt.

Right: W.O.T.2., 15 cwt Infantry truck (W.O.T.2E version). Featured are all weather steel cab doors, sides and floor, canvas canopy, wooden float with drop sides (top half) and tailboard. Also fitted is a full canvas tilt on steel tubular frame, sand tyres all round with single rear equipment. 106.0 wheelbase. 30 hp. V8 Engine.

Below: W.O.T. 2 Fire appliance for home-front service with the National Fire Service.

W.O.T.3., 30 cwt general service truck (W.O.T.3C version) with enclosed steel cab. Spare wheel carrier behind cab, wooden float, fixed sides, and fully demountable canvas tilt. 10.50 x 16 Cross Country tyres with single rear equipment. 143.5 inch wheelbase. V8 petrol engine.

W.O.T.3., 1 ton open truck (W.O.T.3A version). Closed steel cab, spare wheel carrier behind the cab, wooden float, fixed sides (3 ft) half length canvas tilt, and lurching rails front and sides, chain at rear. 2 tubular seats provided under the tilt. 9.00 x 16 Cross Country tyres with single rear equipment. 143.5 inch wheelbase. 30 hp. V8 petrol engine.

W.O.T.6., 4-wheel drive truck. Fixed sided truck body with full canvas tilt with tubular frame. Used for mobile workshop with overhead hand operated lifting tackle. Road tyres with single rear equipment. 143.5 inch wheelbase. 30 hp., V8 petrol engine. Single nearside masked headlamp and convoy disc on offside.

E917T., six-wheeler truck with fixed sided wooden float and full tilt, and auxiliary transmission, closed steel cab and searchlight unit. Note: Half door with canvas curtain and step on nearside to facilitate side entry. 157.0 inch wheelbase with 42.44 inch bogie centres. 30 hp. V8 petrol engine. 4-speed crash change transmission.

Service workshop for military vehicles. Note: The two W.O.T.2s and the war dressed model 61 forward control waiting servicing.

W.O.T.2. Infantry truck under bombardment in the Middle East theatre of action.

Operations for dismantling W.O.T.6., and W.O.T.8., 4-wheel drive cab, for air portability transport.

1st., Operation – removal of all yellow painted hardware, such as door hinges, lock plates etc., remove doors, remove fixings for bottom of windscreen to front end and top half of cab at the rear, top half is now separated from the lower half.

2nd., Operation – Insert the bars, rear cab panel to windscreen pillar to ensure rigidity of top half of cab.

3rd., Operation – Lift off top half of cab.

This reduces the height of the vehicle which can then be accommodated in transport aircraft for air lift.

Ford E83W mobile canteen of the Y.M.C.A., Voluntary Service. Walk-about inspection by Her Majesty Queen Mary, the Queen Mother. Hundreds of these vans carried out mobile canteen work throughout the country operated by many women's auxiliary services.

Ford 7Y, 5 cwt van., N.A.A.F.I., refreshment van. Her Majesty Queen Elizabeth talking to one of the drivers during an inspection tour of the Home Front Voluntary Services.

Ford sponsored E83W mobile canteens line-up for inspection and presentation.

A number of mobile canteens ready to offer tea and refreshments in blitz. London. This particular location is an area around St. Paul's Cathedral apparently clearing up after a previous night's air raid.

The E83W also played its part well as a fire fighting vehicle, and here displays the variety of equipment it carried in this role.

Finishing assembly of engine and transmission. End of engine and transmission line ready for transfer to the main assembly line for installation into vehicle. This particular engine and transmission is the 250,000th 30 hp. V8 side-valve petrol to be produced since the start of hostilities.

Mounting the cab on a W.O.T.6., four-wheel drive chassis on Ford main assembly line at Dagenham using power winches. This particular W.O.T.6. is recorded as the 25,000th four-wheel drive vehicle to be produced since June 1941.

Illustrations of a selection of Ford Military vehicles built by Ford in Great Britain – 1939 to 1945.

Above left: Ford built Carden-Loyd Bren Gun Carrier backing up the Infantry advancing into action.

Above: Ford built, Carden-Loyd Gun Carriers in action. Desert warfare, Middle East.

Rear view of Carden-Loyd Bren Gun Carrier completely equipped ready to go into action.

Front/offside view of Carden-Loyd Carrier completely equipped ready to go into action.

Carden-Loyd Bren Gun Carriers and crew personnel on inspection parade. These carriers were powered by Ford V8 side valve petrol engine with the Ford four-speed transmission and rear axle spiral bevel drive gear with sprocket wheels fitted on rear hubs, and rigidly mounted in the carrier hull.

4 Peacetime production

There was no immediate changeover from War Office to civilian commercial vehicle production upon the cessation of hostilities, although a slow-down did occur as Ford, like other manufacturers, continued to produce their military vehicle range whilst appropriate government departments sorted out the most urgent civilian transport requirements. Both material and labour shortages (many men had not yet been released from the services) precluded any return to real mass production at this stage anyway, and the W.O.T. vehicles still being produced until remaining stocks of the specialized material and components were exhausted could now be diverted to vital civilian roles. Amongst the Fords finding useful employment were the W.O.T.1 six-wheelers being pressed into service with the Post Office Telephone services, whose Engineering Department used them as mobile workshops and detector vans. W.O.T.2s were converted into fire tenders, delivery vans, and small pick-up trucks.

It was not until late in 1945 that the motor industry was authorised to re-introduce the prewar civilian trucks onto the assembly lines alongside the tail end of War Office vehicle production. These civilian models could only be sold under government contracts, as transport generally was still very much on a wartime footing, with the Ministry of War Transport controlling the movements of all freight throughout the country. This was done by granting haulage contractors and cartage agents with licences and petrol ration permits only where motor vehicle transport was essential for such as demolition work, rebuilding, and the conveyance generally of vital supplies.

These were extremely difficult times for all concerned, with many raw materials being at an absolute premium, and therefore also controlled by a government ministry. It would be a considerable time before European, and other countries overrun by opposing forces would be in a position to supply sufficient quantities of iron ore, timber, rubber, bauxite etc. Combating this, the widespread collection of a variety of scrap materials for recycling was quickly implemented at the Government's instigation. This policy did result in assorted scrap metals enabling the blast furnaces to continue turning out useful quantities of the desperately needed iron and steel. From the operating point of view, petrol shortages were a major difficulty, with the result that many haulage contractors adopted the alternative producer-gas fuel. Running on this gas, engines developed rather less power, with a further drawback being that a producer-gas plant had to be either carried on the vehicle or towed behind on its own trailer, thus somewhat lessening the vehicle's loadability.

Having produced their popular and reliable range of forward control 7V trucks, and E83W vans and light chassis during the war under services and home front contracts, Ford of course faced no problems whatsoever in continuing production of these now. Still wearing the rather drab khaki and grey wartime colours, the new 7Vs were soon contributing greatly to the country's back-to-normal campaign. The austere looking finish however soon gave way to more acceptable colours, at which time the manufacturer's "Fordson" oval nameplate appeared at the top of the radiator grille. Updating the specification, and improving the braking performance by replacing the Ford/Kelsey Hayes self-aligning brake assemblies, came a new Girling braking system mechanically operated by a rod and cable layout. This feature would no doubt be appreciated by drivers, but one which would not, however, was the retention of the carburettor's oil bath air cleaner demanded by ministry requirements during the war; the re-shaped engine cowling to cover the oil bath was such as to create a substantial division in the cab.

Gradually, the full variety of 7Vs were re-introduced; short and long wheelbase trucks, tippers, and two versions of the County Commercial six-wheelers. Widening the 7V scope still further, the company successfully worked on the installation of the Perkins P6 six-cylinder diesel engine. Other ideas in a similar direction were also investigated, one being an endeavour to 'dieselise' the Ford V8 engine whilst the other was to simply provide the big V8 with petrol injection using a modified diesel fuel pump. Poor results in both cases however saw these particular projects abandoned.

In contrast, one project coming to fruition saw the range usefully extended by the addition of an articulated tractor unit. Developed at the request of the Sales Department, the tractor unit was based on the short wheelbase tipper chassis cab. A fifth wheel coupling mounted ahead of the rear axle was a feature in line with the recommendations of semi-trailer manufacturers such as British Trailers, Carrimore Sixwheelers Ltd., Taskers, and Dysons.

Changes announced in March 1946 centred around definitive load capacities. The previously rather vaguely rated 4/5 ton tipper being now replaced by two separate models of 4 and 5 tons capacity. The same split was introduced on the fixed float models with individual 2 and 3 ton, and 4 and 5 ton trucks replacing the 2/3 tonner and 4/5 tonner, respectively. At the same time the 24 hp four-cylinder petrol engine was finally discarded as an option, leaving all petrol-engined models with 3.6 litre V8 power. For overseas markets there was a left-hand drive version, the Model 7VF, with the suffix indicating that this was foreign to the British standard truck. Enhancing the appearance, as wartime austerity receded slightly, replacing the wartime mesh fitting came a new vertically slatted radiator grille complete with a chrome surround; the oval badge, too, acquired a chrome plated finish.

With addition of a 2 ton van, and the availability of long or short wheelbase chassis cab or chassis front end versions on which could be mounted virtually any type of bodywork, the 7V gave remarkably comprehensive coverage. It sold well until its production ceased in March 1949, and continued thereafter to serve its operators very well indeed for many more years. The long wheelbase truck chassis, with 29,859 being produced between September 29th, 1937, and March 29th, 1949, had proved to be the biggest seller overall, whilst the best seller postwar was the tipper. Available in each capacity with either under floor hydraulic rams by Anthony Hoist Ltd., or the front end hydraulic tipping ram by Edbro Tippers, both the 4 and 5 tonners could be had with fixed or drop sided bodies, and the 7V tipping lorries found much work in war-damaged Britain. Throughout the period of rebuilding in London and other major cities the tippers could be seen ploughing their war through the demolished building sites, and, that 5 ton capacity rating notwithstanding, coping manfully indeed with the more usual 8 tons or so of rubble on board.

Also enjoying great popularity in those early postwar years, the much sought after E83W light commercial found itself still in the market place in all its various roles: van, high roof van, pick-up, Utilicon, mobile canteen, ambulance, and of course in chassis front end form for the accommodation of other special bodies. As during the war, the mobile canteen was still a great favourite which could be found on building and demolition sites nationwide. Perhaps the most versatile 10/12 cwt machine around, the E83W would continue in production until September 1957, by which time a total of 188,577 had been built over a 19 year span.

During 1947 the company expanded its engineering department to encompass a staff of approximately fifteen; designers, draughtsmen, and clerks. The system adopted by the design facility, with which to cover the engineering of both cars and commercial vehicles, was to delegate three senior engineers to control passenger car design and two senior engineers to trucks, with both activities under the leadership of a chief designer and assistant chief. When the pressure was on for the introduction of a new passenger car then the remaining staff, draughtsmen and clerks, were employed under the direction of the senior engineers assigned to cars. If however there was a pressing need for a new truck range, then the procedure was similar but with the remainder working under the two senior truck designers, leaving just the other three senior men on passenger car development.

At this time (1947), the pressure was on truck design as there was a need for a replacement for the ageing 7V. Layouts and specifications were schemed out for two new commercial vehicles, these being a 3 ton and 6 ton with various derivatives. The proposals were for an entirely new truck chassis as a basis for a range which would include many design features differing from Ford's past practices – completely new engines, transmissions, open propeller shaft drive line, road springs and both front and rear axles being included, as was a new style cab.

These proposals, together with the estimated costs of development, including tooling and new machinery expenditure, were submitted to the company's Policy Committee. The £6,000,000 estimate however was to result in the project being rejected. An all-new Ford passenger car for the 1950s was also vital, and this too would cost several million pounds to develop. High-level talks taking place between Dagenham and Dearborn indicated that Ford of Britain's ideas for a futuristic car range would get the go-ahead, and so the truck side of the business came off second best as usual with the money going into the new car development. Nevertheless, the Policy Committee were well aware that an updated truck range was necessary to keep abreast of the competition, particularly Bedford. The suggestion from them therefore was that a less radical proposal, utilising major assemblies from the 7V, but with a new modern cab and front end layout would meet with their approval. So, it was back to the drawing board again, to scheme out another re-design of what was still essentially the old Model BB which, it was felt, should have no serious problem in surviving another term in an updated guise.

At that time, Briggs Motor Bodies, who could always find plenty of work in addition to supplying Ford, were in the throes of bringing a new cab into production for the Leyland "Comet" truck. Ford, as usual eager to save undue expense for truck development, viewed the Comet cab as a golden opportunity to do just that. During the same period, the Dodge Division of Chrysler Motors, of Kew, were also designing a new all-British medium truck range. They also approached Briggs, and became interested in the Comet cab. Negotiations between the four; Briggs, Leyland, Ford, and Dodge, regarding tooling costs, resulted in an agreement between them whereby Ford, who would have the largest output, would pay the highest percentage of the tooling costs. New designs were approved for the three differing front end panelwork and radiator grille assemblies necessary to distinguish between the respective cabs; Leyland, Ford, and Dodge.

Whilst the neatly styled cab and front end arrangements gave the appearance of a normal control bonneted type lorry, all three were in fact advertised by their respective manufacturers as semi-forward control types. On the Dagenham model, the Fordson nameplate appeared at the front just above the name Thames which had recently been adopted as the title for all Ford commercial vehicles.

On the Ford, under the skin was the faithful 30 hp V8 petrol engine, the four-speed crash change transmission with the familiar torque tube drive layout to the rear axle. Hydraulic brakes, with those at the rear being operated by the assistance of a single external cylinder through a compensator lever and linkage, were however a notable improvement over the outgoing 7V. As with the 7V, the new range was intended to cater for a wide variety of roles, with payloads once again up to a maximum of 5 tons. In its 5 ton configuration this latest Ford incorporated a new British-designed front axle to accommodate heavy duty 34 x 7 high-pressure tyres.

The full range, designated ET6 (English Truck) and ET7 if fitted with a diesel engine, included left-hand drive models (ETF6/7), and consisted of: long wheelbase (157 inches) suitable for a 172 inch float; short wheelbase (128 inch) 2 ton chassis with 132 inch truck float, or a van body; 122 inch wheelbase 4 cubic yard tipper with either fixed or drop side bodies with underfloor or front end hydraulic ram; and an articulated tractor unit accommodating a fifth wheel coupling, and based on the 122 inch wheelbase model. Maximum all-up weight for the tractor and whatever trailer attached was 29,209 lbs (13,159 kilos). Chassis front end and chassis cab versions were once again available on which could be mounted such bodies as tankers, refuse collectors, horse boxes etc., and an interesting 5 ton telescopic U-shaped ejector body known as the Jekta.

A County Commercial-designed Sussex double-drive bogie six-wheeler was again on offer, available in long or short wheelbase form with a $42^1/2$ inch bogie with a centrally mounted pivot and 16-leaf rear springs, heavy duty double acting shock absorbers, and servo assistance for the hydraulically operated brakes. Maximum laden weight in this instance was 25,300 lbs (11.430 kilos). The previous County Commercial single-drive bogie six-wheeler was not included in the new range.

Entering production on March 2nd, 1949, alongside the 7Vs with which there was to be a production overlap so as to ensure continuity, the first ET was a petrol engined (ET6) long wheelbase truck. The first production diesel (ET7) followed on March 31st. Many operators did prefer diesel power, and the unit chosen for the ET7 was the Perkins P6 six-cylinder engine, which produced 70 bhp at 2200 rpm with maximum torque output of 184 lbs ft at 1000 rpm. Easy starting, and freedom from diesel knock was claimed for this version of the P6 which featured a newly developed combustion chamber known as the Aeroflow. An alternative diesel considered during the design stage was a unit of Rushton and Hornsby's manufacture, but the reasons why this engine lost out to the Perkins unit are not clear today.

Although by no means radically new, the ET series did offer useful improvements in certain respects; it had a far more comfortable cab than its predecessor, and it was a very pleasingly styled lorry. Some operators however were unhappy about the move away from full forward control, fearing that this would mean a reduced load length. In fact there was very little difference between the new range and the 7V in this respect as both long and short wheelbases had been appropriately lengthened for the ET models. Load lengths quoted for the 7V short and long wheelbase models were $136^1/2$ inches and $172^1/2$ inches, with the corresponding figures for the ET being 132 inches and 174 inches. Whilst the fully forward control layout of the 7V gave better weight distribution between the two axles, this did often result in the front wheels digging down into the soft muddy ground on building sites when unladen 7V tippers attempted to move out. This was a problem experienced with many forward control tippers, but which was largely overcome by the ET models on which the front wheels carried less of the total vehicle weight.

The new range was soon being seen in action, and inevitably found its way into the hands of many of the so-called cowboy operators who then, as now, are only interested in shifting the greatest possible tonnage with the least number of journeys, irrespective of the vehicle's maximum all-up weight as determined by the manufacturer. Usually, it was the top capacity vehicles which came in for the worst abuse, and in Ford's case now it was the new 5 tonner and 4 cubic yard tipper which suffered greatly. Especially on semi-forward control and normal control vehicles, frame stresses at the rear of the cab have always been a problem, and excessive overloading on the ETs was resulting in chassis sidemembers developing cracks at this point. To overcome the problem, Ford engineers developed a frame reinforcement which increased the depth of the sidemembers in such a manner as to increase the strength of the chassis frame around the problem area. The fact that this modification was made available on the 4 and 5 ton trucks and the 4 cubic yard tipper, when requested by the operator for heavy duty work, implies Ford's tacit acceptance that many operators would continue to ignore maximum vehicle weight limits.

A further problem arose in the transmission line on the 4 cubic yard tippers due to overloading to such an extent which necessitated constant running in bottom gear. The problem was the breakage of the rear axle pinion teeth, but confined to the 7.6:1 ratio crownwheel and pinion set. After analysis it was found that when cutting the 5-tooth pinion the bottom of the teeth were cutting too deep into the pinion shank, and with the excessive overloading which some vehicles were being subjected to causing maximum torque to be transmitted to the final drive gears for extremely long periods, tooth breakages became inevitable. A modification to the gear cutting process eliminated the undercutting and cured the problem.

In view of the responsibility being given to Ford of Britain to engineer and manufacture its own vehicle ranges, it had been necessary to establish a larger and more efficient engineering department, and to include the recruitment of additional experienced staff. The fact that some applicants attending interviews had then turned down the opportunity to work for Ford, citing poor conditions and surroundings as their reasons, had prompted the company to re-house its design/engineering facility. The lease was acquired on a disused three storey factory in nearby Rainham, and following total refurbishing and installation of new equipment, the car and truck design engineering staff settled down here. During 1949 the truck and passenger car combined engineering facility had separated into two divisions, with one senior engineer being delegated to each. The existing chief designer took control of passenger car development, whilst his former assistant had been promoted to lead the truck engineering team.

Looking well ahead, and always bearing in mind anticipated new developments by the rival Bedford concern, the Ford marketing and sales staff were now putting pressure on the management for an entirely new all-British truck range. It was felt that the next generation following the ET would have to break away from certain Ford traditions now regarded as out of date, such as the torque tube enclosed propeller shaft, double shackled rear springs, and the non-synchromesh crash change gearbox. In any case, Dearborn had already discarded these features in the design of its O1T model range, so there could be no argument now about Dagenham independently taking a similar line. An entirely new range was at last agreed upon, and to indeed be all British without any Dearborn influence being brought to bear. This would be the first assignment for the Truck Engineering Division as a separate organisation.

Work commenced on the design of a 6 ton truck chassis as the first stage. A four-speed synchromesh gearbox, hypoid bevel gear driven rear axle wth banjo type axle housing, and new front suspension and axle were all amongst the objectives. Initially, as no new power units were available, the old faithful V8 would power early prototypes, but a new engine range was being developed by a newly formed engine section. Two prototype 6 tonners were completed quickly and a thorough testing routine proved these to be very satisfactory.

Meanwhile, the Sales Division had been busily engaged on a market research programme which included visits to various operators. During one of these visits, the sales department, handling vehicle sales to the armed forces and the Civil Services, obtained a contract as part of a larger contract for the supply of military vehicles to be divided between Ford, Bedford, Commer, and Austin.

The Ford part of the deal was for 5000 four-wheel-drive truck chassis, but, unlike Bedford who had retained their 4 x 4 in production as a civilian model, Ford had no standard model they could offer. The company's Policy Committee therefore quickly approved the inclusion of a four-wheel-drive chassis in the new truck development programme. Advising the ministry of their decision to offer a 4x4 military vehicle based on their projected new truck range, the company received confirmation of the contract plus the welcome news that part of the tooling costs would be borne by the ministry. Timing however was a crucial factor; the ministry could not simply wait for the eventual outcome of Ford's truck development programme.

Briggs Motor Bodies were working on a new Ford cab, codenamed "Atlantic", but this was far from complete and so an alternative was sought. The cab fitted to the Karrier Bantam, and supplied by Motor Panels of Coventry, proved to be suitable and was therefore adopted. Slight modifications were made under the supervision of Briggs to enable the mounting of this cab on the Ford chassis, and to incorporate a new design of front panelwork and grille. For the new range there was already an agreement whereby the latest American Warner 8 MTH four-speed transmission would be manufactured at Dagenham, as would also a hypoid bevel final drive assembly originally designed by the Timken Detroit Axle Co., a division of the Rockwell Standards and Steel Corporation. However, to guarantee the military contract delivery dates two Ford of Britain engineers crossed the Atlantic to check out and approve the immediate acquisition of the 5000 gearboxes and 10,000 final drive assemblies for the army lorries. The front and rear axles, less the final drive assemblies, and the auxiliary transfer gearbox necessary for the four-wheel-drive arrangements were designed by Dagenham's truck engineers.

Another problem was that Dagenham only built the basic 3.6 litre V8 engine, and this produced insufficient power to guarantee the performance requirements laid down in the ministry contract. To overcome this, 5000 of the larger-bored versions of the sidevalve V8 engines were shipped to Dagenham by Ford of Canada. These were of 3.92 litres, with 95 bhp and 170 lbs ft torque against the English Ford's 85 bhp and 150 lbs ft.

After prototypes had successfully undergone rigorous tests at the Service Proving Ground at Chobham, the four-wheel-drive military model entered production on June 4th, 1952. The contract called for three versions, these being: Model 2E, General Service Truck complete with power winch, 1408 examples (production 4th June 1952 to 5th February 1953); Model 3E, Ambulance, 782 examples (production 16th June 1952 to 11th February 1953); Model 4E, Stores Bin Vehicle, 2810 examples (production 23rd July 1952 to 24th February 1953).

1953 also saw the debut of Ford of Britain's own design truck engines, with the four-cylinder petrol and diesel units, both of 3.6 litres capacity and featuring overhead valves, being the first to go into production. The petrol engine developed 70 bhp at 2800 rpm, with the corresponding figure for the diesel being 60 bhp at 2400 rpm. Six-cylinder units, a petrol engine of 4.88 litres and 112 bhp at 3600 rpm, and a 5.4 litre diesel of 105 bhp at 2500 rpm were to follow.

With the availability of the new overhead valve "fours", which would offer useful fuel economy gains over the existing V8 engine, now was the time to review the ET line up. Advertised as the "Cost Cutter" range, came revamped ET models in 2, 3 and 4 ton truck capacities and a 2 ton van, all available with either the petrol or diesel four-cylinder unit. The ET designation disappeared from these, being replaced by 500E (petrol) and 502E (diesel). Left-hand drive versions were 501E and 503E. The 5 tonner remained as before with the V8 petrol engine.

With the ET/500E models offering good coverage on the commercial vehicle market, and now greater economy of operation from the Cost Cutter engines on all but the top payload model, there was no desperate urgency for the projected replacements. Nevertheless, following trials with the early 6 ton prototypes, and the development from these of the 4 x 4 military vehicles of 1952, chassis design for the new range which would eventually emerge as the Thames Trader was now almost finalised. Management approval had not in fact yet been given for the full programme as submitted by truck engineering, only stage one having been given the production go-ahead. This was for a forward control range of 30 cwt, 2 ton, 3, 4, and 5 ton capacity models, with the new six-cylinder engines included for the 4 and 5 ton variations. However, although design was coming on well, there was still no sign of a suitable cab. Briggs Motor Bodies, who were acquired by Ford during 1953 to become the Ford Body Division, had submitted several designs including the previously mentioned "Atlantic" which bore some resemblance to the ET; none however were considered suitable.

Dagenham's Director of Engineering during this period was a colourful American character, seconded to Ford of Britain to act in an advisory capacity during the time the company changed over to producing all-British models. He now suggested a cab design in which the windscreen featured a reverse slope (similar to the rear window of the 105E Anglia car of 1959), his idea being based upon that of the pilot's cockpit screen of an American fighter plane. Prototypes to this configuration were built and tested, but the results were far from satisfactory. Each report from drivers and observers complained that reflections of all road markings ahead travelled up the windscreen, so causing considerable confusion for the driver. After several modifications which were to no avail the design had to be abandoned, much to the Director's disappointment. So, it was back to a more conventional forward control cab design, but with distinctive styling to be incorporated if possible providing that the interior dimensions ensured a comfortable driving position, easily reached controls and easily read instrumentation.

The result of what had proved to be a lengthy development programme was at last seen at London's White City in March 1957 with the announcement there of the Thames Trader range to all Ford dealers, hauliers, and other transport operators. A particular feature of the announcement was the demonstration by mechanics of the ease and extraordinarily short time in which the engine could be removed for either overhaul or replacement.

The 30 cwt, 2 and 3 ton models were powered by the four-cylinder engine in either petrol or diesel configuration, and available only on the short wheelbase (138 inch) chassis, whereas the 4 and 5 ton trucks, which featured six-cylinder power, could be supplied in both short (138 inch) and long (160 inch) wheelbase lengths. A 5 cubic yard tipper on a 108 inch wheelbase once again featured the underfloor ram by Anthony Hoist Ltd., or the Edbro Tippers front end ram. Also on this wheelbase (108 inches) was a new articulated tractor unit for combination weights of up to 29,000 lbs. The tippers and the tractor featured either of the six-cylinder engines, petrol or diesel, as standard equipment. The Trader entered production alongside the elderly ET/500E series four-cylinder models which were to continue for some time yet as attractive low-cost trucks, albeit somewhat outdated now.

The overloading problems which had afflicted the earlier range were soon evident with the newcomers. Investigations into major component failures, on the Trader 5 tonner and 5 cubic yard tipper in particular, drew the obvious conclusion that serious overloading was still widespread. A heavier capacity truck was obviously needed, and realising this now, Ford management approved the second stage of the originally submitted truck programme. This second phase covered a 7 ton truck chassis, 6 cubic yard tipper, an articulated tractor unit for greater maximum combination weights, and two six-wheelers. The design involved a deeper chassis frame, heavier suspension, and a new heavy duty front axle; the remaining mechanical elements, and alternative wheelbases were as on the 5 ton Trader. Chassis cab and chassis front end versions were to be available for the mounting of special bodies.

The views of operators were now sought as part of a thorough review on the design and suitability of six-wheel trucks. Two models were under consideration. One for normal road duty, including both long distance haulage and light tipping operations, whilst the other was for the real heavy duty work such as that involved in off-road and site operations.

Design work for the new generation of normal duty six-wheelers was carried out in conjunction with County Commercial Cars Ltd., whose previous design as used on the 7V and ET series was not now considered suitable for further development. The result of investigations into several possibilities was that the four-spring non-reactive suspension type was decided upon. The four springs were attached to the rear axles in the usual manner, but with the rear end of the foremost spring being connected to a shackle and a pivot arm at the centre whilst the front end was attached to the frame by the usual spring bracket. The front end of the rearmost spring was attached to the centre pivot arm bracket in a similar manner as with a conventional bracket, with the rear end to a shackle and rear pivot arm bracket. Two connecting rods, one each side, were attached at their front ends to a lever on the central pivot arm shaft inside the frame sidemembers, and the rear ends to a similar lever inside the sidemembers on the rear pivot arm shaft. With this arrangement, as one axle rises to surmount an obstruction the other axle is automatically subjected to heavy downward forces by the connecting rods, and therefore providing maximum traction.

Collaboration with All Wheel Drive Ltd., of Camberley, Surrey, was undertaken in respect of the proposed new heavy duty off-road six-wheel design, in which it was essential that the rear bogie would have sufficient articulation to virtually walk over the extremely rough ground so often encountered on development sites. To achieve this a two-spring design, already in widespread use on heavier vehicles elsewhere in Britain and the United States, was adopted. Each spring is mounted longitudinally between the fore and aft axles, and attached to these at its extremities, whilst being mounted at its centre point to a centre pivot bracket attached to the frame sidemembers. Additionally are four torque reaction rods, two per side, one linked to the foremost axle and the bottom of the spring centre bracket, and the other likewise from the rearmost axle.

Although it had originally appeared in the new truck programme, the military four-wheel-drive model had not been developed to become an integral part of Ford's civilian truck range. However, Ford had procured the services of All Wheel Drive Ltd. to produce such a model as a "special build", utilising major assemblies such as the front-wheel-drive axle and the auxiliary transfer box designed for the military truck. Now based on the 7 ton chassis, this became available in the three wheelbase lengths of 108, 138 and 160 inches.

Extending the scope of the Trader range further, as a result of demand, a long wheelbase tipper chassis was announced. This was based on the regular 138 inch wheelbase chassis but with the rear of the frame shortened to suit the required tipping pivot location. As this particular chassis length had not been originally designed to accommodate tipping bodies, Ford approval was only granted for bodies where appropriate sub-frames were fitted.

Ford's marketing division was now requesting transmission options in the form of five-speed gearboxes, whilst two-speed final drive assemblies were also being considered with which to give the flexibility of performance desirable in hilly districts. Although by this time the truck engineering staff numbered twenty individuals it was not considered that they were in a position to undertake the design from scratch, and the development of any new major assemblies within a suitable period of time. In any case, the Dagenham plant didn't have the capacity either to manufacture any additional large assemblies. Therefore, a thorough investigation was carried out regarding the suitability of available transmissions within the industry, with the products of David Brown, E N V, Turner-Newall, and Meadows all being reviewed. Eventually, after arduous testing, it was the Turner five-speed synchromesh type which was chosen, albeit with modifications, particularly in respect of the synchromesh, which had been necessary to gain Ford's approval.

The Timken Detroit Axle Co. already supplying Ford with the normal hypoid bevel rear axle assemblies in use, also had available a two-speed gear set. This design was an arrangement of spur gears which could be fitted straight into the existing rear axle casing. However, there was another option which was to prove more attractive. This was the Eaton two-speed axle of epicyclic gear train design. A less cumbersome and usefully lighter assembly than the Timken, the Eaton possessed the added advantage that it was being manufactured in Britain by both Rubery Owen and E N V. As only a slight modification was required to the existing axle housing in order to accommodate the Eaton two-speed set, this was the type selected.

Early 1959 saw a further extension of the Trader theme with the introduction of a new low-frame chassis in the regular payload categories from 30 cwt through to 5 tons, but no provision had as yet been made to supplement the 2 ton van still available in the old semi-forward control 500E range. Market research indicated a requirement for an easy entry and exit design, virtually a walk in and walk out type of vehicle for such purposes as mobile

shops etc. Working this time in conjunction with commercial vehicle body builders, Garner Motors Ltd., of Acton, London, the Ford Truck engineering Division developed a walk-through design. The basis for this vehicle was the short wheelbase 2 ton low-frame chassis, but with relocated control pedals. On to this was mounted a new front end which nevertheless retained the Trader's established styling features and radiator grille. This front end, complete with cab floor and driver's seat was developed by Garners who supplied the completed front ends to Ford.

For line production of this model a "special build" system was inaugurated on an "Add and Delete Vehicle List" basis. This list accompanied an appropriate chassis which then received the special treatment necessary, such as the relocating of the control pedals which was required before the addition of the special Garner front end. This system allowed final assembly of low-volume derivatives to take place on the same lines as the regular models.

Prior to the introduction of the Trader, Ford of Britain had maintained the use of the American Budd type wheel fixing, which for the dual rear wheels had a double nut arrangement. This had now been abandoned in favour of the British and European Standards of wheel fixing so that wheel interchangeability could be international. Supplies of these were available to Ford from both Sankey and Ford's own subsidiary the Kelsey Hayes Wheel Co. who were encouraged to adopt this type. In co-operation with Ford's truck engineering staff, Kelsey Hayes made many improvements in wheel design around this time, during which the development of truck tubeless tyres with drop centre wheel rims took place, resulting in this feature becoming yet another Trader option.

Truck production was now at the rate of 100 per day, this figure being greater than at any time previously for Ford of Britain commercial vehicles, and a notable achievement indeed as production of these was based on sales in advance. Nevertheless, this popularity notwithstanding, there were continuing complaints regarding failures from both domestic and overseas users. Investigations again showed that these were often due to overloading, and paricularly so in third world countries where vehicle ill-treatment was commonplace and much of the usage was over unmade roads and very rough terrain.

In an effort to combat these apparent inevitabilities, a complete review of the Trader range was carried out; improvements were incorporated, and the range was re-introduced as the Mk2 series. Featured on those models of 5 tons capacity and above in the Mk2 range was the Hydrovac braking system involving direct vacuum assistance to the hydraulic brakes. This replaced the upright Clayton servo-assisted arrangements incorporating a mechanical linkage which were being retained on the lighter models. Other improvements were the introduction of the Simms Minimec fuel injection pump along with new fuel nozzles as optional equipment to the Bosch and CAV injection systems; the availability of the Turner five-speed transmission as standard equipment on certain models; the introduction of an increased capacity rating rear axle of 18,500 lbs., and some improvements to the cab.

To identify the improved series the badging arrangements were changed so that just the word "Thames" appeared along the lower edge of the short bonnet, whilst the word "Trader' was now featured in large letters in the lower grille between the headlamps. Further identification within the range was now by two digits: 15 for the 30 cwt, 20 for the 2 ton, and so up to the 7 ton model designated 70. These designations appeared within a circular badge located on the radiator grille. As a result of further market research an additional top of the range Trader 75 also appeared. This was in effect the basic 70 model but equipped with stronger road springs and larger, low-pressure tyres, and therefore capable of handling a $7^1/_2$ ton payload.

Late in 1961, production of the bonnetted type ET-based 500E/502E was discontinued, so bringing to an end the line which could be traced right back to the introduction of the Model BB in 1932. A normal control model within the Trader range had not been envisaged, but a market research exercise carried out now suggested a sales potential which although not high, would just about justify production of such a vehicle now. A request was submitted to Truck Engineering for their proposals for such a range. The Sales Division suggested a similar market coverage to that of the forward control Trader; 30 cwt, 2, 3, 4, and 5 ton truck chassis with accommodation for float lengths of 132, 150, and 180 inches.

New frames were designed incorporating a slight sweep over the rear axle in order to provide a lower frame height overall. There were to be three wheelbase lengths: 132 inch for the 30 cwt, 2 and 3 ton; 146 inch for the 2 to 5 ton inclusive; and a 166 inch wheelbase to be available on the 3, 4, and 5 ton trucks. A new front axle with lowered spring seats was compatible with the lower-slung chassis, whilst to maintain a comfortable steering wheel rake a universal joint was introduced into the steering column just beneath the steering wheel. The various capacity rear axles were specified to suit the axle loadings expected with the normal control set-up. A departure from past Ford practice was the introduction of Lockheed hydraulic brakes to the commercial vehicle line in place of the Girling system employed by the forward control models. Lockheed's own suspended vacuum servo arrangements featured on those models up to 4 tons capacity, whilst the new 5 tonner was to retain the Clayton Hydrovac type. The existing four-cylinder petrol and diesel engines were employed.

There remained the question of a new cab, and suggestions that this could be based on either that of the forward control Trader but with a suitably lengthened bonnet, or that of the ET/500E with a restyled front end and grille were considered. However, Ford of Germany had recently ceased truck production and had available a reasonably new normal control cab which Ford of Britain were requested to adopt. Cologne shipped a number of cabs, panels, and tooling to the Body Division at Dagenham for evaluation, with the result being that this design was decided upon. Considerable modifications however were necessary, not least of which was the adaptation to right-hand drive for the British market whilst of course retaining left-hand drive for sales in Dagenham's export territories. Secondly, was the need to provide mounting points to suit the British chassis, and thirdly a revamp of the front end panelwork and grille to the Dagenham stylist's liking and to accommodate relocated lamps conforming to the British Construction and Use regulations. The words Thames and Trader were to occupy similar positions at the front to those of the forward control Trader.

As production of the walk-through had ceased after only a few pilot-build examples, the idea was revived now with the availability of these lower normal control chassis, of which the 132 inch wheelbase version was considered to be better suited to the special-build arrangements with the Garner front end and floor assembly. Production commenced with a complete range of these vans embracing the 30 cwt, 2 and 3 ton categories. Thus, the Trader range was complete, with designations being: forward control, 508E consecutively to 530E; normal control, 622E consecutively to 660E.

The normal control Trader was announced at London's Grosvenor House Hotel. Here, a panel consisting of marketing, sales, production, product planning, and truck engineering staff representing the company faced an audience of representatives of Ford dealerships, various trades, transport operators and hauliers, so as to answer questions relative to the merits being claimed for this new normal control Trader range.

As a whole, the Trader range offered considerable scope for operators within that 30 cwt to $7^1/2$ ton payload, and, as with all previous Fords, bodywork was available from many outside concerns with which to satisfy the needs of the operator requiring something other than the regular Ford models. Chassis modifications, too, could be carried out to order. Primrose, of Clitheroe, Lancashire, offered a twin steer six-wheel conversion for the Trader 75, in addition to a more conventional six-wheel conversion on the 75 and other models. BAICO, as was their speciality, would carry out both wheelbase extensions or chassis shortening if required.

Remaining in production until February 1965, the normal control Trader reached a production total of 19,708, for a yearly average of 6350. This did not compare so well with the 15,232 annual rate of the forward control models over the production period May 1957 to July

1965, which had resulted in the 121,353 examples setting the highest production rate so far for a Ford of Britain commercial vehicle.

Soon after the introduction of the normal control Trader, as a result of the entire production capacity at Dagenham being required for the ever expanding passenger car production, truck assembly operations there had been terminated. An old aircraft factory at Langley, in Buckinghamshire, from where wartime Hawker Hurricane fighter planes had once emerged, was to be the new commercial vehicle assembly plant. Leased by Ford some years previously for other uses, 300,000 square feet of hangar space was now cleared for Thames Trader production. It was decided to install the Truck Engineering Division here too, thus forming a complete truck organisation at Langley, although it was rumoured that this move may well be a short term affair as discussions were being held regarding the possible complete reorganisation of both car and truck engineering divisions. Suggestions leaked out, including one on the transfer truck engineering to Canada, indicating that Ford of Canada would become responsible for Ford's world-wide truck development. However, this proved to be incorrect, perhaps in part due to the objections raised by both staff and trade unions in Britain. Even the move to Langley was called off at the last minute, only to be followed some time later by a move which saw the members of the truck engineering facility occupying space at the company's Aveley parts depot. This, too, was said to be a short term measure until such time as suitable modern premises could be found elsewhere. In fact, conditions at Aveley proved so totally unsuitable that a return to Rainham quickly took place, and it was not until 1964 that the Truck Engineering Division took up residence in a new multi-storey building at Gants Hill in Ilford.

The Trader range had not of course been the only Ford commercial vehicle line in production during this time. As we have seen, towards the lower end of the market the prewar designed 10 hp E83W model had continued to serve Ford extremely well in the early postwar period, in fact remaining remarkably popular well into the 1950s. However, developments elsewhere were such that Ford would have to replace this model with something modern in order to keep their market share in this sector. Market research by the company's Product Planning Department indicated the need for a van which could cope with 10, 12, and 15 cwt payloads, and with a reasonable cubic capacity utilising the maximum space possible within compact external dimensions. With these requirements set as the main objectives, the idea of an entirely new van range was approved by the company's top management.

Unfortunately, truck engineering staff at Rainham were not able to cope with such a programme whilst still paying attention to the new truck range (Trader) then under development. Overcoming this problem was the acquisition of premises in Birmingham to house another research and design facility, with this being staffed under the direction of one of the truck division's senior engineers.

Studies were made of the competition in this sector, with the Morris Commercial 10 cwt and 15/20 cwt models, of prewar design; Austin 10 cwt, and later their 25 cwt; Trojan 15 cwt van; and the Bedford 10/12 cwt model all coming in for scrutiny. One proposal, backed by Dearborn, was that the American Ford Econoline van should go into production at Dagenham, thus eliminating any design problems whilst also saving considerably on development costs. This model had however one very serious drawback in that its extremely forward-mounted, and rather heavy engine, resulted in what was considered by some at Ford of Britain to be a dangerous weight distribution in the unladen state. In this state, if firm braking was applied, the rear wheels could be lifted clear of the road on level ground, and it was felt by some that the Econoline could easily somersault end-over-end if an emergency stop was attempted on a down grade.

A new British range was therefore decided upon, to be of the forward control type and of monocoque construction for the van, but based on a ladder type chassis for the pick-up truck and some other variants. A wheelbase of 84 inches was chosen, upon which was accommodated a van body of 180 cubic feet capacity. After some discussion, independent front suspension was sanctioned, but not of the MacPherson strut type which Dagenham had pioneered in the monocoque passenger car applications for which it had been specifically designed in the first place. This system was considered, but its inclusion in the forward control, forward entrance van would, primarily because of the strut height, have placed serious restrictions on cab design particularly in respect of entry. Instead, a system of coil springs and transverse wishbones was agreed upon, and as in this respect the Econoline checked out satisfactorily according to Ford of Britain, a set of drawings of the Econoline's coil and wishbone system was obtained from Dearborn.

An ideal engine and transmission existed amongst Dagenham's passenger car range, this being the Consul's 1703 cc ohv engine, with its associated three-speed gearbox with synchromesh between the upper two ratios and a column gearchange mechanism, and the two pinion differential three quarter floating final drive. The low compression (6.9:1) version of this engine, developing 53 bhp at 4400 rpm was chosen, with the Consul's regular high compression cylinder head (7.8:1) being optional on the new van. A further option was to be the Perkins 4/99 diesel, this being a 1.6 litre four-cylinder unit producing only 42 bhp, therefore somewhat marginal from a performance viewpoint but offering useful long-term economies over the petrol engine.

Production commenced in September 1957, with the model being announced as the Thames 400E series. A bold Thames nameplate appeared on the front beneath which was a circular emblem containing the appropriate figure identifying the vehicle's capacity class. The new model quickly met with widespread approval, and passenger transport use was soon being catered for with the availability of an 8/10-seater estate car derivative, and a 12-seat minibus based on the 15 cwt model. The success of the estate car variant was such that it later became available in a De Luxe configuration, complete with chrome plated overriders for its front bumper, chrome side mouldings and window trims, and dual exterior mirrors.

Within only a short space of time a wide variety of special bodies was available from outside suppliers, with Ford approval for these being confirmed in many cases by their inclusion in the Ford Motor Company's official glossy brochures. Mobile shops, milk floats, ambulances, flat platform trucks with generators or compressors, Luton vans, box vans, and the popular pick-up trucks all appeared. The latter became a bestseller, and by 1961 was listed by Ford as a standard model. Other popular variations of the 400E were the motorised caravans, with those of M. Calthorpe (Coachbuilders) Ltd.; Airborne Service Equipment Ltd.; Kenex Coachworks Ltd.; Moortown Motors Ltd.; M.T.S. & Co. Ltd.; Peter Pitt; and Martin Walter Ltd., all appearing in Ford's "Holiday Adventurers" brochure dealing exclusively with motor caravans.

Left-hand drive 400E models were available from the start, thus ensuring healthy overseas sales, with one of the many European countries taking the 400E van being Denmark where the Ford Motor Company did have an assembly plant. Ford of Denmark sales staff requested authority from Britain to market an increased wheelbase chassis cab version of the 400E to meet specific local demands, and a senior truck engineer from Rainham travelled to Ford's Copenhagen plant to investigate the possibility. Danish Ministry of Transport approval was also necessary, and all testing on their behalf was carried out at the University of Denmark's laboratories. Appropriate care had been taken in lengthening the chassis frame, and after the lengthened propeller shaft had successfully undergone testing which would have revealed any shortcomings such as vibration due to run-out, or critical whirling speeds the conversion received the approval of the Danish ministry and Ford of Britain's senior truck engineer.

During 1963, updated versions of the 1703 cc petrol engine became available, with both low and high-compression ratio versions having improved power outputs in line with the uprated unit as fitted to the Zephyr 4 passenger car which had replaced the Consul. With the high-compression engine now came the passenger car's new four-speed all synchromesh gearbox, and a heavy duty rear axle unit with a four pinion differential. Production of the range continued until September 1965, by which time a total of 187,000 had been built.

Meanwhile, during 1961, the parent company had taken over the full control of Ford of Britain by purchasing all the shares held here by anyone outside the company, and even those held within by Ford employees in Britain. This was, according to Detroit, to protect all Ford interests in the United Kingdom, and there were assurances that there was no intention to dictate to Ford of Britain, policy, designs, and markets in which the company would compete.

Nevertheless, it was not long afterwards that American engineers began to infiltrate both car and truck engineering divisions, whilst other American staff came into finance, product planning, production, marketing, and even into junior management positions. Dearborn was not completely satisfied that Ford of Britain had the number of experienced engineers necessary, or the sound marketing knowledge, to build and promote a really successful commercial vehicle range. They hinted that in their opinion the Thames Trader range was not a success, in spite of its relatively high sales performance. There certainly was some justification for these views as, unlike their strongest competitors in the truck business here, prior to World War Two Ford of Britain had less than a handful of experienced engineers, and even these were primarily car men. The company's own experience of truck development and engineering had only really been gained over the relatively short period of the development and production of the Trader range, as before this, as we have already seen, Dagenham's trucks had been little more than copies of the prewar American series. Additionally, over the entire period, Ford of Britain's management had not been particularly commercial vehicle minded, their thoughts and concentration having been first and foremost on what was always considered to be the company's main bread and butter product, passenger cars.

Many truck complaints by customers had been dealt with under warranty whether justified or not, simply due to the fear of losing buyers. Certainly, some complaints were legitimate in respect of both quality and some design features. The majority, however, were the result of maltreatment due, primarily, to excessive overloading. The 5 ton Trader and 5 cubic yard tipper models had suffered greatly from this form of misuse prior to the advent of the 7 ton model, after which rather less overloading took place on the 5 tonners, but with the practice continuing now on the 7 ton range! Other complaints arose simply due to the use of unsuitable vehicles for particular operations, as many trucks were being purchased on the basis of vehicle cost alone. In respect of this situation the company could perhaps take some of the blame, as little correct marketing had been accomplished in respect of advising operators on selecting the right vehicle for the job; the number of sales had seemed to be the only important consideration.

Naturally, fully aware of their overloading, and in some cases other obvious misuse, many operators were almost rubbing their hands with glee at Ford's warranty payments. It was more economical to buy a cheaper model, overload it from the start and get any failed components as a result replaced free before the guarantee period expired, then work it into the ground before replacing it with another cheap model on the same basis. In fact, it is reckoned that Ford actually gained sales as a result of their leniency over warranty claims – but at what cost?

Clearly, this situation could not be allowed to continue, and the American attitude was that if Ford of Britain wanted to go into the truck business, then it must *go* into the truck business, not half-heartedly as before; go from the bottom to the top, learn the market and cater for it fully. The criticisms were accepted by Ford of Britain's management, and the parent company's advice was sought regarding a new truck range. The company was facing stiff competition in Britain. Bedford's TK range had held a good portion of the market since its introduction in

1959, and Dodge, Karrier, Commer, Austin and Morris Commercial were all in there and anxious to expand. Additionally were the non mass-producers such as Leyland, Atkinson, Seddon, Foden, and ERF still holding a reasonable part of the market. Nevertheless, Dearborn agreed to a new British truck, but with one reservation: if this new range was not a complete success then Ford of Britain would withdraw from the commercial vehicle market.

American engineers were to assist in planning the new range, and a new section, Advanced Truck Design, was set up within the truck engineering division, to be supervised by an American but still under the overall control of the current chief truck engineer. The programme was to be in two distinct phases, and was to give Ford of Britain's salesmen the most comprehensive range of vehicles they had ever known; it was aimed from the beginning at nothing less than market leadership. The range would be identified as the D series, with the load capacity being indicated by the first figure following the D: D 200 = 2 ton. Forward control was to feature throughout the range in the interests of maximum float length, always a most important marketing point, on the shortest appropriate wheelbase, with the best possible front and rear axle weight distribution determining the wheelbase measurements. Excellent driver visibility and vehicle manoeuvrability are also a natural outcome of the forward control layout.

Phase one was to deal with the lower payload models ranging from 2 to 8 tons, with the range consisting of: D200, 300, 400, 500, 600, 700, 750, and D800 trucks; D500, 600, 700, and D800 articulated tractor units; D750 and D800 tippers; and D800 six-wheelers in both 6 x 2 and 6 x 4 configuration. The float lengths and corresponding wheelbases were: 168 inch on 120 inch wheelbase; 192 inch on 134 inch; 220 inch on 156 inch; 258 inch on 182 inch; and 288 inch on 260 inch, all on the four-wheeled chassis. The tippers, of 6 and 7 cubic yard capacity, with underfloor or front end hydraulic rams and either drop- or fixed-sided bodies, were both on a 108 inch wheelbase. The six-wheel chassis cab, single drive on/off road model was available in 138 inch, 154, 178, and 190 inch wheelbases, whilst the cross country double-drive was in just three wheelbase lengths of 146, 178, and 190 inches. The articulated tractor units were purpose-built on a short wheelbase length of 94 inches.

Each model was packaged with its appropriate front axle, suspension, engine, transmission, braking system, and tyre sizes to suit general road operation.

A new range of Dagenham built diesel engines, based on the current designs but with various improvements were released, these being inclined and therefore able to provide a better cab floor line by keeping the engine cowling intrusion to a minimum. This engine range comprised the 240 four-cylinder in-line of 3964 cc, and 82.5 bhp at 2800 rpm; 330 six-cylinder in-line, 5416 cc, 115 bhp at 2800 rpm; and the 360 six-cylinder in-line of 5945 cc and 128 bhp at 2800 rpm. In view of the comparatively few petrol engined vehicles being sold by this time it was decided to withdraw the Dagenham built petrol engines, and to satisfy the requirements for this type of engine now by substituting two readily available American Ford in-line six-cylinder units. These were the 240, of 3933 cc and 129 bhp at 3800 rpm; and the 300, of 4916 cc and 149 bhp at 3800 rpm.

For the drive line there were three basic transmissions, one being a Ford four-speed synchromesh, whilst the other two were five-speed gearboxes of Turner design and manufacture. The choice of rear axles extended to six, four of these being Ford single-speed hypoid bevel types, with the other two being Eaton two-speed spiral bevel assemblies.

Two new front axles of different ratings were allied to front suspension of the conventional semi-elliptic leaf spring type with the springs shackled at their rear end. For models up to and including the D400 conventional rear suspension also consisting of semi-elliptics shackled at their rear end prevailed. However, for the D500 to D800 trucks and tippers came a new form of rear suspension, the radial leaf with slipper ends sliding in the front and rear brackets. This system consisted of a semi-elliptic main spring with slipper ends, with the addition of a radial leaf spring of two or three quarter elliptic leaves sandwiched between the main spring and the spring seat on the rear axle, with the top radial leaf attached to the front rear spring bracket by means of a pivot pin. The claim was that the system had variable rate characteristics in that the spring effective length varied between laden and unladen conditions of load, thus eliminating the need for helper springs. The six-wheeler suspension arrangements remained as before with the four spring system for on/off road operation and the two spring system for cross country work. For the articulated tractor units there was to be no change from the standard conventional semi-elliptic leaf springs front and rear.

The braking equipment was tailored to suit each model, ensuring that each came within the legislative requirements, and encompassed the following systems: vacuum servo with mechanically operated parking brake; single air hydraulic with power assisted parking brake; dual line air over hydraulic with power assisted parking brake and emergency brake for the articulated tractor units.

To provide the operator with exactly what he wanted a great deal of optional equipment was essential, with this being divided into two categories. In the first of these are what are termed Regular Production Options (R.P.O.), which have a reasonable market sufficient to justify being included on the main Ford assembly line when specified, whilst in the other category are casual options which can either be fitted by an authorised Ford agent, or in some cases by the operators themselves.

The new cab was pleasantly styled, providing accommodation for driver and two passengers, and with the underfloor engine gave easy access to the driving seat from either side of the vehicle. Daily servicing was hopefully assured by the hinged access panels at the front of the cab for checking brake and clutch fluid reservoir levels. Access to the electrical system fuses and the wiper motor was also gained through these panels, whilst an additional inspection cover inside the cab between the seats revealed the engine oil dipstick and gave access for routine engine adjustments. For major servicing and overhauls the cab could be tilted forward, leaving the engine and drive line fully exposed. After first removing all loose items from the cab the procedure was to then place the gearlever in a position where it would clear the cab floor during the tilting movement, remove the safety clamp bolt located inside the cab at the rear, and finally, outside the cab after ensuring all doors are closed, the release of the locking catch at the rear of the cab. The cab would then tilt slowly by the assistance of torsion bars which then held it securely in its maximum tilt position. For non-tilt cabs and front ends there was an access panel on top of the seat pan and engine cowling for servicing etc.

More than a hundred pre-production D series vehicles of a wide variety were built and offered to operators for a trial period. As can be imagined, this met with widespread approval in the transport world, and there was no shortage whatsoever of haulage contractors, goods manufacturers operating their own truck fleets, and one-man owner/operators volunteering to try out the new Fords. With such a number of vehicles covering all manner of operations with the Evening News, British United Airways, Birds Eye Frozen Foods, Horne Brothers, and many more, all kinds of comment and criticisms were fed back to truck engineering by a group of engineers sent out into the field to work with the operators during the trial period. These comments and criticisms were acted upon wherever necessary before the actual production commenced.

The complete D truck range was announced at a Ford Commercial Vehicle Show held in the Exhibition Centre at the Grand Hotel in Brighton. Truck engineering representatives who were present on the first day were congratulated by the company's management on their achievement in providing such an extensive and comprehensive range of new commercial vehicles.

The complexity of the range was such that the Sales Division produced a salesman's handbook with which he could familiarize himself with all aspects of the D series, and therefore be able to point out to his prospects the merits of the various models and their suitability for particular operations. The opening passage in the handbook remarked: "The

'D' Series, as the name implies, is constituted by a number of features, options and benefits. Memorizing and applying them to your operator's requirements is a big task. Only practice in the use of a planned method of presenting them will ensure that you cover all the points that matter. The following '7 Step Walkround' is one such method. By getting into the habit of organising your presentation along these lines you will be able to handle your prospect's questions in their right place by keeping your control over the selling situation''. The '7 Step Walkround' was a system devized in which the salesman with his customer view the vehicle first from the front, then proceeding around the offside, to the rear, and then along the nearside of the vehicle pointing out all the features.

With such a comprehensive range within Phase 1, there was a great demand for the mounting of special bodies and conversions. Ford of America had encountered such requests for special vehicles from within their truck ranges and having studied the subject decided that this special vehicle business could be a money spinner – why should the outside vehicle conversion specialists have all the profits? Having therefore established a Special Vehicle Organisation, building specials based on standard production models to their own customer's individual requirements, Dearborn now suggested to Ford of Britain that they set up a similar operation. This resulted in a Special Vehicle Options organisation with its own marketing, engineering, and special build being created and housed at the Langley plant.

It was during the development of the first phase of the new truck programme that pressure within the company had seen the Truck Engineering Division take up residence in their new premises at Gants Hill, and here they settled down to the next phase of the D series development which would complete the range. With the designation D1000 covering all models, this phase was to deal with trucks, tippers, and articulated tractor units from 15 tons gross, to 28 tons gross vehicle weights.

Of 15 tons and 16 tons gross were two new tippers with underfloor or front end hydraulic tipping rams, and either fixed- or drop-sided bodies, the wheelbases for these were 120 inches and 147 inches for the 15 and 16 tonners, respectively. Rated at 16 tons gross vehicle weight was a truck chassis available in four wheelbase lengths, these being 147 inches, 165, 188, and 206 inches, upon which could be accommodated float lengths of 177 inches, 201, 234, and 264 inches, respectively. Able to cope with gross combination weights of 24 tons and 28 tons came two articulated tractor units both on a 144 inch wheelbase, and with fifth wheel coupling positioned in the recommended position ahead of the rear axle.

Initially, the power unit was the Cummins Mark V 'Vale' 470 diesel, a V8-cylinder engine of 7702 cc developing 170 bhp at 3000 rpm in its basic tune, with a higher output version developing 185 bhp at 3300 rpm also available on these Fords. Later, Ford introduced a further diesel engine as an alternative to the Cummins. Also available in two power rating, 170 bhp at 2600 rpm and 185 bhp at 2600 rpm, this 8336 cc V8 unit was developed by Ford in conjunction with Perkins, and marketed as the Ford 511. For the drive line there were three transmissions, two of these being heavy duty Turner five-speed synchromesh gearboxes, and the other a ZF six-speed synchromesh unit. A Ford single-speed hypoid bevel axle, or one of either two Eaton two-speed spiral bevel final drives completed the power train.

As with the smaller models, the D1000s were eached packaged with the appropriate front axle, suspension, tyres and braking systems to suit general road operations. Two new front axles of 9500 lbs and 14,000 lbs rated capacity were in conjunction with the conventional front suspension of semi-elliptic leaf springs shackled at their front end. All models were equipped with a radial leaf suspension system at their rear, and full air operated braking arrangements. The same degree of optional equipment was available as on phase 1 models, with special vehicles being accommodated by the Special Vehicle Options organisation. To distinguish the D1000 models was a chrome plated horizontally ribbed grille on the cab front panel above the radiator grille.

Continuing to operate alonside the D series, the normal control Trader models underwent a market re-alignment to be re-introduced as the K series truck. Three models were announced, a 6 ton and a 7 ton truck chassis, and a 7 ton tipper. Re-designed K150 and K700, these normal control vehicles lost their former Trader identification completely, with the name FORD now appearing in large letters in the centre panel of the radiator grille. Engineering responsibility for these was transferred to Special Vehicle Engineering at Lanley. During the same period the Clearway walk-through van range was also re-aligned as the M series, with models, M150, M200, and M300.

In 1968 Ford of Britain introduced another six-cylinder diesel engine, based upon the 360 (5945 cc) unit, but with the addition of an exhaust driven Holsted turbocharger with which it developed 150 bhp at 2400 rpm. This new version was made available for the D1000 16 ton gross truck and the D800 20 ton gross combination weight articulated tractor units as an alternative powerplant. The tandem six-wheeler range was now uprated from a maximum 17 tons to 24 tons gross, with designations DT1400 (20 tons), DT1500 (22 tons) and DT1700 for the 24 ton gross vehicle weight model. The Ford turbocharged "six", or either of the two V8 engines could be specified.

The Special Vehicle Option packages developed included roadsweepers, crew cabs, automatic coupling conversions for articulated tractor units, tanker body mounting, wheelbase extensions, twin steer conversions, self-loading crane mounting, fire fighting equipment in line with legislation, 17 inch wheel and tyre fitting to comply with the Guernsey overall width regulations, automatic transmission, and many more. Thus, the Ford truck range now offered suitable vehicles for virtually any transport operation.

In order to ensure that new models conformed with overseas regulations, and were acceptable to other countries' government's transport departments, a special section was established. Known as the Homologation Engineering Group, this consisted of a number of senior engineers and clerical staff delegated to work in conjunction with similar establishments in the many other Ford organisations throughout the world. These arrangements ensured that new models and modifications to existing ranges were always fully documented, and able to meet the type approval standards in force wherever Ford exported.

During 1969, problems were becoming frequent due to incorrect body mounting. With so many special bodies and special features available it was becoming difficult to maintain a check on the mounting of various bodies from outside concerns. Combating this, Ford's Quality Control Division formed a team of quality inspectors and engineers to investigate the situation by travelling throughout the country visiting various body building concerns, where body mounting procedure was inspected and advice given regarding the relevant aspects of the Ford chassis. The problems were not just confined to the home market, but extended to overseas countries in Europe where the D series was being exported. The Quality Control Division recommended that truck engineering should issue a booklet to explain, by means of descriptive matter and illustrations, the correct methods which should be adopted for mounting all types of bodies: general floats, tankers, mobile cranes, Luton vans, container bodies, etc., and the mounting points and options available. When completed, the booklet was introduced at a London hotel to representatives of Ford main agents, the Quality Control Division, Ford's European plants, and a wide spectrum of body building specialists. Including examples of bad mounting and the results experienced, in addition to details of correct mounting points and procedures, the book was widely accepted and became the body mounting "bible" to which the company would expect all to conform.

During 1971 the range was reviewed, with the result being several marketing and engineering changes. A new identification coding system was adopted which did now give an indication of both gross vehicle weight and the power unit, consisting of the letter D followed by a four figure number. A new engine range was introduced to replace the current 'Dorset' range. The 240 (3964 cc) was replaced by the 254 (4161 cc); the 330 (5416 cc) was deleted; the

360 (5945 cc) developing 128 bhp was replaced by the 363 (5948 cc) developing 113 bhp, with the former 360 turbocharged variant remaining but also now designated 363. An additional unit now was the 380 (6224 cc) six-cylinder developing 123 bhp. To conform with the new vehicle coding the entire diesel engine range was further re-designated as follows; 254 to 07 (4.2 litre), 363 to 10 (6 litre), 380 to 11 (6.2 litre), 363 turbo to 14 (6 litre turbo), Ford 511 to 16 (8.4 litre low output) and 17 (8.4 litre high output), and the Cummins to 18 (8.3 litre).

The new coding commenced with the D0507, this indicating a 5 tons gross vehicle weight truck with the 4.2 litre engine, and continued up to D1618. For the articulated tractor units the letters DA appeared, with tractors ranging from DA1610 to DA2818. Six-wheeler tandems were designated from DT1711 to DT2418.

Ford of Britain now embarked upon the design, development and manufacture of its own heavy duty commercial transmissions, of four-, six-, and eight-speed type with the internals housed in vertical split cases. The designations for these were 4-410 four-speed, 6-600-S six-speed close ratio, 6-540-S six-speed high ratio, and 8-570-S for the eight-speed unit.

By 1978 the petrol engines had been deleted from the D series trucks, and the low-volume production K series and M series Clearway range were now phased out. The bottom of the range D0507 was also discontinued in favour of the D0607 which was now marketed in two gross vehicle weights of 5.8 tons, and 6.3 tons. The D series cab received a new grille and a redesigned interior featuring passenger car type appointments which provided greater comfort for all occupants.

For the heavier of the tandem six-wheelers a new twin spring bogie made its appearance, consisting of two centrally pivoted minimum leaf springs at each side of the frame, with one above the pivot and one below. The rear axles were attached to the spring eyes by rubber-bushed gimbals. With this arrangement the driving and braking forces are fed directly into the frame at all degrees of articulation with minimum bogie steer effect, and control of bogie wheel movement is therefore at an optimum in both on or off-road conditions. This bogie was available for the 6 x 4, 22 and 24 tons gross six-wheelers. The advent of the Ford designed transmissions saw the deletion of the Turner and ZF gearboxes, with two four-speed, two six-speed, and one eight-speed Ford transmissions being in use. Eight Ford single-speed, and four Eaton two-speed axles were available to complete the drive line, and there were now five differently rated front axles and three braking systems, 'Airpak' air/hydraulic, dual line air/hydraulic, and a full air braking arrangement.

With the D series development completed and phase 1 already in production, and with the phase 2 range ready to start on the assembly lines at Langley another move had been planned for the Truck Engineering Division, but this time not on their own; this move included the Car Engineering Division also.

Ford of Britain had been thinking for years about the possibility of creating a first class car and truck engineering and research centre, but it was not until the parent company had given them a push in this direction that any firm decision was reached. At last, in 1967, a new Ford of Britain Engineering Centre opened at Dunton at the cost of eleven million pounds, for both car and commercial vehicle design development, research and testing, with separate establishments within the concept.

During the American invasion of Ford of Britain's engineering departments they brought with them the American systems. The adoption of these split the division into component specialists under a supervisor responsible to a manager of a group under the leadership of a component engineering executive. Commercial vehicle design was also split into two sections, light vans and trucks, and medium and heavy trucks, each under an executive with the overall control by a chief engineer.

The complicated paperwork system also introduced additional sections in the division of clerical staff; one such section was product engineering timing. This section had the responsibility of ensuring that managers kept within the estimated timing programme

throughout the whole project to Job 1 production date. The system catered for original marketing requirements, product planning and research of competition in any particular marketing, timing of every stage within a programme, a financial controller to study development and design costs including manpower, management acceptance of estimated costs, production engineering process sheets for production manufacturing, purchase of prototype materials and specialised machinery. All to achieve one objective – a predetermined Job 1 production date.

During the time truck engineering accepted the D series project, the advanced engineering section were studying further projects, with a new van range well to the fore.

Ford were confronted wth two huge markets, the Common Market (EEC) of some 200 million people, and the European Free Trade Association (EFTA) consisting of the outer seven countries with a population of 100 million. Reduced internal tariffs and, generally, expanding economies were a feature of these organisations which represented a great opportunity for manufacturers such as Ford. Whatever Britain did in the long term, Ford would have to build up its operations within the EEC. That this was happening in the early 1960s was plain to see, Dearborn and Cologne were co-operating on a new compact passenger car, the front wheel drive Taunus, there was a new Ford factory at Genk, in Belgium, in 1962, to be followed by a tractor plant at Antwerp.

Meanwhile, Ford of Britain was continuing to develop independently, its new Cortina passenger car of 1962 being of similar style and size to the new German Taunus but in fact differing completely in that it shared no components with the German car and retained the conventional rear wheel drive arrangements. The fact that the Cortina was a spectacular success, unlike the front wheel drive German model which was a relative failure, could not however secure Ford of Britain's independence. Rationalisation was inevitable if Ford were to be strong contenders in Europe now, and so the first attempt at a common European Ford range got under way, with Britain and Germany entering into close co-operation in the development of a completely new van.

Dearborn, naturally, took an interest, and approved the name "Transit" which in fact had already been used on a German Ford light commercial range in the past, the models FX1000 and FK1250 light trucks. Dearborn's influence was to be seen too in the design of the new Anglo/German van which was to follow loosely that of the American Econoline, which, itself having gone through continued development was not now being objected to by Ford of Britain in the way it had been some years earlier.

From the outset, this new range was planned around two wheelbase lengths in order to provide the maximum market coverage for this type, the aim being to cover everything the operator required. Convenience in respect of loading/unloading was to be carefully studied in an effort to provide a van with which wherever it stopped to collect or deliver, nearside, offside or the rear, the operator should be able to load and unload from the nearest approach. There were to be two trim and equipment levels, with the Custom version for those who required a rather more impressive appearance and greater cab comforts than the norm for this type of vehicle.

Designated LCX in its short wheelbase (106 inch) form, and LCY with a 118 inch wheelbase, the Transit van would offer 178 cubic feet or 261 cubic feet of load space depending upon which length was chosen. Derivatives of the basic van were a bus and a kombi; the latter being in effect a van with side windows and seat mounting points in the load compartment for the fitting of seats when required. Chassis cab and chassis windshield versions were available for the mounting of special bodies. The LCX catered for 12 cwt, 17 and 22 cwt payloads for the van, kombi, and chassis cab/windshield models, and 9 or 12-seat buses, with the LCY providing for payloads 25, 30 and 35 cwt for the vans etc., and 15 seats in the bus. Dual rear tyre equipment was standard on the LCY.

The power units were the four-cylinder versions of Dagenham's new V configuration ohv petrol engines which, in four-cylinder form were extremely short, thus allowing a normal control layout within an overall length little greater than a forward control model. The LCX featured the 1663 cc unit which developed 73 bhp at 4750 rpm, with the LCY being powered by the 2 litre (1996 cc) version developing 85.5 bhp at 4750 rpm. Initially the Perkins 4/99, but after a short period the Perkins 4/108 four-cylinder in-line diesel engine of 1.7 litres and 52 bhp at 4000 rpm was an option on the LCY 30 and 35 cwt models for restricted applications. Being an in-line "four", the Perkins was of greater length than the Ford V units, and Transits so equipped featured a slightly lengthened nose centre section to accommodate the diesel engine. Completing the drive line on both models was a four-speed all synchromesh gearbox with floor mounted gearchange, an open propeller shaft, and three quarter floating spiral bevel rear axle of various ratings to suit the load capacities. In contrast to the independent front end set up of the preceding 400E, and the Econoline, the front axle and suspension considered to be the most suitable in respect of ground clearance, and to cope with all conditions worldwide was the rigid non-independent I beam axle with semi-elliptic leaf springs assisted by hydraulic telescopic shock absorbers. The conventional semi-elliptics also featured at the rear.

The van was of monocoque construction, and some consideration was given to the possibility of using this method for a light truck variation by using the lower part of the van up to the waistline as the truck body sides, with an inserted back panel behind the driver to form a cab. However, this concept would not have catered for the conventional wooden float, and the box vans which had proved to be a popular fitting on the 400E chassis cab, and therefore a separate chassis was finally decided upon. This was once again of the ladder type, with box section side and cross-members, and with cruciform members inserted in the centre of the frame on the long wheelbase model ensuring adequate rigidity was maintained over the greater length. The chassis windshield version included the whole of the cab floor, which gave added strength to the front of the frame, and was complete with driver's seat ready for delivery to the body builder.

On the vans, two rear loading doors were standard equipment, along with a forward-hinged side loading door on either side in addition to the hinged cab doors. Optional sliding side loading doors were available, as were sliding cab doors; but with the latter the side loading doors were omitted. A lift up tailgate was a further option highlighting the versatility of this van range.

Introduced in September 1965, the Transit quickly met with widespread approval, which was not surprising when it is realised that with engine options, body options, Custom trim, left-hand drive etc., more than 80 different models were available, and taking into account other extra-cost options etc., over 1000 variations were possible.

In 1966, a parcels van, based on the chassis windshield in both wheelbase lengths, gave either a 290 cubic feet or 390 cubic feet capacity. Of walk-through design, this model featured a glass fibre roof panel, large sliding doors and built in side steps, and could be specified with all three engine options. During 1967 Borg-Warner automatic transmission became available as a production line fitted option on all LCX models, and also on the LCY 25 cwt diesel. Uprated road springs enabled improved payload ratings of 14 cwt and 18 cwt (previously 12 and 17 cwt) to be announced on the two lowest capacity rated short wheelbase models in October 1969. At the same time the combined flashing indicator and sidelamp units gave way to separate indicators, with the side and headlamps now being combined units.

MkII Transits were announced in January 1971 with model numbers approximating to the metric gross vehicle weights being applied, with the range now comprising Models 75, 90, 100, 115, 125, 130, 150, and 175. The bus models were now of 12, 14, or 15 seat capacity, and were joined by a new series of assembly line built crewbuses with 13, 16, or 17 seats. The 2 litre V4 engine could now be specified on certain LCX models (short wheelbase), and a long wheelbase LCX Model 100 was available to apparently confuse the issue. This was in effect an

LCY, but with the small engine and single rear tyre equipment previously exclusive to the short wheelbase (LCX) range.

In the short wheelbase configuration in particular, the Transit attracted the attention of many builders of motor caravan bodies, with several well-known makers gaining Ford's approval, and warranty, for their Transit-based motor caravans. One of the most interesting of these was the Walker Suntrakker, a demountable caravan body for attachment to the LCX chassis. With this easily removable body the Transit could be used as a commercial vehicle with pick-up type bodywork during the week, and be quickly converted to its leisure role at the weekend.

The range expanded considerably during the early 1970s, and included a Transit articulated tractor unit with a semi-trailer box van of 2000 cubic feet; this was a Special Vehicle Engineering project in conjunction with P.E.M. Trailers. A high-roof van on the regular models was another variant, featuring a glass fibre roof height extension of 19 inches. The Ford Body Division designed its own steel floats in two sizes to suit the two wheelbase lengths; factory built and mounted, these featured drop sides and tailboard, and a replaceable hardwood floor. Replacing the Perkins diesel installation in 1972 came a new diesel engine of Ford design. This was the York, a 2.4 litre ohv in-line four-cylinder unit developing 61 bhp at 3000 rpm.

The name Transit was now almost a household word, with the model being in use for every conceivable type of delivery work, goods or people, and in use with the police, the AA and RAC, welfare organisations etc., in addition to a multitude of trade applications.

During 1975 the 1.7 litre (1663 cc) V4 engine gave way to the 1598 cc version of the in-line four-cylinder Kent engine which had enjoyed truly enormous success in the company's passenger cars. Developing 62 bhp at 5000 rpm, the Kent offered greater fuel economy with but little dimunition in performance, and so successful was this installation that in 1976 it gained Ford an industrial award for technical achievement. The 2 litre V4 remained for the LCY range, and a special order option now was a low-rated (100 bhp) version of the passenger car 3 litre V6-cylinder unit. 1976 was notable also as in September that year the one millionth Transit was produced, the milestone vehicle being built at Ford's Southampton assembly plant which now supplemented the Langley operation.

Restyled front ends appeared in March 1978, with a new full width plastic grille incorporating the headlamps; vertically stacked sidelamps and flashing indicators were situated at the front corners in line with the grille. A deep front bumper was now also of moulded plastic. As an alternative choice to the 1.6 litre Kent engine now was the 1.6 litre four-cylinder in-line overhead camshaft unit first seen on the Mk 3 Cortina passenger car in the early 1970s, with the 2 litre version of this ohc unit now replacing the V4 2 litre in the Transit range. Power outputs were 65 bhp and 78 bhp for the 1.6 and 2 litre units, respectively, with an "economy" low-output version of the 2 litre available as an option. The York diesel remained an option on all models. Automatic transmission could be specified only with the regular 2 litre petrol engine.

New coding representing the average payload in metric tonnes was adopted:- Model 80 = 0.80 metric tonnes. The LCX short wheelbase range now consisted of the 80, 100, and 120, with the parcels van being available in Model 100 configuration only, and a 100 long wheelbase variant for both van and kombi. The LCY long wheelbase series comprised models 130, 160, 175 and 190, with the parcels van in this range being based on the 160. Chassis cab versions were available from Model 100 upwards. With two wheelbases, six basic body styles, thirty-two door combinations, five engine options, manual or automatic gearboxes, and six rear axle ratios, the permutations seemed endless, but it didn't end just there. Special Vehicle Operations had developed other packages for low-volume markets, one of these being a kit for a chassis windscreen version with a half floor specially prepared for the mounting of ambulance bodies.

The Transit had of course been launched in Germany as well as in Britain, but although each country's versions were identical in appearance, largely due to the previous autonomy enjoyed by Dagenham and Cologne they had differed in several detail respects, and so had not featured the overall use of common parts regarded as the ideal. Nevertheless, as a European rather than just a British, or German Ford, the Transit had proved to be the very successful first step in co-operation between major Ford outfits which would eventually lead to total integration throughout Western Europe. In Britain, thanks to the Transit, Ford's market share in this sector had risen from 23 per cent in 1965 to a commanding 35 per cent by 1970.

Comprehensive though the Transit range was, there existed a gap between it and the appreciably larger D series trucks, and the decision was taken to develop a "go between" range which emerged as the new A series in September 1973. There had been no problem in designing a new chassis frame and front axle for this model, and there were sufficient mechanicals such as engines, transmissions, brakes etc., from elsewhere in the Ford range. However, the cab would have to be new, and in an effort to save tooling costs here there was a submission that the front end of the Cortina passenger car, complete with its windscreen pillars and front doors be adopted, with a closure panel behind the driver's seat. This certainly would have provided a sleek looking cab, but as it became clearer just what was wanted the idea was abandoned as there would have to have been considerable tooling modifications. Also, of course, was the fact that any new Cortina would almost certainly be totally restyled and therefore the exercise would have to start all over again. Another submission by the Body Division was simply to use the Transit cab in its entirety and widen it with an insert in the centre. Thus, the problem was solved, 7.1 inches inserted provided a new cab of $84^1/4$ inches width. This was allied to an appropriately wider and slightly longer bonnet also of similar style to the Transit, with a newly styled radiator grille completing what was a very well-proportioned front end/cab design.

At a gross vehicle weight of 7,700 lbs (3,500 kilos) were models A0406, A0407, A0409, and A0410; at 10, 120 lbs (4,600 kilos) were A0506, A0507, A0509, and A0510 at the slightly heavier all-up weight of 11,000 lbs: at 12,320 lbs (5,600 kilos) came models A0606, A0609, and A0610. AA0709 was an articulated tractor unit, with fifth wheel coupling, catwalk behind the cab, and a three-line braking system. The wheelbases were two each for the A0406 and A0407, of 120, and 145 inches; two each for the A0409 and A0410, of 130, and 156 inches; and three each for all models A0506 to A0610, 130, 145, and 156 inches. The articulated tractor unit, and tipper chassis were both on the 120 inch wheelbase.

Four power units were available, the 2 litre ohc in-line "four", and the 3 litre V6 being the petrol engine options, with the two alternative diesels being the 2.4 litre York, and a new 3.5 litre in-line six-cylinder York derivative developing 96 bhp at 3600 rpm. The drive lines were made up from the Ford four-speed 4-310-WR wide ratio, the 4-310-CR close ratio, the Turner T4-150 four-speed, or the ZF-S5-24/3 five-speed gearboxes, in conjunction with either of two hypoid bevel rear axles, the heavier rated of which being the Type 42 Salisbury design.

Included in the range were Ford factory built truck floats with drop sides and tailboard. Special bodies could be mounted on a chassis cowl version, and based on the A0407, 145 inch wheelbase model was a large parcels/delivery van of 350 cubic feet capacity bodied by Strachans. Other body builders were soon supplying van bodies, but the A series failed to achieve widespread popularity, and in an endeavour to improve its market penetration the range was re-aligned in 1977. This resulted in the 2 litre petrol engined models, A0407 and A0507, including the parcels vans being deleted. Like the 350 cubic feet models, the articulated tractor unit had also failed to gain significant sales, and so was also dropped from the range. The Turner T4-150 option on the trucks was also deleted, but did remain on the tipper chassis. Thus streamlined, the A series model range continued in production, but unfortunately still could not manage the sales figures which would have made the company happy, and in 1983 production ceased without a replacement model being announced.

With the introduction of the A series models, the Ford commercial vehicle range was covering almost every conceivable payload up to 28 tons, and it was now time to look into the possibility of contesting the real heavyweight market with vehicles of up to 44 metric tonnes. Unlike those of some of the smaller categories however, this was definitely a limited market, and also, Ford were not the only ones with the idea of mounting a challenge, as Bedford were feeling their way in the same direction with the help of General Motors. There was also very keen competition from the well established British and German heavy goods vehicle manufacturers – Foden, Fowler, ERF, Leyland-Scammell, Seddon-Atkinson, MAN, Deutz, and other European and Scandinavian makes. Additionally was the factor that this market was not one in which there was a consistent sales potential requiring a constant production level.

Nevertheless, an assault was decided upon, and in the initial stages thought was given to the market preparation of selected models from Ford of America's W series, examples of which in both normal, and forward control were obtained for trial. However, despite reaching the preparation stage of documentation for type approval in Europe, Dearborn's W series was dropped as changes were necessary, the expense of which was not considered justifiable for a limited application; it would be better for Ford of Britain to work out an entirely new design. Work began on what was to become the Transcontinental H series, a range of premium long distance trucks including drawbar trailers and highway articulated tractors available in 4 x 2 and 6 x 4 versions with designed gross vehicle, gross train, and gross combination weights from 38 metric tonnes to the limit of 44 tonnes.

New frames, the heavy duty 15,000 lbs rated capacity front axle from the D series, and semi-elliptic leaf springs front and rear formed the basis, with much of the remaining mechanical elements being bought-out proprietary units; this being especially so for the powertrain with a selection of six-cylinder in-line Cummins diesel units, Eaton-Fuller RT9509-C nine-speed, and RT09513 thirteen-speed transmissions and Rockwell single-speed rear axles and four-wheel-drive rear bogies for the six-wheel models.

All 4 x 2 models (except articulated tractor units) were available in two wheelbase lengths, 155 inches and 177 inches, and featured the nine-speed transmission as standard with the thirteen-speed as an option. The 4 x 2 model series consisted of Model H3824 powered by the Cummins NTE 290 (255) diesel developing 255 bhp at 1900 rpm, GVW (gross vehicle weight) at 16 tonnes, and GTW (gross trailer weight) of 38 tonnes. Model H4427 powered by the Cummins NTE 290 developing 290 bhp at 1900 rpm, with GVW of 16 tonnes, and GTW of 44 tonnes. Models H4432 and H4435 featured the NTE 350 (350 bhp) and NTE 370 (370 bhp), respectively, and were each of 16 tonnes GVW and 44 tonnes GTW. All the series were equipped with the 11.5 tonnes rated capacity R180 rear axle as standard, but could be specified with the heavier rated U180 of 13 tonnes capacity with which a GVW of 19 tonnes was permissible. Gross trailer weights remained the same irrespective of which axle was fitted.

All 4 x 2 articulated tractor units were available in wheelbase lengths of 121 and 138 inches, and featured the same specifications/options, and gross weights quoted for the 4 x 2 trucks of the same numerical designation. The tractors were prefixed HA, and comprised HA3824, HA4427, HA4432, and HA4435.

The six-wheel trucks were of 191 or 209 inch wheelbase, and featured the Rockwell SHD/SHR four-wheel-drive rear bogie. This was of the four-spring non-reactive type similar to that of the six-wheel D series trucks. Gross vehicle, and gross trailer weights of 24.39 tonnes and 44 tonnes were quoted for each of the three models in this series. These were the HT4427 (290 bhp), HT4432 (350 bhp), and the 370 bhp HT4435. The 6 x 4 articulated units HA4427 (290 bhp), HA4432 (350 bhp), and HT4435 (370 bhp) were available only in a short wheelbase of 132 inches, with a GVW of 22.36 tonnes. The mechanical specification was as the 6 x 4 trucks, and the gross combination weight was 44 tonnes.

The H series cab was the result of negotiations between Ford of Britain and the French commercial vehicle manufacturer, Automobiles Marius Berliet S.A., of Lyons, for the purchase of the basic cab used on the Berliet TR range. Outwardly the versions used by Berliet and Ford were similar except for the new heavy front hinged panel and grille fitted to the Ford version. Routine daily servicing could be attended to through the hinged panel, whilst for more serious work the cab could be tilted 70 degrees to reveal the engine. Excellent visibility, a fully adjustable driver's seat, two separate passenger seats, the outer one of which was of armchair style and with adjustable rake and a headrest, were notable features of this cab.

The recommended body lengths were 212 inches for the 155 inch wheelbase, and 240 inches for the 177 inch wheelbase four-wheel trucks, with body lengths of 276 inches for the 191 inch wheelbase, and 295 inches for the 209 inch wheelbase six-wheel models.

Introduced in April 1975, the new Transcontinental H series range went into production at Ford's Amsterdam plant, this location being chosen as the greater part of the Transcontinental's anticipated market was on the continent of Europe. In only little more than a year the 1000th H series model was delivered, thus indicating that Ford had got it right in their first attempt at producing a top-weight commercial vehicle range. Nevertheless, competition was fierce in this sector, and in 1980 the H series underwent a market re-alignment in which the following specification changes took place:

4 x 2 truck models; short wheelbase deleted leaving one wheelbase only on four-wheel models. H3824 at GVW of 16 tonnes and GTW of 38 tonnes, replaced by new model H3424 at GVW of 16.26 tonnes and GTW of 34 tonnes, with Rockwell R170 rear axle replacing R180; H4427 at GVW of 16 tonnes replaced by H4428 at GVW of 16.26 tonnes, with GTW remaining at 44 tonnes; H4432 deleted; H4435 16 tonnes GVW deleted in favour of H4435 of 19 tonnes GVW; other models H3824, H4427, and H4432 at GVW of 19 tonnes deleted.

4 x 2 articulated tractor units; HA3824 at GVW of 16 tonnes and GCW 38 tonnes replaced by new model HA3424 at GVW of 16.26 tonnes and GCW of 34 tonnes, with Cummins NTE 290 (255) diesel and Rockwell R170 rear axle; HA4427 at GVW of 16 tonnes replaced by new model HA4428 at GVW of 16.26 tonnes; HA4432 and HA4435 uprated to GVW of 16.26 tonnes; HA3824, HA4427, HA4432, HA4435 at 19 tonnes GVW all deleted. 6 x 4 truck and articulated tractor models; HT4427 replaced by new model HT4428 with Cummins NTE 290 engine, remainder of specification as before on HT4427: HT4432 and HT4435, uprated front axle. Additionally were the Special Vehicles Options catering for requirements as diverse as the mounting of tanker bodies in line with Home Office recommendations, or perhaps greater driver comfort in the sleeper cab versions.

Sales however continued to fluctuate in the manner which is the norm for the heavy truck industry, and were never very high at their best, and production of the Transcontinental was phased out around 1983 with no replacement model being envisaged.

Fortunately, a little lower down the scale, the picture was completely different. When the D series was introduced in 1965 it had established a pattern which others followed throughout the 1960s and '70s. During its sixteen year production life it had incorporated appropriate changes whenever necessary to deal with ever changing legislation and operating requirements, and when production ceased on December 31st 1981 more than 540,000 D series models had left the truck assembly plant at Langley, with more than fifty per cent of these having gone for export.

After careful appraisal of future market predictions and design studies, the decision was made in 1976 to commence the design and development of a new truck range for the 1980s with which to carry forward the traditions the D series had set. Code named "Delta", the new range eventually appeared in 1981 as the Ford Cargo, the result of a £150,000,000 investment programme. Identifiable by its drag reducing aerodynamically styled cab, the Cargo inherited many of the well established and reliable mechanical elements of the D series, and adopted the latter's four digit coding system which by this time was so well understood. Actual engine codings were changed, which became rather confusing when two particular engines received two codes each yet exhibited no change in specification or power output! The D series 0710, GVW 6706 kilos with 6 litre 113 bhp engine is replaced with the Cargo 0711, GVW 6500 kilos and with the 6 litre engine rated at 114 bhp – the difference being only 1 bhp, yet we have a new engine code. The 4.2 litre with increased power from 81 to 88 bhp had a coding change from 07 to 09; the 6.2 litre with increased power from 123 to 131 bhp had a coding change from 11 to 13; and even the 6 litre turbocharged unit with no quoted power change was recoded from 14 to 15.

By comparison with the D series the number of models increased considerably; 4 x 2 articulated tractor units, from 9 to 13 models; 4 x 2 tippers from 9 to 14 models; and 4 x 2 trucks from 22 to 35 models. Six-wheelers were available in 9 truck versions, including tandem tippers in 6 x 2 and 6 x 4 configurations, and a 6 x 4 tandem chassis for cement mixers. Many of these could be seen as direct replacements of the D series, but at the upper end of the Cargo range were heavier articulated units with a capability somewhere between the D series and the Transcontinental. Some examples of these were; Model 2824C powered by the Cummins 10 litre V6 turbocharged diesel developing 249 bhp at 2100 rpm, with drive line utilising the Eaton-Fuller RT 11609A nine-speed synchromesh gearbox and open drive shaft to an Eaton 23120 single-speed spiral bevel rear axle assembly, 118 inch wheelbase, sleeper cab, and 61,740 lbs (28,000 kilos) gross combination weight; also with this GCW was Model 2820D, powered by the Deutz air-cooled F6L-413-FZ V6 diesel unit developing 206 bhp at 2500 rpm, with the ZF-56-80 GV80 thirteen-speed splitter transmission and the Eaton 23120 axle; at a GCW of 83,790 lbs (38,000 kilos) was the heaviest Cargo, Model 3828 tractor unit with the Cummins 10L 10 litre V8 engine of 283 bhp at 2100 rpm, and drive line comprising the Eaton-Fuller nine-speed gearbox and Eaton single speed axle.

Wheelbases throughout the range were: Models 0609 to 0813 inclusive; 126 inches, 146 inches, $172^1/4$ inches, and 196 inches; Models 0911 to 1013, 121 inches, $141^3/4$ inches, $167^1/4$ inches, and 191 inches. These same wheelbases also applied to Models 1111 and 1317C inclusive, with the addition of a longer wheelbase of $214^1/2$ inches. Models 1513 to 1515 inclusive were on wheelbases of $141^3/4$, $167^1/4$, 197, and $220^1/2$ inches; Models 1613 to 1628C were, $138^1/2$, $167^1/4$, 197, $220^1/2$, and 244 inches. There were up to two wheelbase lengths for the 4 x 2 tippers, up to two also for the articulated tractor units, one wheelbase for the tandem cement mixer, up to three for the tandem tippers, and up to four for the tandem trucks.

With 23 wheelbases, 11 engines, 11 transmissions, 12 gross vehicle weights and 8 gross combination weights the Cargo range extended to no less than 95 models. Given the imprecise, and indeed all too often lax nature of commercial vehicle operations, one cannot but wonder whether all of such a variety was marketable or really necessary.

Early in 1986 Ford of Britain announced that due to heavy losses in the commercial vehicle field the company would cease to market medium and heavy commercial vehicles, and was considering the possibility of a merger with FIAT's associated commercial vehicle company, IVECO. In July 1986 a new company was formed, IVECO-Ford Trucks Ltd., retaining the Langley assembly plant and with new administrative headquarters in Watford.

Wisely, Ford had kept the Transit out of this deal, and so this best-selling light commercial vehicle was to continue as a Ford of Britain product, and was about to appear in its new "fast front" guise which was a visible result of a new Transit development programme which had been underway for some time. Lower front end panelling styled somewhat in the manner of the latest Ford passenger cars is another feature of this aerodynamic Transit range which once again covers the standard van, semi-high-roof van, kombi, bus and crewbus models, and a chassis cab version for pick-up and light truck bodies.

Still designated LCX and LCY in short and long wheelbase versions, the new Transits are of slightly longer wheelbase lengths than hitherto with 110.8 inches (LCX), a 4.8 inch increase, and the LCY with just an 0.9 inch increase to 118.9 inches. The standard van load capacities of 212 cubic feet and 298 cubic feet for the short and long wheelbase models, respectively, represent an impressive 34 cubic feet increase on the LCX and 37 cubic feet on the long wheelbase, LCY.

Individual model designations remain the same as before, with the identification numbers representing (very vaguely) the payload capacity in kilograms. LCX models are; 80, 908 kilogram payload (2002 lbs); 100, 1166 kilogram payload (2571 lbs); 120, 1319 kilogram payload (2908 lbs). Standard power unit for the LCX range is the 1.6 litre ohc in-line four-cylinder engine, driving through a four-speed all synchromesh gearbox to the hypoid bevel three quarter floating final drive assembly. Engine options are the 2 litre ohc unit, and a new 2.5 litre direct injection diesel engine of 70 bhp at 4000 rpm. Transmission options are the five-speed all synchromesh manual gearbox, or, with the 2 litre petrol engine only, the Ford C3 fully automatic transmission.

The LCY model range comprises; 100, 1111 kilogram payload (2449 lbs); 130, 1371 kilogram payload (3023 lbs); 160, 1668 kilogram payload (3678 lbs); and 190, 1928 kilogram payload (4251 lbs). Extended wheelbase versions, 136.7 inches, were available for models 160 and 190, catering for 157.5 inch body lengths. The standard engine/transmission combination for the LCY models is the 2 litre petrol engine with five-speed all synchromesh manual gearbox and fully floating hypoid bevel rear axle. Optional variations are the four-speed manual gearbox, the 2.5 litre diesel engine with five-speed gearbox on all models except 100, and the C3 automatic transmission in conjunction with the 2 litre petrol engine only for models 130, 160, and 190.

Suspension arrangements show a breakaway from the previous Transit at the front on the new LCX models which feature MacPherson struts with coil springs mounted inboard. The LCY continues to use the simple beam axle front end arrangements in conjunction with semi-elliptic leaf springs, as this system is regarded as better able to cope with the heavier all-up weights of the long wheelbase range. Both models retain the longitudinally mounted semi-elliptics at the rear.

Specialised applications of the new Transit include parcels vans, ambulances, welfare buses, security vans, caravan conversions and an interesting 4 x 4 preparation package with which to prepare the Transit for conversion to four-wheel-drive, with that operation being carried out by County Tractors, the successors of County Commercial Cars who carried out so many Ford conversions in the past.

Walls

sausages

Finest because they're fresh!

7032

HERCULITE

INSULATED HYGIENIC MEAT VAN

BODY £560 IN·PRIMER

THAMES 5 ton L.W.B. CHASSIS & CAB £460

FORD MOTOR COMPANY LTD.
DAGENHAM

DESIGNED & BUILT BY
WILSDON & Cº LTD
SOLIHULL WARWICKSHIRE

Photographs on previous pages and above: The Model 7V was quickly back into full production following World War Two; at first with drab paintwork, miniscule headlamps, and wartime plain mesh radiator grille, but soon adopting a brighter finish as postwar austerity receded. These illustrations amply portray the versatility of the 7V range as it got down to the job of aiding Britain's recovery.

Below and Opposite page top: The ubiquitous E83W was also ready to enjoy a new lease of life following the end of hostilities, being used for almost any job with which a compact 10 hp vehicle could cope.

HAYES & HARLINGTON U. D. C.

Below: Ford ET6, model Thames 4 cubic yard tipper. Underfloor hydraulic tipping ram, Anthony Hoist fixed sided steel body. Spare wheel carrier behind the cab. Powered by the V8 petrol engine, four-speed, crash change transmission. 122.0 inch wheelbase. 1949.

Above: Ford ET6 model Thames, 3 ton truck wooden float with drop sides and tailboard. Servo assisted hydraulic brakes. V8 petrol engine. Spare wheel carrier at the rear under the chassis frame. 128.0 inch wheelbase. 1949.

Right: ET6 Thames 4 cubic yard tipper, underfloor hydraulic tipping ram. With body sub-frame. Drop sides and tailboard. Anthony Hoist steel body.

Right: ET6 Thames special underfloor hydraulic ram tipper adapted for grit spraying. Mechanically operated grit depositer driven via a chain arrangement from the rear axle hub end. As the tipper is slowly reversed the chain drive roller deposits the right amount of grit onto the road. 1949-50.

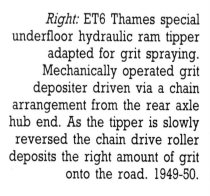

Left: ET6 Thames lhd light fire/rescue truck with pulley/rope operated extension ladder for service in Egypt. 1949. V8 petrol engine. The basic vehicle is the 3 ton 128.0 inch wheelbase chassis cab.

ET6 Thames. Long wheelbase extension with horse box body. Drop side doors, glass visors over windshield, and three passenger compartment with individual entrance door with window. Accommodation for three horses and four grooms. 5 ton chassis.

Below: ET6 Thames 4 x 4 conversions. LHD military type with steel cargo bodies and canvas tilts. Cabs fitted with hip rings in the roof for observer or gunner. Sand tyres on W.D., split disc wheels secured together by the outer ring of nuts and bolts. Spare wheel carrier behind the cab. Extension arms projecting from the front of the chassis frame for additional equipment. V8 petrol engine, four-speed transmission, auxiliary/transfer gearbox. Conversions carried out by Autolifts & Engineering Company Limited, Blackburn, Lancashire. Basic model 4 ton short wheelbase 128.0 inches.

Thames 3 ton 128.0 inch wheelbase. Wooden float with drop sides and tailboard. Farm work with bales of hay or straw. V8 petrol engine powered. 1948.

ET6 4 ton 128.0 inch short wheelbase drop sides and tailboard. V8 30 hp., petrol engine. Delivering wood to saw mill. 1949.

Below: Fordson Thames 2 ton van short wheelbase model ET6 1948. The van is equipped with a driver's sliding door and two wide opening doors at the rear. Powered by the V8 petrol engine and four-speed transmission.

ET6 Thames with telescopic ejector body, the 'Jekta' with 5 ton long wheelbase 157.0 inch chassis. Body consists of three 'U' shaped sections arranged to telescope into each other for the purpose of expelling the load. The movement of the sections on a running rail on top of the sub-frame is obtained by a patented design of double acting hydraulic rams.

Advantages claimed were stresses imposed upon the vehicle frame by normal tipping bodies is eliminated, thus prolonging chassis life. Can be partially discharged as required. 1949.

Left: ET6 Thames with telescopic ejector body. View showing 'load discharged' position.

Below: ET6 Thames 5 ton tipper, underfloor hydraulic tipping ram. Shallow steel tipper body with fixed sides, opening tailgate. 122.0 inch wheelbase. Used mostly by local contractors and councils. 1948/50.

ET6 Thames 5 ton short wheelbase, flat platform truck. Loading with sacks of coal from railway sidings. 128.0 inch wheelbase powered by the V8 petrol engine. 1948-50.

ET6 chassis front end with short coupé pillars, short wheelbase of 128.0 inches plus 42.44 inch bogie, six-wheeler. Double drive complete with delivery floor and seat. V8 petrol engine, single rear tyre equipment, cross country type tyres on the rear with road tread tyres on the front, hence two spare wheels.

Below: 502E chassis cab with drink industry float, with high front headboard and tailboard. Four-cylinder diesel engine. 3 ton short wheelbase 128.0 inch. Note '4D' badge on the front of the radiator grille. 'Thames' badge on front edge of bonnet and side flashes with word 'Ford'. 1953.

Left: ET6 3 ton chassis cab with drinks industry float, with the high headboard and tailboard. Short wheelbase 128.0 inch. V8 petrol engine. 1950.

3E model military 4 x 4 ambulance. 3 ton payload. Powered by the Canadian V8, 32 hp side-valve petrol engine, four-speed synchromesh transmission, open propeller shaft, auxiliary/transfer gearbox, and hypoid bevel gear driven front and rear axles. This vehicle was part of a 5,000 contract from the War Office for four-wheel drive vehicles. Other models were 2E and 4E. 1951/2.

Below: ET6 front view of the vehicle range showing the 'Thames' badge, side flashings 'Ford' and engine designation round discs, these replaced front engine type emblem. 1952.

Below left: ET6 rear view showing drop tailboard, and rear lighting arrangement, also rear located spare wheel. 1950.

4E model, military 4 x 4 Stores Bins Truck. Designed by Ford of Britain and built at Dagenham. Powered by the Canadian V8 32 hp petrol engine. Part of the contract for the War Office. The chassis is basically the same as for the 3E.

2E, 3E, and 4E models military 4 x 4 vehicles. Front view showing front drive axle, head and side lamps, and convoy disc on right-hand side of front panel. 1951/2.

2E, 3E, 4E, military models 4 x 4 vehicles. Three-quarter rear view of chassis. Note the spare wheel carrier behind the cab. Single rear tyre equipment, sand/cross country tyres. Towing hook on the rear of the chassis is mounted on a transverse leaf spring to absorb shocks over rough country. 1951/2.

Right: Model 400E. 15 cwt van. Independent front suspension, four-cylinder petrol engine of 1703 cc. Three-speed synchromesh transmission with steering column gear change.
'Thames' badge on the front panel with payload disc underneath. 1961. All Ford of Britain's commercial vehicle models were under the 'Thames' badge at this time.

Model 400E. 15 cwt van. Three-quarter offside view. Independent front suspension and semi-elliptic longitudinal leaf spring for the rear suspension.

Below left and right: Model 400E. 15 cwt. Independent front suspension, semi-elliptic rear springs. Chassis cab version for mounting of special bodies including pick-ups and light truck float bodies.
Many special bodies were made available. Sliding cab door windows with security locks.

105

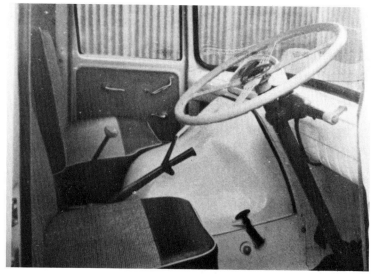

Top: Model 400E. 15 cwt van. Thames badge on front panel with disc indicating payload. This version is 'Van 800' maximum payload of 800 kgs (1760 lbs).

Above left: Prototype cab. Forward control. Code name 'Atlantic'. Prior to the development of the Thames Trader. Styled for a new experimental 6 ton chassis the basis of the four-wheel drive military models 2E etc. 1950. This style of cab was never produced.

Interior of the Thames Trader forward control cab. Simple layout of instruments, panel located above the engine cowling in the centre of the belt rail finish panel. Rubber catches for the interior engine cowling. Lighting switches in the steering column stalk. 1953.

Top: Thames Trader forward control long wheelbase six-wheeler. All Wheel Drive Limited of Camberley, who designed and produced the six-wheeler conversion. Two spring type. On trials at the Bagshot military proving ground with representatives of All Wheel Drive Ltd., and Ford of Britain watching progress. Six-cylinder in-line diesel engine, four-speed transmission and double drive rear axle bogie. Basic model was the Thames Trader 50, 5 ton chassis cab.

Above left: Thames Trader front end with short coupé pillars. Six cylinder in-line petrol engine. Left-hand drive. Note the brake servo, located inside the chassis frame, just below the frame, and the tapering top flange at the front of the vehicle.

Above right: Thames Trader forward control long wheelbase six wheeler chassis cab. All Wheel Drive Ltd., conversion. Trader 50 long wheelbase basic model. Six-cylinder in-line diesel engine with four-speed synchromesh transmission. Spare wheel carrier on the side of the frame operates by a small hand winch.

Below left: Thames Trader 5 cubic yard tipper, in operation on site. Six-cylinder in-line diesel engine, four-speed transmission and hypoid bevel gear driven rear axle.

Below right: Petrol tanker on delivery at a Ford dealer petrol station. The basic vehicle is the Thames Trader 4 ton short wheelbase chassis cab. Tanker body mountings include a sub-frame via rubber insulation. Four mounting points, one near the front, two down the side and one near the rear, for tankers on long wheelbase models, and probably only one point on the side for a short wheelbase.

Bottom: All Wheel Drive Ltd., carried out 4 x 4 conversions to the Thames Trader models. This is one with a standard military steel float, powered by the six-cylinder in-line diesel engine, four-speed synchromesh transmission, auxiliary/transfer gearbox, constant mesh type, and hypoid bevel gear driven front and rear axles. Probably just been photographed at the first stage before being subjected to test trials on the proving grounds of the Fighting Vehicles Research and Development Establishment (F.V.R.D.E.), at Bagshot.

Front end hydraulic telescopic tipping ram operated tipper body by Edbro. On Thames Trader 7 cubic yard tipper chassis. 9.00 x 20 low pressure tyres with dual rear tyre equipment. Cross country tyres on the rear and road tread tyres on the front.

Thames Trader six-cylinder in-line diesel engined powered 7-ton tipper chassis with a cement mixer body mounted. The mixer is operated by a constant mesh gearbox from the power take off of the vehicle's transmission. Note new badging; flashing on side indicating engine type, not having any surround.

Articulated combination, delivery of Ford spare parts. Container type van semi-trailer. Thames Trader articulated combination powered by the six-cylinder diesel engine.

138.0 inch wheelbase 5 ton Thames Trader chassis cab with box type bodies mounted. For the Ministry of Defence. Six-cylinder diesel powered.

3 ton short wheelbase, 138.0 inch. Thames Trader with steel float drop sides and tailboard. Four-cylinder in-line diesel engine, four-speed transmission and hypoid bevel gear driven rear axle.

Below: Thames Trader low frame model, 4 ton forward control, chassis cab. Note the kick-up of chassis frame over the rear axle with the frame rising forwards from the rear of the cab to keep the frame height to a minimum. Spare wheel carrier at the rear under the frame.

Above: Thames Trader normal control 5 ton long wheelbase. Six-cylinder in-line diesel engine with a steel float, drop sides and tailboard. Modified Cologne cab originally designed and produced for Ford of Germany's normal control truck. Ford of Germany ceased production of commercial trucks in early 1950s.

Left: Ford 'K' series (normal control) 7 ton tipper with Edbro underfloor hydraulic tipping ram. Body mounted on brackets attached to the chassis frame without any sub-frame. 'K' series was an updated normal control range to use the same mechanicals as the 'D' series. Thames Trader names were removed and replaced by the 'Ford' in large letters on the radiator grille.

Left: Ford 'K' series 7 ton long wheelbase chassis cab.

Above: Ford 'A' series, intermediate class of commercials between the 'D' series and the Transit light commercials. A0510. Ford 3 litre V6 petrol engine. Alloy float, drop sides and tailboard. Semi-forward control range. Using four-speed transmission and a hypoid bevel gear driven Salisbury type rear axle. 156.0 inch wheelbase.

Ford 'A' series A0610, 3.5 ton capacity semi-forward control. Steel float with drop sides and tailboard. Powered by the V6 six-cylinder petrol engine. 156.0 inch wheelbase.

Right: Ford 'A' series model A0609. 3.5 ton capacity. Chassis cab version with wooden float, drop sides and tailboard. Dual rear tyre equipment. Powered by the Ford 3.5 litre six-cylinder in-line diesel engine with four-speed synchromesh transmission. 1976.

Left: 'D' series. recovery truck. Ford dealer garage, Aberdeen, Scotland. 1965. Operating under trade plates. 4 ton chassis with breakdown body.

Ford 'D' series DT1700 six-wheeler designed for gross vehicle weight at 24 tons. Wheelbase of 237.0 inch. Cummins Vale 470 six-cylinder diesel engine. Flat platform 29 ft truck float built by Garners of Acton, London.

Below: Ford 'D' series trucks leaving Ford Headquarters at Warley, Brentwood, on sales mission to Russia. Export marathon of 10,000 miles trip through Europe 1965. First vehicle is a 5 ton truck, second a 4 ton truck with Ford tractor as the load.

'D' series tipper. 9 cubic yard, designated as D1614. Powered by the turbocharged 6.0 litre six-cylinder diesel engine. Front hydraulic telescopic tipping ram, steel tipper body by Edbro Tippers. 147.0 inch wheelbase. Eight-speed transmission and Eaton spiral bevel gear driven rear axle.

D series Mobile crane, hydraulically operated. Operating on site only, no registration. Plate stating maximum speed replaces licence plate for travelling within the compound. Note jacking legs to stabilize the vehicle when the crane is operated.

'D' series 4 ton short wheelbase. Special vehicle build. Low gear ratio-road marker. Controls fitted for both left-hand and right-hand drive. Enables the driver to view the forward aligning wheel at the kerb side when operating on either side of the road. 1973.

'D' series Phase II. DT2417, 24 ton tandem tipper, 147.0 inch wheelbase. Front end telescopic hydraulic tipping ram. Special vehicle options: low pressure tyres with single rear equipment, front guard grille, custom cab, powered by the Cummins 8.3 litre V8 diesel engine and a Turner 5-speed synchromesh transmission. 1972.

'D' series Phase II. Custom cab. 147.0 inch wheelbase. Powered by the Cummins 8.3 litre V8 diesel engine. Skip loader body. Front towing eyes secured to the front of the chassis frame through the front bumpers.

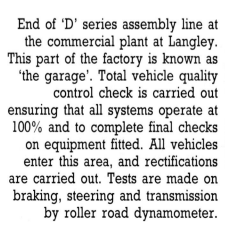

End of 'D' series assembly line at the commercial plant at Langley. This part of the factory is known as 'the garage'. Total vehicle quality control check is carried out ensuring that all systems operate at 100% and to complete final checks on equipment fitted. All vehicles enter this area, and rectifications are carried out. Tests are made on braking, steering and transmission by roller road dynamometer.

Right: D0707, 120 inch wheelbase at 7.37 tons gross vehicle weight. Chassis cab with aluminium box van. Powered by the four-cylinder in-line 4.2 litre diesel engine, four-speed transmission and front towing eyes.

Prototype van and minibus bodywork during the Transit development period, still under the "Thames" and 400E designations. The front end styling would appear to be appreciably more aerodynamic than that eventually chosen for the production Transits of 1965.

Below: Ford Transit – Mark I, four-cylinder diesel L.C.Y. chassis cab with milk float mounted. 118.0 inch wheelbase. Dual rear tyre equipment. Perkins 4/108 diesel engine. 1969. Delivering your daily pinta.

Above: Transit Mark I. L.C.Y. model. 118.0 inch wheelbase. Chassis cab with special delivery float. Using roller shutter system for protection of load. Three-way loading, both sides and the rear. Dual rear tyre equipment. Custom cab. 1969.

Ford Transit – Mark I. LCY model chassis cab with compressor and equipment body. 2.0 litre V4 petrol engine, four-speed transmission. Dual rear type equipment. Used by local contractors and councils for road repairs and other breaking operations. 118.0 inch wheelbase and Custom cab. 1968.

Transit Mark I. L.C.X. van, short wheelbase of 106.0 inches. Newspaper delivery. Single rear tyre equipment. Standard van body. Quite a number of Fleet Street newspapers use the standard Transit van for deliveries.

117

Right: Mark II. L.C.X. standard short wheelbase 106.0 inch van. Single rear tyre equipment. Powered by the V4, 1663 cc petrol engine. New styled radiator grille goes with the Mark II version. 1973.

Transit Mark I. L.C.X. Custom van 106.0 inch wheelbase, single rear tyre equipment. Rescue vehicle for the British Racing and Sports Car Club. V4 petrol engine of 1663 cc. 1967.

Below left: Mark II. L.C.X., short wheelbase 106.0 inch 'Super Van'. Converted by Terry Dury Racing for Ford of Britain Sales Division. It was a Custom Van, equipped with a V8 petrol engine and racing tyres.

Below right: Rear view of Transit Mark II Ford of Britain Sales 'Super Van'.

Mark II. L.C.X. standard van with some extraordinary passengers. Elephants go in two by two. Zoo transportation. Before the elephants were in the van the small one had wandered round to the nearside to see if the side door was easier.

Transit Mark 1 L.C.X. Standard 106.0 inch wheelbase van. London to Katmandu expedition accompanied by a Jeep in 1967. Seems to be some explanation to a security soldier of the Middle East.

Transit Mark II. L.C.X. caravan conversion. Custom cab version provided an extremely good basic vehicle for caravans. Powered by the optional 2.0 litre petrol in-line engine, with four-speed transmission. The extending roof provides for easy sleeping accommodation. 1973.

119

Mark II. L.C.Y. Custom Cab version. 118.0 inch wheelbase chassis cab with a high lift cage hydraulically operated for servicing street lights. This actual vehicle is a demonstration model.

Below: Transit Mark II. Chassis cab with a light truck float body mounted. Consignment of exhaust pipes and silencers being transported from one Ford factory to another at Langley. 1973.

Below right: Mark I. Parcels van, on an L.C.Y. 118.0 inch wheelbase. With sliding driver's door. The easy access into the van for the driver and through the rear wide doors for the loading and unloading made this version an excellent vehicle for express parcels service. Note the full bulkhead behind the driver.

Transit Mark I. L.C.Y. standard van 118.0 inch wheelbase, powered by the Perkins 4/108 four-cylinder in-line diesel engine of 1760 cc capacity. Complete with radiator blind, on low temperature tests in Finland. 1972.

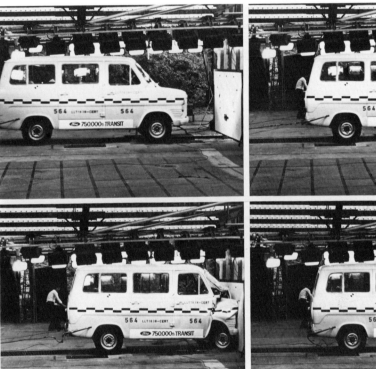

To ensure the public of the strength of the Transit in road accidents, crash tests were conducted. Crashing the vehicle at speed into a solid wall. With instrumentation, various results can be established. This photograph shows the Transit approaching the wall, and the results. The vehicle in question was the 750,000 Transit to be built.

Transit Mark II. L.C.Y. 118.0 inch wheelbase, Luton van mounted on the chassis cab version. Powered by the 2.0 litre V4 petrol engine. Model under the latest designation of numbers, this version is the 175. Operated by Ryder Truck Rental of London is one of many operated by such companies all over the country.

Mark III. L.C.Y. 118.0 inch wheelbase, with a welfare ambulance body mounted by Dormobile in 1980. Powered by 2.0 litre ohv, in-line petrol engine. The Mark III employed a new radiator grille style enhancing the model.

Transit Mark II. L.C.Y. 118.0 inch wheelbase chassis cab converted to an articulated tractor unit. Used in conjunction with a dropped frame box van semi-trailer making a very acceptable small combination. Developed by Ford of Britain's Special Vehicle Engineering in conjunction with P.E.M. trailers. 1972.

Another motorised caravan used on a Transit Mark II. L.C.X. 106.0 inch wheelbase, but with a difference. A demountable caravan body which can be mounted on a Transit pick-up model. The caravan body can be lifted off the pick-up and stored away, enabling the vehicle to be used for business during the week days. The caravan then can be mounted for weekends and holidays. Can be accommodated on both the L.C.X. short wheelbase and the L.C.Y. long wheelbase models.

Above: Transit Mark I. L.C.X. on the right and L.C.Y. on the left of the picture. With Perkins 4/108 diesel engine on high speed test track. Testing at Ford of Germany's proving ground in Genk, Belgium.

Sketch illustrating mechanicals of the short wheelbase L.C.X., powered by the V4 petrol engine.

Special build based on the Ford tipper, 'D' series chassis. The Beaulieu Motor Museum 'General' bus. Conversion was powered by Ford's 6.0 litre six-cylinder in-line diesel engine. It is a representation of a London General Omnibus Company's 1910 type 'B' bus and used for rides around the museum estate.

Cargo chassis cab with special box type van specially styled and prepared for travelling libraries.

Ford's latest truck range, the Cargo. Tandem model 2417C Cement mixer chassis. Specially marketed for the cement industry. Powered by the Cummins 8.3 litre V8 diesel engine, Ford six-speed, 6-450-NW, wide ratio synchromesh transmission and the two-spring tandem bogie.

Below: Cargo 1315 model chassis cab with box van. Shutter type door at front of van side. 141.7 inch wheelbase. Powered by the 6.0 litre turbocharged six-cylinder in-line diesel engine.

Cargo chassis cab with special horse box body mounted. To accommodate horse, grooms and riders. 0811 model 195.8 inch wheelbase. Powered by the 6.0 litre six-cylinder in-line diesel engine, four-speed 4.310.S synchromesh transmission. Gross vehicle weight 16,515 lbs (7,490 kgs).

Cargo articulated combination. 138.5 inch wheelbase. Gross combination weight 71,706 lbs (32,520 kgs). Powered by the Perkins 10.5 litre V8 diesel engine, Eaton-Fuller 9-speed constant mesh RT 11609A transmission. Triaxle pallet loader with side curtains.

Below: Cargo six-wheeler tipper model 2417. 148.9 inch (3.784 metres) wheelbase. Chassis cab version fitted with steel tipper body with front end telescopic hydraulic tipping ram. Powered by Perkins 8.8 litre V8 diesel engine, Ford 6-540-NW, wide ratio, six-speed transmission. Gross vehicle weight 53,779 lbs (24,390 kgs).

Above: Cargo box van with drawbar trailer model 1515. Gross vehicle weight 33,075 lbs (15,000 kgs). Powered by the 6.0 litre turbo charged six cylinder in-line diesel engine. 141.7 inch (3.600 metres) wheelbase.

Cargo truck with alloy float body with drop sides and tailboard. Model 1311 G.V.W. 27,562 lbs (12,500 kgs). Powered by the 6.0 litre six-cylinder in-line diesel engine. 167.3 inches (4.250 metres) wheelbase.

Cargo 0609 model version. G.V.W. 13,230 lbs (6,000 kgs). Powered by the 4.2 litre four-cylinder in-line diesel engine. Alloy float with drop sides and tailboard. 146.6 inch (3.725 metre) wheelbase.

Below: Transit ambulance on L.C.X. model version. Special Vehicle Engineering.

Bottom left: The new Transit range L.C.X. standard van, 80 version. G.V.W. 4,806.9 lbs (2.180 kgs). Single rear tyre equipment. Powered by 1.6 litre ohc four-cylinder in-line petrol engine. 110.8 inch (2.815 metre) wheelbase.

Bottom right: New Transit light truck. L.C.Y. model with double cab. Six personnel as well as working materials can be transported in this Transit double cab.

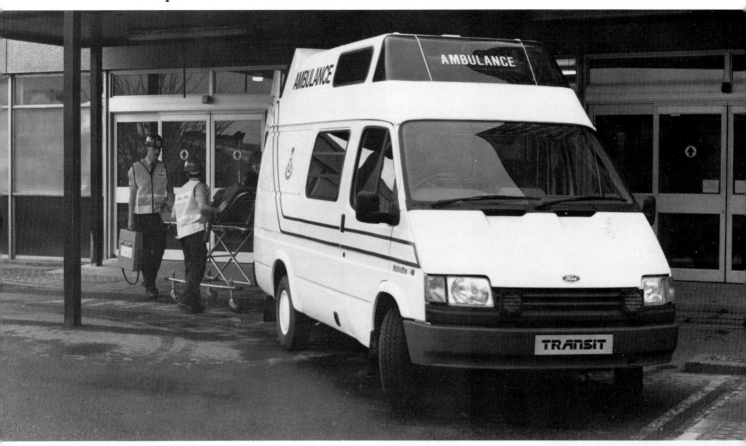

Below left: Transit L.C.Y. standard van 118.9 inch (3.020 metre) wheelbase. Dual rear tyre equipment. 130 model version powered by the 2.0 litre ohc., four-cylinder in-line petrol engine and four-speed synchromesh transmission. G.V.W. 6,460 lbs (2,930 kgs).

Below right: Cargo cab interior trim. l.h.d. shown.

Bottom left: Cargo cab assembly line. Cabs waiting to be trimmed and finished with interior equipment. Southampton Body plant.

Bottom right: Cargo main assembly line at Langley commercial vehicle plant, now under IVECO-Ford Trucks Limited.

Right: Transcontinental 'H' series. Ford of Britain's heaviest vehicle range. Articulated tractor unit 4 x 2 being prepared in the experimental and prototype workshop at the Ford Engineering Research facility at Dunton, Basildon.

'H' series Transcontinental Mark II. With new front panel and radiator grille. 4 x 2 articulated tractor with tanker semi-trailer.

Below: Transcontinental 'H' series articulated combination with tanker semi-trailer. The 'H' series was designed by Ford of Britain and built by Ford of Netherlands in Amsterdam.

5 Light delivery vans

The advent of the 8 hp Model Y saloon in 1932, with which Ford was to quickly establish itself as one of the 'big three' car manufacturers in Britain, also gave the company the opportunity of satisfying the demand for a really economical light delivery vehicle.

This first small Ford was based upon a 90 inch wheelbase chassis frame, which accommodated the front and rear transverse leaf spring suspension arrangements as on the larger Ford cars. A new 933 cc sidevalve four-cylinder engine provided very ample power with which to cope with a 5 cwt payload, with this power being transmitted to the rear wheels via a three-speed gearbox complete with synchromesh between the upper two ratios. Ford's torque tube drive to a spiral bevel rear axle assembly completed the transmission.

The wooden framed, metal panelled body featured a waterproofed fabric roof, and was attached to the chassis frame in the same manner as with the passenger car, with the metal side panels being welded to the chassis frame thus relieving the frame top flange of undue stress. A spare wheel mounted on the offside door panel left the van interior unobstructed, giving a usefully shaped loading area of 50 cubic feet. The lack of a passenger seat provided more load space if required, and gave additional access to the cargo area. Differing from the car only in respect of the van portion of the bodywork, and a set of lower-ratio indirect gears with which to ensure a satisfactory getaway and hill-climbing potential with a full load, the Model Y van was an extremely attractive proposition. Weighing in at less than 12 cwt unladen it came within the lowest commercial vehicle road tax category, therefore qualifying for the £10 only annual payment; there was a genuine 40 mpg economy potential, and at a purchase price of £115 its widespread acceptance was ensured.

Becoming available in February 1933, the production Y type vans differed from the prototypes which had featured running boards and a nearside door only. Two doors were now provided, and the running boards deleted with neat lower valance panels in their place to cover the chassis members. During a production run of almost five years the Y type remained largely unchanged, with only detail revisions usually in line with the passenger cars which included, in October 1933, the longer radiator and valanced mudguards. Unlike on the car, however, the front bumper was deleted from the van at this time. The provision of small rectangular windows in the rear loading doors was a welcome improvement in October 1934. In line with the basic two-door passenger car, the van price was reduced to just £100 in October 1935, remaining so over the next two years during which the only notable change was the repositioning of the spare wheel now on the passenger's (nearside) door in October 1936.

The Model Y range ceased production late in 1937 by which time some 30,000 Y type vans, including 1225 in CKD form for overseas assembly had been produced.

A completely restyled 8 hp Ford appeared in October 1937, designated Model 7Y, and again including a light van derivative with a 5 cwt payload rating. A feature of the roomier bodywork on this model were the front-hinged driver's and passenger's doors which were regarded as appreciably safer than the rear-hinged variety of the Y type and many other cars of the period, should the doors be inadvertently opened with the vehicle in motion. 'Easy clean' wheels, of the disc type replaced the wire spoked type of the earlier model, and although the mechanical elements remained virtually unchanged, altogether the 7Y could be seen as a worthwhile improvement over the preceding range. A change in the mechanical specification took place early in 1939 when the engine acquired a timing chain in place of the fibre timing wheels.

A redesigned bonnet and rather upright radiator grille applied to the 8 hp passenger car during 1940 resulted in a new designation, E04A, and the introduction of the name "Anglia" which would grace several generations of small Fords. The van however did not acquire this new front end styling, instead continuing in production as the 7Y with the existing sloping front end design which in the opinion of many was more attractive than that of the latest passenger car. Production of the 7Y van ceased in November 1941, by which time 12,000 examples had been produced.

When it reappeared in 1945 following the resumption of civilian production, the van still retained the sloping front, but did now adopt the designation E04C bringing it into line with the E04A Anglia car. As the name 'Fordson' was now being applied to Ford commercial vehicles, this now appeared just above the grille on the E04C van.

As part of the postwar export drive a North American special-build was developed which resulted in both the Anglia and the van being equipped with left-hand drive, and with the 10 hp engine as standard equipment. Headlamp lenses and bulbs, and rear/stop lights were deleted to allow for these items to be fitted in the United States in line with individual State Laws. Designated E03CF in this configuration, the 5 cwt van also featured the Anglia's chrome front bumper with overriders.

During 1949 the Anglia reverted to the sloping frontal styling once more, but with a twin aperture rather than the previous single aperture grille, and was now designated E494A. The van also received the twin aperture grille, becoming the E494C in the process, and continuing in production as such for another five years before being replaced in July 1954 by the van derivative of the new 100E Anglia and Prefect cars.

Designated 300E in their commercial vehicle variations, and featuring the word 'Thames' on the bonnet for the first time on a small Ford, these new Fords were quite revolutionary by comparison with their predecessors. Of monocoque construction, this new 5 cwt van consisted of the entire front end panelwork of the Anglia car allied to a van rear end of 66 cubic feet capacity. The front wing styling lines were continued through to the rear of the van bodywork which also featured the neatly flared wheelarches of the passenger car, and as this modern full-width styling necessitated removing the spare wheel from its door-mounted position, that item was now accommodated in an upright position in the nearside of the van body. All of this resulted in a thoroughly modern looking light commercial vehicle under the skin of which also could be found much modern thinking. The Ford front and rear transverse leaf spring layout had disappeared completely, to be replaced with, at the front the MacPherson strut independent front suspension system first seen on the Consul/Zephyr cars, and by a pair of longitudinally mounted semi-elliptics at the rear. Hydraulically operated brakes were also making their first appearance on a small Ford model.

Although the 100E/300E marked the end of the 8 hp sidevalve engine, the sidevalve arrangement, and the 1172 cc capacity of the 10 hp engine remained as features of an otherwise completely new engine for the 100E range. This unit, much of which could be produced on existing tooling used in the manufacture of the old "ten", developed 36 bhp at 4500 rpm, sufficient to propel these new Ford vans at up to 70 mph. A hydraulic clutch was also new, whereas the gearbox followed established Ford practice in the provision of only three speeds, and as before synchromesh was provided between the upper two ratios only. Gear selection was by a long direct-acting floor-mounted lever. An open propeller shaft and spiral bevel rear axle assembly completed the drive line.

Slight changes in specification during 1955 were, in January, an increase in the brake drum diameter from 7 to 8 inches, and in April the lowering of the indirect gear ratios, whilst in

September that year appeared a 7 cwt De Luxe model. This featured an extra leaf in the rear springs and lever arm, instead of telescopic rear shock absorbers. The De luxe equipment included such items as the Prefect car's chrome grille and headlamp surrounds, "aeroplane" bonnet mascot, and chromed bumpers. A standard 7 cwt van without these embellishments followed just one month later.

Slight trim and decorative changes in line with the Anglia and Prefect cars occurred in October 1957, as the 300E vans continued to enjoy great popularity amongst a variety of users ranging from the self-employed tradesman, small retail and wholesale merchants, to large fleet operators. When production ceased early in 1961 more than 195,000 examples had been built.

With the introduction of the new 105E Anglia in September 1959, small Ford development had taken another great step forward. A completely new short-stroke ohv engine of 997 cc replaced the venerable sidevalve units, and was mated to an excellent new four-speed gearbox with synchromesh between second, third, and top gears. Another small, but nevertheless very welcome improvement, was the adoption of electric windscreen wipers in place of the vacuum operated variety so long favoured by Ford, but which never seemed to work satisfactorily on the small four-cylinder models. The suspension arrangements followed closely those of the preceding 100E/300E range.

The expected light van variations duly arrived in June 1961, being designated 307E and available in both 5 cwt and 7 cwt configurations. A front passenger seat was an optional extra in both versions, although the 7 cwt did otherwise feature a rather more de luxe finish than the lower rated model. A small, but particularly useful feature of these vans was the curved bottom edge to the driving compartment doors, thus allowing the doors to open fully when the vehicle was parked on a steeply cambered road edge adjacent to a high kerb. Apart from this altered door line, the front end was once again exactly as on the passenger car in respect of panelwork. Late in 1962 an 1198 cc version of the Kent engine became optional, and with this installation also came wider brake drums with which to cope with the extra performance provided. Thus equipped, the vans were designated 309E. This new optional package came straight from the new Cortina passenger car, with the almost immediate availability on the Anglia car/van series serving to illustrate the interchangeability of components which existed between the Ford small/medium ranges.

With the introduction of the D series trucks in March 1965 the Thames name was dropped from all Ford commercial vehicles, and so the light delivery vehicle now became the more logically named Anglia van. Some 205,000 of this generation of Thames/Anglia vans had been produced by the time the Anglia name disappeared early in 1968 with the announcement of the new Ford Escort light car range.

April 5th 1968 saw the release of the new Escort vans, with an 82 cubic feet capacity and improved payload ratings now of 6 cwt and 8 cwt; these loads were amply catered for by a new 1098 cc, and the existing 1298 cc (Cortina Mk2) versions of the Kent engine. Both units featured Ford's crossflow cylinder head design, and brought with them new levels of performance and economy to the light delivery van field. A servo-assisted braking system, with discs at the front, was a standard feature of the 8 cwt model, on which version only, the Borg-Warner type 35 automatic transmission quickly became an option. The Escort settled down to a lengthy production run before restyled Mk 2 models appeared early in 1975.

Apart from the introduction of a dual line braking system, these Mk 2 Escorts were essentially as before under the skin, but were now advertised as the Model 30 (1098 cc engine), and the Model 45 (1298 cc), rather than by the old payload in hundredweights ratings. In fact, depending upon weight distribution, maximum payloads were up quite substantially, with the Model 30 being advertised as being capable of handling up to 818 lbs (7.3 cwts) payload, whilst the 45 came with a 1078 lbs (9.7 cwts) rating. Custom trim packs came with both models, consisting of chromed front and rear quarter bumpers, overriders, hazard flashers, reversing lamps, halogen headlamps, improved seat trim, a full width under facia parcel shelf, and a dipping rearview mirror.

Differing greatly by comparison with what had gone before, Ford's light van range for the 1980s consisted of appropriate variations of the company's phenominally successful hatchback light car series of front wheel drive, transverse-engined models comprising the Fiesta and new Escort range. With these, Ford are still to the fore, offering the sort of value for money first seen in this field 55 years ago with the little Y type, and maintained throughout by successive generations of small Ford vans.

Catalogue photograph of the model 'Y' 5 cwt Van. Ford of Britain's first light van. Late model with nearside spare wheel mounting.

Catalogue photograph of the cover for model 'Y' 5 cwt van, 1934.

Right: Model 'Y' 5 cwt van. Price £100. 8 hp (933 cc) four-cylinder in-line petrol engine and three-speed synchromesh transmission. Oct 1935 onwards.

1937 Model 7Y 5 cwt van. Demonstration model with suggested designs of sign writing for the local grocer.

Below: 1937 Model 7Y 5 cwt van. Demonstration model with suggested designs of sign writing for the local fishmonger.

Below: 1937 Model 7Y 5 cwt van. Demonstration model with suggested designs of sign writing for the local butcher.

Bottom left: 1949 Model E493C/B, 5 to 7 cwt l.h.drive chassis for export to the U.S.A., with 10 hp. side-valve, four-cylinder in-line petrol engine and three-speed synchromesh transmission.

Bottom right: 1949 model E493C chassis front end with long coupé pillars. Equipped with disability controls on the steering column. For special van body.

1948 model E93C chassis front end long coupé pillars for special van body. Powered by the 10 hp. side-valve four-cylinder in-line petrol engine, and three-speed transmission.

1949 model E494C chassis front end with long coupé pillars and windshield, r.h.drive ready for the mounting of a special van body.

Model 300E, Thames 5 cwt van, based on the 100E Anglia passenger car. 1172 cc four-cylinder side valve petrol engine. Late model with mesh grille, 1957 onwards.

Above: Model 302E Thames 7 cwt van, 1954, 10 hp, 1172 cc four-cylinder in-line petrol engine.

Left: 1987 'Escort' 'Combi. 42.4 cubic feet loading space.

Below left: Model 307E 'Anglia' 5 cwt van, 1961. 997 cc four-cylinder ohv in-line petrol engine. The name Thames was removed from the vans in 1965.

Below: 1987 'Escort' van with 80 cubic feet loading space.

Right: 1987, view of 'Escort' Combi with rear tailgate open showing access entrance for loading.

1987, view of 'Escort' van with the rear doors open showing access entrance for loading.

Bottom right: Ford Fiesta van 'L' version. Powered by either 950 cc, 1100 cc, or 1600 cc four-cylinder petrol engine. 34.3 cubic feet of loading space. Ford of Britain's smallest commercial vehicle.

Bottom left: Interior view of the 'Escort' Combi 'L' trim 1987.

6 Public service vehicles

The earliest Ford public service vehicles of any significance were those based upon the Model TT truck chassis, with their char-a-banc bodies built by outside concerns. These had become quite a common sight during the 1920s as they conveyed their passengers on seaside trips and countryside outings, their popularity being such that with the advent of the new Models A and AA Ford advertised chassis specifically for the mounting of passenger carrying bodywork.

These chassis were based very closely on those of the corresponding 14.9 hp 10 cwt van, and the 24 hp 30 cwt truck, being of the same wheelbase lengths of $103^1/_2$ and $131^1/_2$ inches, and utilising the same mechanical elements and running gear. In addition to its usefulness as a compact all-weather saloon coach, the smaller model was suitable as a hotel station wagon and for hackney carriage work, whilst the 20-seater Model AA found favour with the tour operators. In the previously mentioned Ford booklet of approved bodywork applications some 16 types of suitable bus and coach bodies were illustrated.

The ultimate of the prewar Ford motor coaches however was without doubt that based on the Model BB long wheelbase (157 inches) 2 ton chassis powered initially by the 24 hp four-cylinder engine, but available from 1933 onwards with the 30 hp V8 unit. Also designed to accommodate 20-seat bodies, this model, even when fully laden, would usually be well within the 2 ton payload rating, thus ensuring good performance at all times. The shock absorbers fitted all round, rather than just at the front as on the previous model, would doubtless be very much appreciated by the passengers, just as was the very smooth and quiet operation of the V8 engine. Nevertheless, the Ford did not find favour with all coach operators, and it was the rival concerns of Bedford and Commer who were to dominate this market during the 1930s, and to such an extent that with the subsequent Model 7V Ford no serious attempts appear to have been made to attract coach operators to this chassis.

The Postwar ET6 did prove quite popular as a crew bus with such outfits as Wimpey and other construction companies, but this model and its 500E derivatives were never taken seriously by the tour operating industry, and it was not until 1956 that Ford decided upon a real attempt to enter the public service vehicle market when, in conjunction with Messrs. Duple Bodies Ltd., of Hendon, they began work on a chassis designed specifically for the job.

During development of this there were discussions regarding the possibility of producing an additional variation of Ford's six-cylinder diesel engine which would be installed flat in the chassis, thus improving the floor line. However, Ford management were not prepared to allocate additional funds for specific engine developments such as this for what was thought by them to be an uncertain market, and so the standard upright engine was to be utilised. This was the 330 six-cylinder in-line diesel of 5.4 litres and 108 bhp, although the 112 bhp 4.8 litre petrol "six" was to be available as an option. Completing the power train was the four-speed gearbox with synchromesh engagement between the upper three ratios, and an open propeller shaft to a fully floating hypoid bevel final drive.

On a wheelbase of 212 inches, the low-built chassis swept up over the rear axle, terminating after only a short rear overhang. At the front, the overhang was necessarily long in order to mount the engine as far forward and as low as possible so as to comply with the minimum body entrance dimensions as required by law.

Initially, the 41-seater bodywork was, of course, by Duple, although some time later Plaxtons, of Scarborough, also supplied 41/42-seat bodywork for mounting on this chassis. Surprisingly, for what was Ford's first purpose-built job in this field, the name "Thames" which by this time was synonymous with heavy haulage nevertheless appeared on the front of the new motor coach. Although announced at the White City alongside the Thames Trader range in March 1957, the coach was temporarily withdrawn as Ford management had a change of mind regarding the venture, but then relenting some months later and authorising production to commence. Any fears about the model's sales potential were quickly dispelled as the Thames coach soon established itself as a worthy competitor to the Bedford which held much of this market.

For those operators requiring a rather more compact coach Ford now offered a short wheelbase 4 ton Trader chassis suitably modified in line with the Construction and Use regulations for Public Service Vehicles, on which could be mounted 20-seater coach bodies.

One of the 41-seat production models, after operating for some time with Excelsior Motorways, undertook an interesting tightly scheduled journey to Moscow as part of a sales-drive. Modifications for the lengthy trip included a reduced seating capacity in order to provide on-board kitchen and toilet facilities. The coach left Victoria Coach Station for Europe, then it was overland to Moscow before returning once more to Victoria Coach Station 45 hours later.

Following legislative changes allowing motor coach bodies of greater overall length, Ford decided upon a new coach chassis with a 226 inch wheelbase to accommodate the more commodious bodies now possible. This was developed at the company's Birmingham research and design facility, but under the overall guidance of truck engineering at Rainham, some of whose staff worked at Birmingham during this particular development. The 5.4 litre diesel engine and drive line were as before on the shorter wheelbase model. Duple, Plaxton, and others offered passenger coach bodies, whilst the chassis also found customers amongst those operating large mobile shops, horse boxes, and racing car transporters. Of the latter category was an interesting vehicle purchased by Lotus for the transport of their Formula 1 racing cars. This could accommodate two racers, one at floor level, with the other being slung from up above. The crew cabin featured many refinements including fully adjustable aircraft type reclining seats.

With the introduction of the D series trucks feasibility studies were carried out regarding the possibility of installing the new truck's inclined diesel engine in both the coach chassis and that of the normal control K series trucks, thus utilising one class of diesel engines throughout the whole commercial vehicle range. However, it transpired that the new engine would not offer any significant improvements in respect of the legal minimum body entrance measurements on the coach chassis, and because of the anticipated short remaining production life of the normal control K series truck the front end and cab modifications here to accommodate the new unit were not justifiable. Therefore, it was decided that the upright diesel would remain in production until at least the demise of the K series truck.

Due to the seasonal nature of motor coach operations production of the PSV chassis was inevitably inconsistent, with most operators requiring delivery during the autumn/winter period in readiness for the touring season beginning in the following spring. As a result of this factor and the special engineering requirements exclusive to the PSV chassis the responsibility for these was handed over to Special Vehicle Engineering at the Langley assembly plant. Without this facility the coach chassis, despite its relative success, would not have remained a really viable proposition to such a mass-production outfit as Ford; as it was the company were able to remain quite competitive in this field throughout the 1970s. By this time, the coach range consisted of the R series, these being, initially, the R1011 short wheelbase (192 inches) and the 226 inch wheelbase R1111. The powertrain consisted of the 330 6.2 litre six-cylinder diesel (upright version), the Turner T5-3017 five-speed synchromesh gearbox, with the T5-3018 overdrive version as an option, and pen propeller shaft to a fully floating spiral bevel rear axle. With the introduction of the 360 six-cylinder 5.9 litre turbocharged diesel came two additional models powered by the upright version of this engine, these being the R1014 and R1114 short and long wheelbase models.

Ford six- and eight-speed transmissions eventually replaced the five-speed Turner gearboxes, and an R series chassis equipped with the D series inclined diesel unit was also later marketed by Ford after a successful conversion was engineered by Tricentrol Chassis Developments, an associated company of the well known Ford main agents.

During its final years, 1979 – 1981, the R series consisted of just two home market models, the R1014 and R1114 now powered by the inclined version of the 6 litre turbocharged diesel unit developing 150 bhp at 2400 rpm. The gearbox was the Ford 6-600-S six-speed, or the 8-570-S eight-speed transmission in association with the Eaton fully floating spiral bevel rear axle as optional equipment. The R1011 and R1111 chassis were now export models retaining the upright 6.2 litre engine but with the drive line as on the R1014 and R1114 models. The advent of the Cargo truck range in 1981 spelled the end of the big Ford motor coaches as, never too happy about relatively low-volume production vehicles, the company now decided against PSV derivatives of their heavy-transport chassis.

Ideal as crew buses for the transportation of company employees, and as welfare service vehicles were the 18 to 25-seat capacity buses based on the A series chassis windshield, many of which can still be seen in operation today. These were the A0609 and A0610 models, powered by the 3.5 litre ohv in-line six-cylinder diesel engine, and the 3 litre V6 ohv petrol engine, respectively. The standard drive line consisted of the Ford 4-310 wide-ratio four-speed gearbox, with the close-ratio version of this, or the ZF-55-24/3 five-speed transmission as optional equipment. An open propeller shaft to a fully floating spiral bevel final drive assembly completed the arrangements. Wheelbases of 130, 145, and 156 inches were available, with gross vehicle weights of 12,320 lbs (petrol) and 13,860 lbs (diesel). Amongst those offering passenger carrying bodywork for these A series chassis was Tricentrol Chassis Developments, whose attractive 25-seater "Unibus" on the A0609 chassis was to find employment with Hull City Transport.

At long last plugging the gap left by the demise of the original Model A and AF saloon coaches of 30 years earlier, came the Transit PSV models in October 1965 as an integral part of the new Transit light commerical vehicle range.

These were available in either 9- or 12-seat configuration on the short wheelbase (106 inch) LCX chassis, and with 15 seats on the long wheelbase (118 inch) LCY model. All seats were forward facing on these rear-entrance models which featured full PVC headlining, interior lights, rubber floor covering and hinged rear quarter windows. A standard or Custom model could be specified, with the latter including an interior heater/demister, full width chrome front bumper, rear chrome quarter bumpers, and a full gloss enamel finish.

The power for the 9- and 12-seater models was provided by the new V4 1.7 litre ohv petrol engine developing 73 bhp at 4750 rpm, with the gearbox being the four-speed all synchromesh unit as used on the similarly powered passenger cars. An open propeller shaft transmitted the power to a three-quarter floating spiral bevel rear axle. The 15-seat bus was equipped with the 85 bhp 2 litre V4 petrol engine, mated to the same gearbox as the smaller models but with a fully floating hypoid bevel final drive assembly in this case. The Borg-Warner Model 35 automatic transmission was optional throughout the range, and on the LCY model could be specified in conjunction with the optional diesel engine; this being the Perkins 4/108 four-cylinder cylinder ohv in-line unit producing 52 bhp at 4000 rpm. With this engine installed, the maximum number of passengers permitted was reduced to 14.

Changes through the years to the Transit vans was reflected wherever appropriate in the corresponding bus models. In 1979 the 9-seater bus was deleted, but the range overall was extended now by the addition of 13-seat and 17-seat crew bus versions based on the regular 12-seat and 15-seat LCX and LCY models. Basic power unit for the 12-seater now was the 1.6 litre overhead camshaft in-line four-cylinder petrol engine, developing 69 bhp at 4750 rpm. A four-speed all synchromesh gearbox, open propeller shaft and three-quarter floating hypoid bevel rear axle completed the drive line. Optional power units were the 2 litre ohc four-cylinder in either normal or economy tune, and a 2.4 litre ohv four-cylinder diesel. The Ford C3 automatic transmission could be specified with these larger units. Gross vehicle weights were 5292 lbs and 5623 lbs for the petrol and diesel, respectively. Apart from being equipped with a heavier duty fully floating hypoid bevel rear axle the 13-seat crew bus featured the same mechanical specifications as the 12-seat model.

In both 15- and 17-seat (crewbus) configurations the standard power unit was the 2 litre ohc petrol engine developing 83 bhp at 4500 rpm, with the 2.4 litre diesel being an option. The drive line again consisted of the four-speed gearbox and the heavier duty type final drive. Gross vehicle weights with either seating capacity were 6385 lbs for the petrol engined model and 6946 lbs with the diesel option.

Forward facing seats in either four of five rows or three seats per row gave the 12 and 15 seat capacity in the normal bus models, whilst inward facing bench seats running lengthwise, plus additional seating alongside the driver were a feature of the crew bus versions. The custom trim option with features as on the previous models was available on the normal buses only.

Public service buses and the crew bus variants are amongst the present day Transit range which, with its sloping front styling, makes for a very striking light passenger transport vehicle. These buses are based on the semi-high roof van body, with access by both sliding side door with integral step in addition to the normal rear doors. Seating capacities, and arrangements, follow the pattern of the previous Transits, with the PSV model again being available as a standard model or with an improved trim option, the latter now being the "L" trim. Although still within the LCX and LCY groupings, both wheelbase measurements are slightly longer than before, now being 110.8 inches and 118.9 inches. The suspension arrangements differ considerably now between the short and long wheelbase models, with the former boasting independent front suspension of the MacPherson hydraulic telescopic strut principle, but with coil springs mounted inboard of the struts minimising interior protrusion. On the long wheelbase model the front end arrangements consist of an I-beam axle with a pair of asymetric longitudinally mounted semi-elliptics. Also longitudinally mounted are the long rear semi-elliptic leaf springs on both models, and completing the suspension are double-acting telescopic shock absorbers all round on the larger bus, and at the rear on the short wheelbase model in conjunction with its MacPherson strut type up front.

Power units now are the 2 litre ohc petrol engine as standard, with the new 2.5 litre direct injection diesel unit as the optional equipment. Four- or five-speed all synchromesh transmissions are available to choice on the 12-seat bus, with the five-speed gearbox being standard on the larger version. The Ford C3 automatic remains an option and once again the hypoid bevel final drives are of the three-quarter floating, and fully floating type, on the 12- and 15-seat models, respectively. The mechanical specifications for the 13-seat and 17-seat crew bus variants are as on the corresponding PSV Transits.

As a builder of public service vehicles of all categories at some time or another, Ford of Britain has experienced some, but by no means total success, as much of the market fell to those PSV specialists who could concentrate wholly on the specific market requirements. Nevertheless, the R series sold reasonably well over a number of years, giving good service to both coach tour operators and some municipalities. But the company's real success in this field lies in the lightweight category where the long-running Transit series has proved to be a popular choice, and remaining so today as Ford of Britain's only contender.

Above: An early example of a Ford motor coach. 18-seater bodywork mounted on the 24 hp Model AA long wheelbase 2 ton chassis.

26-seater coach body mounted on a Thames Trader 4 ton short wheelbase chassis. The Trader instrumentation and the steering wheel with the lighting operating stalk switches have been retained. With single sliding door entrance. This type of coach is very acceptable for smaller parties. 1961.

Duple bodied Ford P.S.V., 212 inch wheelbase chassis. At Victoria Bus Station before departing for Moscow. It was driven through Europe to Moscow and returned to be greeted with enthusiasm at Victoria Coach Station after 45 hours from departure. A number of seats were removed and replaced by a chemical toilet and food bar. 1964.

Specially built double deck body by Strachens mounted on the Ford P.S.V. chassis of 212.0 inch wheelbase to carry both bicycles and their riders for Dartford tunnel transport. The bicycles were stacked in the lower deck with the riders up on the upper deck. The venture was unsuccessful and later abandoned. 1963.

Luxury 54-seat coach body by Duple Motor Bodies mounted on the Ford 11 metre coach chassis, 1963. In 1965 a Duple-bodied 11 metre Ford coach won the prestigious Coach of the Year award at the annual Brighton Motor Coach Show.

Below: Scottish highlands bus destination, Inverness, operated by the Highlands Omnibus Limited. Mounted on Ford 'R' series P.S.V. 192.0 inch wheelbase. 1973.

Above: District service coach operated by Doncaster City Transport. Duple body 52-seater mounted on Ford 'R' series model R1114, P.S.V. 226.0 inch wheelbase chassis. 1973.

Transit Mark II L.C.Y. Dial a Ride bus and taxi service. L.C.Y. chassis 118.0 inch wheelbase. Dual rear tyre equipment. Picking up from Maidstone prison. 1973.

Transit L.C.Y., Mark II long wheelbase, 118.0 inch 15-seater bus. Powered by 2.0 litre ohv. petrol engine. Side opening door entrance. Dual rear tyre equipment. 1973.

Transit L.C.Y., long wheelbase, 15-seater bus. Powered by 3.5 litre six-cylinder in-line diesel engine. Dual rear tyre equipment. 1974.

R series, R1011, 192.0 inch wheelbase P.S.V. chassis with Eastern coachwork, single deck bus body. Operated by the National Bus Corporation under Alder Valley area. Powered by 6.0 litre six-cylinder in-line diesel engine. 1974.

Transit Mark II, L.C.Y., long wheelbase. Welfare Dormobile Pacemaker Social Service bus body. Loading wheelchair patient. Dual rear tyre equipment. 1980.

R series, R1114, 226.0 inch wheelbase. Powered by 6.0 litre turbocharged six-cylinder diesel engine. 54-seater coach. 1980.

New Transit 15-seater L.C.Y., bus on private hire. Long wheelbase 118.9 inch, dual rear tyre equipment. Quite a number of this size of Transit bus are being operated by municipal transport regions. 1986.

New Transit, 12-seater. L.C.X., short wheelbase of 110.8 inches. Independent front suspension should improve the ride as compared with the previous Transit range. Powered by either the 2.0 litre ohc., four-cylinder petrol engine or the latest 2.5 litre ohv. D.I. (direct injection) four-cylinder diesel engine. 1986.

New Transit 15 seater, L.C.Y. bus. Long wheelbase of 118.9 inches. Side loading hinged type door. Powered by either the 2.0 litre ohc., four-cylinder petrol engine or the latest 2.5 litre ohv D.I. (direction injection) four-cylinder diesel engine. 1986.

Front view of the 'R' series P.S.V. chassis showing front end bulkhead ready for the building of either a coach or bus body. 1963.

Offside to rear view of the 'R' series P.S.V. chassis showing extended exhaust tailpipe, and the location of the battery. Also the kick-up of the chassis frame over the rear axle. 1963.

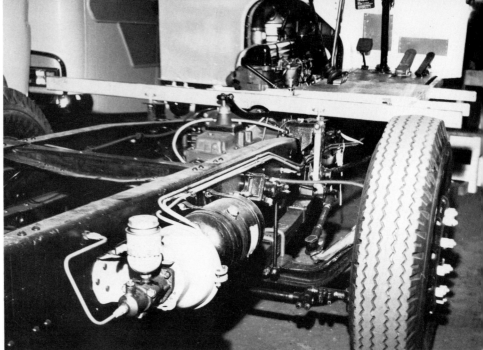

Offside to front view of 'R' series P.S.V. chassis showing the power braking system, air assisted hydraulic brakes. Awaiting mounting of bus or coach body. 1963.

General view of the 'R' series P.S.V. chassis facing forwards. Showing the mechanicals. 1963.

7 Power and drivelines

All the Ford four-cylinder side-valve petrol engines installed in British built Fords from the Model T through to the 8 and 10 hp vehicles, and the big V8-cylinder sidevalve units were of Detroit design.

In the case of the Model T and the Model AF some of these units were supplied by Henry Ford & Son Ltd., Cork, Ireland, but in the 1930s all were being built at Dagenham to Detroit's specifications and detail drawings. Although some research into the possibility of designing an all-British Ford petrol engine did take place during the 1930s, the onset of war curtailed these tentative studies. During the war however, when Ford of Britain had settled down to the war effort, some technical studies were made with a view to the design and development of British Ford engines, both petrol and diesel, under the supervision of a newly recruited senior member of the engineering staff who possessed considerable experience in engine design and development work.

After hostilities had ceased, serious work did commence in this direction, but principally aimed at passenger car units, although no specific categories could be visualised at this stage as company plans were still somewhat vague, and particularly so in respect of commercial vehicles.

Experimental single-cylinder petrol and diesel engines were built simply in order to establish the most efficient combustion chamber shapes, overhead valve layouts, and piston designs. Much was also learned by studying automobile literature and scaling specialist engine manufacturer's engine arrangement drawings which appeared therein, so accumulating much useful comparitive data and information.

The company's first all-British power units were the short-stroked (oversquare) ohv four and six-cylinder engines for the new Consul/Zephyr passenger cars which appeared in the latter part of 1950, but development work on new commercial vehicle engines was now going ahead for the projected new truck range which would eventually emerge as the Thames Trader. As we have seen in an earlier chapter, the first of these were the four-cylinder petrol and diesel units which were introduced into the specification of the ET6 models in 1953. The six-cylinder versions followed in the Trader, and were not without their troubles at first, with problems being experienced with tappets, camshaft, and valves. These problems were however quickly overcome and the engines settled down to give very satisfactory operation. By this time the four-cylinder units had amassed many miles in service under a variety of operating conditions, and undergone assessments in respect of operating economies by comparison with the side-valve V8 petrol engine and the Perkins P6 diesel. Overall, the results were encouraging, and in the 1960s a separate Truck Engine Engineering section evolved, and continued the development of large capacity diesel power units, with the next generation of these being for the D series trucks. Rather than develop engines for limited applications however, suitable proprietary units were obtained, with the heavy end of the D series featuring Cummins V6 and V8 diesel power in addition to the Ford/Perkins V8 engines.

Cummins, with their V8 8.3 litre, and two versions of their 10 litre six-cylinder turbocharged unit; Deutz, with their air-cooled 9.5 litre V6; and Perkins with their 8.8 litre and 10.48 litre V8 diesels provide the power for the heavy range of Ford Cargo trucks. Cummins alone provided the power units for the Transcontinental H series, all of which featured an appropriate version of the 14 litre in-line six-cylinder NTE range of engines.

In contrast, the small capacity diesels used in the Transit were all of Ford manufacture, these being the York 2.4 litre (four-cylinder) and 3.5 litre six-cylinder units, and the latest 2.5 direct injection four-cylinder engine.

The petrol engines were all of Ford manufacture, and apart from the two large capacity six-cylinder units provided by Dearborn for the petrol engined D series models, were all in production in Britain as passenger car units. The first thoroughly modern design to see service in the commercial vehicles was the Mk2 Consul engine in the 400E van. This was an oversquare ohv unit already into its second generation in the passenger car range. The small capacity ohv engines in the light delivery vans were versions of Dagenham's now legendary Kent series of engines, whilst the overhead camshaft units have their origins in the Pinto range of engines first seen in Ford of America's sub-compact cars.

The V configuration ohv units first seen in the Transit were also the power units for the Corsair and, in 2 litre form, the Zephyr V4 cars, whilst the six-cylinder versions of these were initially the source of power for the Mk4 Zodiac and Executive range, and later the 3-litre Capri and Granada models, albeit in a considerably higher state of tune than the commercial vehicle applications.

As had been the case with the petrol engines, early transmission systems used in the British Fords were of American design, with the earliest, the Model T, being unique amongst these as it was of epicyclic two-speed design. With the Model A came the conventional three-speed sliding gear type, but devoid of synchromesh. The next three-speeder, for the Model B, saw the introduction of synchromesh engagement for second and top gears, with this arrangement also being a feature of the small three-speed gearbox which came in 1932 for the 8-hp, and later the 10 hp models.

The four-speed non-synchromesh gearbox of the Model BB trucks was based on the American Warner T98 which remained in production right through to the ET models of the postwar period. This was followed by the Warner four-speed T98A, designated by Ford as the 8MTH and in production from the Trader to the present day Cargo range, but now designated as the Ford 4-310 with improved components such as the strengthened reverse idler gear and first gear train, and the offer of both wide and close ratio gears.

A number of proprietary transmissions were also purchased for use in the early Trader, early D and R series, and the A series, such as; for the A series, the Turner T-150 four-speed synchromesh, and the ZF gearbox ZF-S5-24/3 five-speed as optional equipment; for the D series, the Turner T5C-3017 and T5C-3018 five-speed units; and for the early phase 2, D 1000 models the Turner T5C-4007 and T5C-4008 five-speed units, and the ZF-56-70-3 six-speed gearbox.

However, during the late 1950s a senior design engineer who had specialised in transmission design started a separate section which was to concentrate on the development of transmissions, including rear axle drive gear and differential assemblies. As a result, eventually came the new Ford four, six, and eight-speed all synchromesh transmissions, housed in vertically split cases for ease of assembly and repair. These replaced the Turner five-speed gearboxes, and in many cases became standard equipment for the D series and subsequent Cargo range, although the latter has seen the introduction to Ford of another ZF transmission, the ZF-S5-35/2 five-speed unit.

For the heavier vehicles making up the Cargo range are the Eaton Fuller nine-speed synchromesh transmissions types RT 6609 and RT 11609A, together with another ZF type. This is the ZF-56-80 GV80 splitter, a twelve-speed splitter transmission with six main speeds and two splitter speeds – low at 1:1, and high at 0.836:1. The advent of the Transcontinental H series trucks saw the introduction of two further transmissions into the Ford range, these being the Eaton Fuller RT 9509C nine-speed, and RTO 9515 thirteen-speed constant mesh.

Once again, up to the introduction of the Thames Trader, the rear axles like the engines and gearboxes were of American Ford design, with the Model T featuring a semi-floating spiral bevel gear driven type with a two pinion differential, whilst the Model TT 1 ton truck was equipped with an overhead worm gear drive arrangement.

A three-quarter floating design was adopted for the Model A, giving improved road wheel support, whilst the Model AA initially continued with the overhead worm type before it too received the spiral bevel drive which was to be a feature of Ford commercials until the Thames Trader introduced the hypoid bevel assemblies.

The fore and aft vertical split axle housing was another feature of the torque tube drive Fords up to and including the ET range, whereas with the hypoid bevel axles came a new design of housing. This was the pressed steel banjo type with a separate drive gear and differential carrier which could simply be withdrawn from the axle housing without the axle first having to be removed from the vehicle as with the vertical split type.

The three-quarter floating arrangements where a single hub bearing is mounted on the hub end of the axle housing arm, and therefore relieving the half shafts of any load was normally used on light commercials and passenger cars. However, the fully floating type as introduced on the Model BB is preferred for the medium and heavy vehicles, with the two bearings mounted on the rear hub end of the axle arm being spaced a distance apart to provide stability to the wheel mounting and relieving the axle half shafts of any load bearing stresses, leaving them to provide rotary power to the wheels thus taking torsional loads only. On the heavier models of the Transit the Salisbury type rear axle is employed in which the gears and differential are mounted in the nose of the integral gear carrier and axle housing, with a removable back cover for assembly and gear adjustment. Car type three-quarter floating axles are used on the short wheelbase Transit models, with the Salisbury type being confined to the long wheelbase range.

The hypoid bevel gear and differential carrier assembly follows the design of the Rockwell Axle Division originally designed by one of the subsidiary companies, Timken Detroit Axle Company. This was adopted for the Trader and has continued in production for the D series and the Cargo range. Optional equipment for the D series and Cargo however are the Eaton single-speed with spiral bevel crownwheel and pinion, and the Eaton two-speed epicyclic spur gear assembly.

Ford single-speed drive gear and differential carrier units are designated as follows; 13A, 14B, hypoid bevel gear drive; 15C, 16A, and 16C, spiral bevel gear drive. Mounted in rear axles of differently rated capacities the designations for the complete axle assemblies become, for example; 14B/165, a maximum 14 inch crownwheel diameter and 16,500 lbs capacity; 15C/195, a maximum 15 inch crownwheel diameter and a 19,500 lbs capacity. Similar designations are used for both the Eaton single and two-speed versions; 18300/225 Eaton single-speed carrier with 22,500 lbs capacity; 16220/225 Eaton two-speed carrier and 22,500 lbs capacity axle. For the Transcontinental, Rockwell heavy duty rear axles of the hypoid bevel type were chosen.

For the County Commercial double drive six-wheelers a crownwheel and two pinions arrangement was used for the foremost rear axle, this continuing the drive to a standard Ford axle in the rearmost position, whilst on the D series and Cargo six-wheel models an Eaton foremost axle with spiral bevels and spur gears produces through drive to a standard Ford or Eaton single-speed axle in the rear. The six-wheel Transcontinental models featured the Rockwell hypoid bevel types in both foremost and rearmost positions.

Appendix 1 Ford model identification codings

Ford vehicle models initially were identified as: model 'T' and 'TT', model 'A' and 'AA', and model 'B' and 'BB' with no other form of designation.

Model coding system relative to actual information regarding the model commenced around 1935.

Model	Year	Type	Engine
50	1935	15 cwt van	30 hp V8 petrol
50E	1935	15 cwt van	22 hp V8 petrol
51	1936	Truck range	30 hp V8 petrol
61	1936	25 cwt F/C	22 hp V8 petrol
67	1936	15 cwt van	30 hp V8 petrol
73	1937	15 cwt van	22 hp V8 petrol
77	1937	15 cwt van	30 hp V8 petrol
79	1937	Truck range	24 hp 4 cyl/30 hp V8 petrols
7V	1937	Truck range	24 hp 4 cyl/30 hp V8 petrols

According to these codes the first digit did denote the year with the exception of the model 51 range which was not adopted by Ford of Britain till 1936. The second digit did not seem to represent anything positive, the only set which did was the 1937 where 73 denoted 22 hp V8 15 cwt van, 77 the 30 hp V8 version and 79 the truck range. It was not until 1938 when the full coding system digits represented something associated with the model or model range.

It was a four digit or five digit if the Country of production was involved in any deviation from the standard Detroit model.

Representation of the coding is:

1st	Year in which the model commenced
2nd	horse power of the engine
3rd	the wheelbase
4th	type of vehicle
5th	country in which model or modifications to the standard model is peculiar. Thus:-
1st	Year – indicated by 8 – 1938, 9 – 1939, 0 – 1940, etc.

2nd   hp of engine by:

1 – 30 hp V8	6 – 36.4 hp
2 – 22 hp V8	7 – 27.4 hp 4 cyl
3 – 10 hp 4 cyl	8 – 24 hp 4 cyl
4 – 8 hp 4 cyl	9 – 32.5 hp V8

3rd   Wheelbase, only if specially indicated by digit. Absence indicates standard wheelbases included.

4th   Type of vehicle:

A – passenger car.

C – Normal control light Commercial (15 cwt Van etc.).

N – Tractor.

T – Normal control truck.

U – Tipper.

W – Forward control truck, or cab over engine.

5th   Country to which the model is peculiar or modified from the standard American design or production.

Initial letters thus:

A – Australia.   C – Canada,   E – England,   Q – South Africa.

Examples of coding:

E817T = England (E), 1938 (8), 30 hp, engine (1), 157″ W/B (7), truck (T).

O1T = 1940 (O), 30 hp, (1), truck (T).

E88W – England (E), 1938 (8), 24 hp (8), forward control (W).

Prefixes

The prefix to a part number normally consists of the symbol number of the model for which it was originally designed. In this way, the correct classification of models by their numbers may often provide useful information in regard to parts designed for models from 1938 to 1945, even when there is no previous knowledge of the model concerned.

Additional information may be conveyed if the prefix to a part number, indicates that the part is 'foreign' to 'domestic' production. In most cases (but not every case) the differences between 'foreign' and 'domestic' parts is one of R.H. (right-hand) or L.H. (left-hand) drive.

Where there is no 'peculiar-country' letter at the beginning of the prefix, American design is indicated, in which case a peculiar R.H. drive will be indicated by the addition of an 'F' to the prefix as American domestic production is L.H. drive. On the other hand, where an initial 'E' is the prefix indicates English design, it is the peculiar L.H. drive part which has the final 'F' in its prefix as our production is R.H. drive.

Examples:

81TF = R.H. drive (or other variation from American domestic production).

E93AF = L.H. drive (or other variation from English domestic production).

However the model 7V did not come into the designation coding. The 7 might denote 1937 when the model range was released, but the 'V' does not seem to mean anything, except perhaps the V8 engine as the premier power unit, leaving the 24 hp, as the option with no designation. Similarly from 1948 the models ET6 and ET7 do not follow the system. It is believed that 'E' = English, 'T' = truck and the '6' or '7' the vehicle range number.

Another system was evolved after the ET6 and ET7, in which a group of numbers was released to indicate passenger cars, vans, trucks, tractors, etc.

200 – 299   passenger cars.

300 – 399   light vans (car derivatives).

400 – 499   medium vans (10, 12 cwts).

500 – 599   forward control trucks, including the ET6 with the four cyl. engine, semi-forward control.

600 – 699   trucks normal control.

700 – 799   tractors.

Examples:

Anglia van 5 cwt – 300E RHD., 301E LHD.

Thames Trader – 508E RHD. 6 cylinder petrol, 509E LHD. version; 510E RHD.

6 cylinder diesel, 511E LHD. version, etc.

ET6 with the four cylinder petrol and diesel engines redesignated 500E 4-cylinder petrol, RHD, 501E LHD. version; 502E 4-cylinder diesel RHD., 503E LHD. version, etc., up to 508E.

10, 12 and 15 cwt vans – 400E RHD. petrol, 401E LHD. version; 402E RHD. diesel, 403E LHD. version, etc., up to 499. The prefix 'E' for England still remained.

This system did not last long. It was replace by a further coding system commencing with the 'D' series truck range.

Four digit number, the first two digits indicated the model gross vehicle weight in tons and the last two digits denoted the engine by its bhp.

Example:
D0607 – 06 for 5.8/6.3 tons G.V.W., 07 for 74 nett bhp four-cylinder diesel engine.
D1010 – 10 for 9.84/10.5 tons G.V.W., 10 for 106 nett bhp six-cylinder diesel.
This system remained for the identifying of models by weight and engine power, continuing in the Cargo range of trucks.
However, the Transit models were coded similarly but only by payload, with a three digital code number. Identification by payload in kilograms.

Examples:
Model 160, gross vehicle weight for the petrol model of 3,100 kilos and payload of 1661 kilos- coding 160 using the nearest three digits.

Appendix 2 Commercial vehicle production 1931 to 1986

Ford of Britain commercial vehicle production 1931 to 1986; 55 years
The following production figures include the models specified during each year.

Year	Models	Production
1931	AA, A	4,569
1932	AA, BB, B, 19Y	13,651
1933	BB, B, 19Y	16,137
1934	BB, B, BBE (F/C), 19Y	19,127
1935	BB, B, BBE (F/C), 19Y, 50F	18,054
1936	BB, BBE (F/C), 51, 19Y, Tug Artic, 61	19,182
1937	7V, 79, BBE, 7Y, 73, 77, 67, 61	16,335
1938	7V, BBE (F/C), 79, 817T, 887T, E88W, E83W, 73, 77, 67, 81C, 82C, E88C, 7Y, 61	16,770
1939	91C, 7V, E83W, 81T, 88T, 7Y, WOT2, WOC1, 61, E88W, WOT3	17,356
1940	81T, 88T, 01W, 018W, 61, E88W, 7V, E83W, 7Y, 91C, 92C, 98C, WOT1, WOT2, WOT3, WOC1, RO1T, RO18, O1Y, O1T, 018T	28,483
1941	018W, 61, E88W, 7V, WOT1, WOT2, WOT3, 01T, 018T, WOT8, E83W, 01Y	29,574
1942	61, E88W, 7V, WOT1, WOT2, WOT3, WOT8, WOT6, E83W, AOP Carrier	38,310
1943	7V, WOT1, WOT2, WOT3, WOT6, E83W, AOP Carrier, Loyd Bren Gun Carrier, Universal Carrier	41,942
1944	7V, E83W, WOT1, WOT2, WOT3, WOT6, Loyd Bren Gun Carrier, Universal Carrier	37,505
1945	7V, EO4C, WOT1, WOT2, WOT6, Universal Carrier, E83W	26,577
1946	7V, E83W, EO4C, EO3CF/A	33,822
1947	7V, E83W, EO4C	35,832
1948	EO4C, E83W, E494C, EO3CF/A, E493C/B, 7V	37,289
1949	7V, ET6, ET7, E493C/B, E83W	39,693
1950	ET6, ET7, E493C/B, E83W	43,891
1951	ET6, ET7, E83W, E493C/B	41,551
1952	ET6, ET7, E83W, E493C/B, 2E, 3E, 4E	38,671
1953	ET6, ET7, 500E, E83W, 2E, 3E, 4E	43,474
1954	ET6, ET7, 500E, 502E, 501E, 503E, E83W, E493C/B, 300E	41,946
1955	ET6, ET7, 500E, 502E, 501E, 503E, E83W, 300E, 302E, 304E	65,398
1956	ET6, ET7, 500E, 502E, 501E, 503E, E83W, 300E, 302E, 304E	57,092
1957	ET6, ET7, 500E, 502E, 501E, 503E, E83W, 300E, 302E, 304E, Trader, 404E, 400E	57,601
1958	Trader, 300E, 302E, 304E, 404E, 500E, 502E, 503E, 400E, 408E	74,485
1959	Trader, 300E, 302E, 304E, 404E, 408E, 500E, 503E, 502E, 400E	87,374
1960	Trader, 300E, 302E, 304E, 404E, 408E, 500E, 502E, 503E, 400E	100,353
1961	Trader, 300E, 302E, 304E, 404E, 400E, 408E, 406E, 500E, 502E, 503E, 307E, 309E, 310E	88,151
1962	Trader, 402E, 400E, 406E, 404E, 408E, 410E, 307E, 308E, 310E, Trader N/C	88,893
1963	Trader, 402E, 400E, 406E, 404E, 408E, 410E, 307E, 308E, 309E, 310E, Trader N/C	83,381
1964	Trader, 400E, 402E, 404E, 406E, 408E, 410E, 307E, 308E, 309E, 310E, Trader N/C	92,170

Year	Models	Production
1965	Trader, 400E, 402E, 404E, 406E, 408E, 410E, 307E, 308E, 309E, 310E, Trader N/C, D series, Transit, R series	85,317
1966	D series, Transit, 307E, 308E, 309E, 310E, R series, K series	113,623
1967	D series, Transit, 310E, 307E, 308E, 309, R series K series, H series	93,860
1968	D series, Transit, Escort van, R series, H series	108,986
1969	D series, Transit, Escort van, R series, H series	134,792
1970	D series, Transit, Escort van, R series, H series	141,517
1971	D series, Transit, Escort van, R series, H series	121,260
1972	D series, Transit, Escort van, R series, H series	143,519
1973	D series, Transit, A series, Escort van, R series, H series	137,209
1974	D series, Transit, A series, Escort van, R series, H series	131,268
1975	D series, Transit, A series, Escort 30, Escort 45, R series, H series	128,502
1976	D series, Transit, A series, Escort 35, Escort 45, R series, H series	141,628
1977	D series, Transit, A series, Escort 35, Escort 45, R series, H series	148,380
1978	D series, Transit, A series, Escort 35, Escort 45, R series, H series	106,472
1979	D series, Transit, A series, Escort 35, Escort 45, R series, H series	167,248
1980	D series, Transit, Escort 35, Escort 45, Cargo series	138,373
1981	Cargo series, Transit, Escort 35, Escort 45	86,182
1982	Cargo series, Transit, Escort 35, Escort 45, Fiesta van	115,637
1983	Cargo series, Transit, Escort 35, Escort 45, Fiesta van	96,852
1984	Cargo series, Transit, Escort 35, Escort 45, Fiesta van	94,211
1985	Cargo series, Transit, Escort 35, Escort 45, Fiesta van	101,407
1986	Cargo series, New Transit, Escort 'Combi', Escort 35, Escort 55, Fiesta 950, Fiesta 1.1, Fiesta 1.6D	93,860

1960 Ford of Britain achieved the magical figure of just over 100,000 commercial vehicles in one year's production. This was an all-time record.

1965 the introduction of the 'D' series to 1980 reached the all-time record of truck sales for one range of 540,000 for Ford of Britain.

1976 reached more than all-time records, it gained the gold when the Transit topped the one million mark.

From the early days it was obvious that the light commercial vehicles, such as the E83W 10 cwt proved to be the most popular with production of over 180,000.

However, a considerable number of these vans were produced during the Second World War under the direction of the government and were not under normal individual sales circumstances.

Appendix 3 **Specifications**

The following specifications show major assemblies and are those of standard equipped vehicles. No options have been included as these are too numerous to quote for the whole of Ford of Britain's commercial vehicles since 1912.

The new Cargo models have been selected to endeavour to give an overall picture of the model range which has more than seventy models and variants.

These specifications show the enormous selection of commercial vehicles manufactured by Ford of Britain over the years in an endeavour to meet operators' requirements.

The development of the major assemblies grew rapidly after the introduction of the all British designed Ford commercial vehicle range, the Thames Trader. From 1950 to 1986 there were ten petrol and seven diesel Ford engines, eight Ford transmissions and fourteen Ford rear axles.

Engines – Petrol

1	20 hp, four cylinder in-line, side-valve – Model 'T' and 'TT'.
2	30 hp, V8. side-valve.
2A	22 hp, V8. side-valve.
3	32.5 hp, V8. side-valve. (Canadian Ford engine).
4	8 hp, four-cylinder in-line, side-valve.
5	10 hp, four-cylinder in-line, side-valve.
6	24 hp, four-cylinder in-line, side-valve, (40 bhp).
7	24 hp, four-cylinder in-line, side-valve, (52 bhp).
8	3.6 litre, four-cylinder in-line, OHV.
9	4.88 litre, six-cylinder in-line, OHV.
10	1.7 litre V4, OHV.
11	2.0 litre V4, OHV.
12	1.1 litre four-cylinder in-line, OHV, (Low compression and high compression).
13	1.3 litre four-cylinder in-line, OHV, (Low compression and high compression).
14	1.6 litre four-cylinder in-line, OHV.
15	1.6 litre four-cylinder in-line, OHC.
16	2.0 litre four-cylinder in-line, OHC (Economy, Regular, and Heavy duty versions).
17	3.0 litre, V6, OHV.
18	5.0 litre, six-cylinder in-line, OHV, (Ford U.S.A.). (Early 'D' series).

Engines – Diesel

19	3.61 litre four-cylinder, in-line, OHV.
20	Perkins P6, six-cylinder, in-line, OHV.
21	4.730 litre six-cylinder, in-line, OHV.
22	Cummins Vale, 470 C.I.D. V6, OHV, (170 bhp).
23	Cummins Vale, 470 C.I.D. V6, OHV, (185 bhp).
24	Deutz, 9.6 litre, V6 Air-cooled (F6L – 413 – FZ).
25	Perkins 640, 10.5 litre, V8, OHV.
26	2.4 litre four-cylinder, in-line OHV.
27	3.5 litre six-cylinder, in-line OHV.
28	4.2 litre four-cylinder, in-line. OHV, (inclined version).

29	6.0 litre six-cylinder, in-line, OHV, (inclined version).
30	6.2 litre six-cylinder, in-line, OHV, (inclined version).
31	6.0 litre turbocharged, six-cylinder, in-line, OHV (inclined version).
32	Cummins 8.3 litre, V8, OHV.
33	Ford 8.8 litre, V8, OHV, (also Perkins 540).
34	2.5 litre, four-cylinder, in-line, OHC, (D.I.) direct injection.
35	Cummins L10, 10-litre, six-cylinder, in-line turbocharged OHV.
36	Cummins L10A, 10-litre, six-cylinder, in-line turbo charged, OHV.
37	Perkins 4/108, 1.76-litre, four-cylinder, in-line, OHV.
38	Cummins NTE 290, (255), 14-litre, six-cylinder, in-line, turbocharged, OHV.
39	Cummins NTE 290, 14-litre, six-cylinder, in-line, turbocharged, OHV.
40	Cummins NTE 350 (335), 14-litre, six-cylinder, in-line, turbocharged, OHV.
41	Cummins NTE 370, 14-litre, six-cylinder, in-line, turbocharged. OHV.

Transmissions

1	Ford model 'T' and 'TT', epicyclic transmission.
2	Three-speed synchromesh, truck transmission.
3	Four-speed, crash change, truck transmission.
4	Ford 8 – 570 – S eight-speed, synchromesh in forward gears.
5	Ford C3, automatic transmission.
6	Four-speed synchromesh, A, B, C, and D. versions.
7	Ford 4 – 410 – S, four-speed synchromesh in all forward gears.
8	Ford 6 – 600 – S, six-speed, close ratio (6 – 600 – SO) and wide ratio (6 – 540 – SW).
9	Turner four-speed, T4 – 150, close and wide ratio versions, synchromesh.
10	ZF five-speed, ZF – S5 – 24/3, synchromesh.
11	Ford 4 – 310 four-speed, close and wide ratio versions, synchromesh.
12	Turner, five-speed synchromesh, T5A – 3017.
13	Turner, five-speed synchromesh, T5A – 3018.
14	Turner, five-speed synchromesh, T5C – 4008.
15	Turner, five-speed synchromesh, T5C – 4007.
16	ZF six-speed, ZF – 56 – 70 – 3, synchromesh.
17	ZF twelve-speed, ZF – S6 – 80 GV80 Splitter.
18	Ford auxiliary/transfer transmission (for 4 x 4 vehicles).
19	ZF, five-speed, ZF – S5 – 35/2, synchromesh.
20	Eaton-Fuller, nine-speed constant mesh, RT – 6609.
21	Eaton-Fuller, nine-speed constant mesh, RT – 11609A.
22	Eaton-Fuller, nine-speed constant mesh, RT – 9509C.
23	Eaton-Fuller, thirteen-speed constant mesh, RTO – 9513.

Rear axles

1	Eaton two-speed axle-driving gear and differential assembly.
2	Ford single speed-axle, types 15C, 16A and 16C. Driving gear and differential assembly.
3	Ford light commercial vehicle axle, types 24, 27, 32, 34, 42, 52 and 53, driving gear and differential assembly.
4	Ford single-speed rear axle – hypoid bevel gear. Type 13A. Driving gear and differential assembly.
5	Ford single-speed axle – hypoid bevel gear. Type 14B. Driving gear and differential assembly.
6	Rockwell single-speed rear axle-Type R170. Driving gear and differential assembly.
7	Rockwell single-speed rear axle – Type R180. Driving gear and differential assembly.
8	Rockwell single-speed rear axle – Type U180. Driving gear and differential assembly.

9   Ford single-speed rear axle. Split type axle housing. Spiral bevel. Driving gear and differential assembly. Model 'AA'.

10   Ford single-speed rear axle. Split type axle housing. Spiral bevel. Driving gear and differential assembly. Model 'BB' to '79'.

11   Ford single-speed rear axle. Split type axle housing. Spiral bevel. Driving gear and differential assembly. Models 7V, ET6, and ET7.

Tandem rear axles

1   Ford tandem double drive axles. Six-wheelers. (Ex-County Commercial Cars Ltd).

2   Eaton tandem axles 38DT/18220 (Bogie type 410). Six-wheelers ('D' series and Cargo).

3   Eaton tandem axles 30 DS/Ford 15C and Eaton 38DS/Ford 16C (Bogies types 300/358/410).

Front drive axle

1   Ford front drive axle assembly. W.O.T.6., & W.O.T.8, 3 ton and 30 cwt 4 x 4 trucks.

Petrol Engines

Model T 20 hp   – Spec 1

No of cylinders	4 in-line.
Bore	3.75 in (92.25 mm).
Stroke	4.0 in (101.6 mm).
Displacement	2896 cc (176.7 cu in).
Power	20 bhp at 1,600 rpm.
Nett torque	–
Valves	Side valves, cam operated.
Main bearings	3, replaceable inserts.
Fuel system	Gravity feed.
Lubrication	Splash type. Oil collected on flywheel. No oil pump.
Ignition	Magneto & coils – 6 volt timing mechanically controlled coil fitted in magneto.

R.A.C. Rating at 22 hp.   – Spec 2A

No of cylinders	8 V90°.
Bore	2.6 in (66.04 mm).
Stroke	3.2 in (81.28 mm).
Displacement	2.23 litre (135.9 cu in).
Compression ratio	6.64:1
Gross power	46.1 kW (62 bhp) at 4,200 rpm.
Nett power	–
DIN power	47.6 kW (63.8 PS) at 4,200 rpm.
Gross torque	67.9 Nm (92 lb ft) at 2,200 rpm.
Nett torque	–
DIN torque	–
Engine weight (inclusive of clutch and transmission)	380 lb (172.3 kg).
Main bearings	3, replaceable inserts.
Valves	Side valves.
Fuel system	Lift pump, mechanically operated by push rod.
Lubrication	Pump circulation. No filter.

Ford V8 petrol engine   – Spec 2

Ford of Britain V8 used in Dagenham produced commercial vehicles. 30 hp.

No of cylinders	8 V90°.
Bore	3.0625 in (77.97 mm)
Stroke	3.75 in (95.25 mm).
Displacement	3622 cc (221 cu. in).
Compression ratio	6.15:1
Gross power	85 bhp at 3,500 rpm.
Nett torque	150 lbs ft at 1,500 rpm.
Engine weight (dry)	458 lb (207 kg).
Main bearings	3, replaceable inserts.
Valves	Side valves.
Fuel system	Lift pump, mechanically operated by push rod from rear of camshaft.
Lubrication	Pump circulation. No filter.

– Spec 3

V8, Canadian produced for Ford of Britain's 4 x 4 model 2E, 3E and 4E Military vehicle 1950/52.

No of cylinders	8 V90°.
Bore	3,1875 ins (81.03 mm).
Stroke	3.75 ins (95.25 mm).
Displacement	3920 cc (239 cu. ins).
Compression ratio	6.8:1
Gross power	95 bhp at 3,600 rpm.
Nett torque	170 lb ft at 2,100 rpm.
Engine weight (dry)	468 lb (212 kg).
Main bearings	3, replaceable inserts.
Valves	side valves.
Fuel system	Lift pump. Mechanically operated by push rod from rear of camshaft.
Lubrication	Pump circulation. No filter.

Ford Model 'Y' 8 hp   – Spec 4

No of cylinders	4 in-line.
Bore	2.23 in (56.64 mm).
Stroke	3.64 in (92.5 mm).
Displacement	933 cc (56.9 cu in).
Compression ratio	6.4:1
Gross power	17.1 kW (23 bhp) at 4,000 rpm.
Nett	–
DIN power	17.68 kW (23.7 PS) at 4,000 rpm.
Gross torque	49.32 Nm (36.4 lb ft) at 2,300 rpm.
Nett torque	–
DIN torque	–
Engine weight (dry)	185 lb (83.9 kg).
Main bearings	3, replacement inserts.
Valves	Side valves.
Fuel system	Fuel pump. Mechanical.
Lubrication	Full flow. No oil filter.

Ford Model 'C' 10 hp   – Spec 5

No of cylinders	4, in-line.
Bore	2.5 in (63.5 mm).
Stroke	3.644 in (92.56 mm).
Displacement	1172 cc (71.55 cu in).
Compression ratio	6.6:1
Gross power	23,8 kW (32.5 bhp) at 4,000 rpm.
Nett power	–
DIN power	24,57 kW (32.96 PS) at 4,000 rpm.
Gross torque	71.3 Nm (52.6 lb ft) at 2,350 rpm.
Nett torque	–
DIN torque	–
Engine weight (dry)	207 lb (93.87 kg).
Main bearings	3, replaceable inserts.
Valves	Side valves.
Fuel system	Fuel pump. Mechanical.
Lubrication	Full flow. No oil filter.

Ford 24.0 hp 'AA' Model   – Spec 6

No of cylinders	4, in-line.
Bore	3,875 in (98.4 mm).
Stroke	4.25 in (108.0 mm).
Displacement	–
Compression ratio	–
Gross power	29.8 kW (40 bhp) at 2,200 rpm.
Nett power	–
DIN power	29.83 kW (39.2 PS) at 2,200 rpm.
Gross torque	–
Nett torque	–
DIN torque	–
Engine weight	
Main bearings	3, replacement inserts.
Valves	Side valves.
Fuel system	Fuel pump. Mechanical.
Lubrication	Full flow. No oil filter.

Ford 24.0 hp 'BB', '51' & '7V'   – Spec 7

No of cylinders	4,. in-line.
Bore	3.875 in (98.4 mm).
Stroke	4.25 in (108.0 mm).
Displacement	–
Compression ratio	–
Gross power	38.8 kW (52 bhp) at 2,600 rpm.
Nett power	–
DIN power	40 kW (53.6 PS) at 2,600 rpm.
Gross torque	–
Nett torque	–
DIN torque	–
Engine weight (dry)	–
Main bearings	3, replaceable inserts.
Valves	Side valves.
Fuel system	Fuel pump. Mechanical.
Lubrication	Fuel flow. No oil filter.

Ford 3,610 cc petrol – 4 cylinder   – Spec 8

No of cylinders	4 in-line.
Bore	3.937 in (100 mm).
Stroke	4.520 in (115 mm).
Displacement	3610 cc (220 cu. in).
Compression ratio	6.0:1
Gross power	52.2 kW (70 bhp) at 2,800 rpm.
Nett power	48.5 kW (65 bhp) at 2,500 rpm.
DIN power	48 kW (67.9 PS) at 2,800 rpm.
Gross torque	223.5 Nm (165 lb ft) at 1,500 rpm.
Nett torque	214.1 Nm (158 lb ft) at 1,500 rpm.
DIN torque	–
Engine weight (dry)	–
Main bearings	5, replacement inserts.
Valves	ohv push rods.
Fuel system	Fuel pump. Mechanical,
Lubrication	Full flow, replacement oil filter element.

Ford 4,888 cc petrol – 6 cylinder   – Spec 9

No of cylinders	6 in-line.
Bore	3.74 in (95 mm).
Stroke	4.52 in (115 mm).
Displacement	4,888 cc (300 cu in).
Compression ratio	6:1
Gross power	83.5 kW (112 bhp) at 3,000 rpm.
Nett power	–
DIN power	77 kW (107.PS) at 3,000 rpm.
Gross torque	–
Nett torque	–
DIN torque	–
Engine weight (dry)	–
Main bearings	7, replaceable inserts.
Valves	ohv pushrods.
Fuel system	Fuel pump. Mechanical.
Lubrication	Full flow, replaceable oil filter element.

Ford 1.7 litre V4 petrol — Spec 10

No of cylinders	4. V formation.
Bore	3.69 in (93.7 mm).
Stroke	2.38 in (60.4 mm).
Displacement	1663 cc (101.5 cu in).
Compression ratio	7.7:1
Gross power	54.5 kW (73 bhp) at 4,750 rpm.
Nett power	47.0 kW (63 bhp) at 4,760 rpm.
DIN power	53.8 kW (76 PS) at 4,750 rpm.
Gross torque	123.3 Nm (91 lb ft) at 3,000 rpm.
Nett torque	114.5 Nm (84.5 lb ft) at 3,000 rpm.
DIN torque	113.6 Nm (11.6 mkg) at 3,000 rpm.
Engine weight (dry)	–
Main bearings	3, replaceable inserts.
Valves	ohv push rods.
Fuel system	Fuel pump. Mechanical.
Lubrication	Full flow, replaceable oil filter element.

Ford 2.0 litre V4 petrol — Spec 11

No of cylinders	4, V formation.
Bore	3.69 in (93.7 mm).
Stroke	2.85 in (72.4 mm).
Displacement	1996 cc (121.8 cu in).
Compression ratio	7.7:1
Gross power	63.7 kW (85.5 bhp) at 4,750 rpm.
Nett power	55.6 kW (74.5 bhp) at 4,500 rpm.
DIN power	65.8 kW (89.3 PS) at 4,750 rpm.
Gross torque	154.4 Nm (114 lb ft) at 2,750 rpm.
Nett torque	145.0 Nm (107 lb ft) at 2,750 rpm.
DIN torque	142.6 Nm (14.5 mkg) at 2,750 rpm.
Engine weight (dry)	–
Main bearings	3, replaceable inserts.
Valves	ohv pushrods.
Fuel system	Fuel pump. Mechanical.
Lubrication	Full flow, replaceable oil filter element.

Ford 1.1 litre ohv low compression — Spec 12

No of cylinders	4
Bore	3.188 in (80.98 mm).
Stroke	2.098 in (53.29 mm).
Displacement	1098 cc (67 cu in).
Compression ratio	8:1
Gross power	33.9 kW (45.5 bhp) at 5,800 rpm.
Nett power	30.6 kW (41.0 bhp) at 5,500 rpm.
DIN power	32.4 kW (44.0 PS) at 5,500 rpm.
Gross torque	69.6 Nm (51.3 lb ft) at 3,000 rpm.
Nett torque	66.7 Nm (49.2 lb ft) at 3,000 rpm.
DIN torque	70.6 Nm (7.2 mkg) at 3,000 rpm.
Engine weight (dry)	240 lbs (109 kg).
Valves	ohv pushrods.
Main bearings	6, replaceable inserts.
Fuel system	Fuel pump. Mechanical
Lubrication	Full flow, replaceable element oil filter.

Ford 1.1 litre ohv high compression

No of cylinders	4
Bore	3.188 in (80.98 mm).
Stroke	2.098 in (53.29 mm).
Displacement	1098 cc (67 cu in).
Compression ratio	9:1
Gross power	36.7 kW (49.2 bhp) at 5,800 rpm.
Nett power	33.4 kW (44.8 bhp) at 5,500 rpm.
DIN power	35.4 kW (48 PS) at 5,500 rpm.
Gross torque	72.1 Nm (53.2 lb ft) at 3,000 rpm.
Nett torque	69.3 Nm (51.1 lb ft) at 3,000 rpm.
DIN torque	73.6 Nm (7.5 mkg) at 3,000 rpm.
Engine weight (dry)	240 lb (109 kg).

Ford 1.3 litre ohv low compression — Spec 13

No of cylinders	4
Bore	3.188 in (80.98 mm).
Stroke	2.480 in (62.99 mm).
Displacement	1298 cc (79.2 cu in).
Compression ratio	8:1
Gross power	40.9 kW (54.9 bhp) at 5,700 rpm.
Nett power	37.6 kW (50.4 bhp) at 5,500 rpm.
DIN power	39.8 kW (54PS) at 5,500 rpm.
Gross torque	83.4 Nm (61.51 lb ft) at 3,000 rpm.
Nett torque	80.8 Nm (59.6 lb ft) at 3,000 rpm.
DIN torque	85.4 Nm (8.71 mkg) at 3,000 rpm.
Engine weight (dry)	242 lbs (110 kg).
Valves	ohv push rods.
Main bearings	5, replaceable inserts.
Fuel system	Fuel pump. Mechanical.
Lubrication	Full flow, replaceable element oil filter.

Ford 1.3 litre ohv high compression

No of cylinders	4
Bore	3.188 in (80.98 mm).
Stroke	2.480 in (62.99 mm).
Displacement	1298 cc (79.2 cu in).
Compression ratio	9:1
Gross power	43.3 kW (58.0 bhp) at 5,700 rpm.

Nett power	39.7 kW (53.2 bhp) at 5,500 rpm.
DIN power	42.0 kW (57 PS) at 5,500 rpm.
Gross torque	89.0 Nm (65.6 lb ft) at 3,000 rpm.
Nett torque	86.0 Nm (63.4 lb ft) at 3,000 rpm.
DIN torque	91.2 Nm (9.3 mkg) at 3,000 rpm.
Engine weight (dry)	242 lbs (110 kg).

Ford 1.6 litre ohv — Spec 14

No of cylinders	4
Bore	3.188 in (80.98 mm).
Stroke	3.056 in (77.62 mm).
Displacement	1598 cc (97.5 cu in).
Compression ratio	8:1
Gross power	–
Nett power	46.5 kW (62.3 bhp) at 5,000 rpm.
DIN power	46.5 kW (63.2 PS) at 5,000 rpm.
Gross torque	–
Nett torque	104.1 Nm (76.8 lb ft) at 2,500 rpm.
DIN torque	110.0 Nm (11.2 mkg) at 2,500 rpm.
Engine weight (dry)	245 lb (111 kg).
Main bearings	5, replaceable inserts.
Valves	ohv, push rods.
Fuel system	Fuel pump. Mechanical.
Lubrication	Full flow. Oil filter-disposable.

Ford 1.6 litre ohc — Spec 15

No of cylinders	4
Bore	3.448 in (87.6 mm).
Stroke	2.598 in (66.0 mm).
Displacement	1593 cc (97.2 cu in).
Compression ratio	8.1:1
Gross power	50 kW (67 bhp) at 4,750 rpm.
Nett power	–
DIN power	48.0 kW (65 PS) at 4,750 rpm.
Gross torque	112 Nm (82.8 lb ft) at 2,500 rpm.
Nett torque	–
DIN torque	114.0 Nm (11.0 mkg) at 2,800 rpm.
Engine weight (dry)	265 lbs (120 kg).
Main bearings	5, replaceable inserts.
Valves	ohc.
Fuel system	Fuel pump. Mechanical.
Lubrication	Full flow oil filler – disposable.

Ford 2.0 litre ohc Economy — Spec 16

No of cylinders	4
Bore	3.574 in (90.8 mm).
Stroke	3.031 in (77.0 mm).
Displacement	1993 cc (121.6 cu in).
Compression ratio	8.1:1
Gross power	44 kW (60 bhp) at 4,000 rpm.
Nett power	–
DIN power	43.0 kW (58 PS) at 4,000 rpm.

Gross torque	127 Nm (93.7 lb ft) at 2,800 rpm.
Nett torque	–
DIN torque	127.0 Nm.
Engine weight (dry)	286 lbs (130 kg).
Main bearings	5, replaceable inserts.
Valves	ohc.
Fuel system	Fuel pump. Mechanical.
Lubrication	Full flow oil filter – disposable.

Regular

No of cylinders	4
Bore	3.574 in (90.8 mm).
Stroke	3.031 in (77.0 mm).
Displacement	1993 cc (121.6 cu in).
Compression ratio	8.1:1
Gross power	60 kW (80.6 bhp) at 4,500 rpm.
Nett power	–
DIN power	57.0 kW (78 PS) at 4,500 rpm.
Gross torque	–
Nett torque	–
DIN torque	146.0 Nm (15 mkg) at 2800 rpm.
Engine weight (dry)	286 lb (130 kg).
Main bearings	5, replaceable inserts.
Valves	ohc.
Fuel system	Fuel pump. Mechanical.
Lubrication	Full flow oil filter-disposable.

Heavy Duty

No of cylinders	4
Bore	3.574 in (90.8 mm).
Stroke	3.031 in (77.0 mm).
Displacement	1993 cc (121.6 cu in).
Compression ratio	8.1:1
Gross power	58 kW (77 bhp) at 4,850 rpm.
Nett power	–
DIN power	55.0 kW (75 PS) at 4850 rpm.
Gross torque	137 Nm (101 lb ft) at 3,000 rpm.
Nett torque	–
DIN torque	137 Nm (13.9 m kg) at 3,000 rpm.
Engine	286 lb (130 kg).
Main bearings	5, replacement inserts.
Valves	ohc.
Fuel system	Fuel pump. Mechanical.
Lubrication	Full flow oil filter-disposable.

Ford 3.0 litre V6 — Spec 17

No of cylinders	6. V60°
Bore	3.69 in (93.6 mm).
Stroke	2.85 in (72.41 mm).
Displacement	2992 cc (182.6 cu in)
Compression ratio	8:1
Gross power	74.7 kW (100.2 bhp) at 4,750 rpm.
Nett power	70.1 kW (93.3 bhp) at 4,650 rpm.
DIN power	74.6 kW (100.0 PS) at 4,650 rpm.
Gross torque	182.2 Nm (134.3 lb ft) at 2,500 rpm.
Nett torque	180.2 Nm (132.7 lb ft) at 2,100 rpm.

DIN torque	190.3 Nm (19.4 mkg) at 2,100 rpm.
Engine weight (dry)	428 lb (194 kg).
Main bearings	4, replaceable inserts.
Valves	ohv push rods.
Fuel system	Fuel pump. Mechanical.
Lubrication	Full flow oil filter-disposable.

Ford 5.0 litre (USA-FORD)   – Spec 18

No of cylinders	6 in-line.
Bore	4.00 in (101.6 mm).
Stroke	3.98 in (101.1 mm).
Displacement	4918 cc (300.1 cu in).
Compression ratio	7.9:1
Gross power	97 kW (130 bhp) at 3,400 rpm.
Nett power	87.3 kW (117 bhp) at 3,400 rpm.
DIN power	91.3 kW (124 PS) at 3,400 rpm.
Gross torque	330.8 Nm (244 lb ft) at 1,600 rpm.
Nett torque	320.0 Nm (236 lb ft) at 1,600 rpm.
DIN torque	335.4 Nm (34.2 mkg) at 1,600 rpm.
Engine weight (dry)	623 lb (283 kg).
Valves	ohv, push rods.
Fuel system	Fuel pump. Mechanical.
Lubrication	Full flow oil filter-disposable.

Diesel Engines

Ford 3610 cc 4 cylinder   – Spec 19

No of cylinders	4. in-line.
Bore	3.937 in (100 mm).
Stroke	4.52 in (115 mm).
Displacement	3610 cc (220 cu. in).
Compression ratio	16.0:1
Gross power	–
Nett power	44.76 kW (60 bhp) at 2,400 rpm.
DIN power	46.0 kW (61.8 PS) at 2,400 rpm.
Gross torque	203.0 Nm (150 lb ft) at 1,600 rpm.
Nett torque	–
DIN torque	–
Engine weight (dry)	–
Main bearings	5, replacement inserts.
Valves	ohv push rods.
Fuel system	Injection pump – Simms in-line.
Lubrication	Full flow, replaceable oil filter element.

Perkins P6 – 6 cylinder   – Spec 20

No of cylinders	6. in-line.
Bore	3.5 in (88.9 mm).
Stroke	5.0 in (127 mm).
Displacement	4730 cc (288.7 cu in).
Compression ratio	16.5:1
Gross power	–
Nett power	52.2 kW (70 bhp) at 2,200 rpm.
DIN power	53.7 kW (72 PS) at 2,200 rpm.
Gross torque	249.6 Nm (184 lb ft) at 1,000 rpm.
Nett torque	–

DIN torque	239.7 Nm (24.44 mkg) at 1,000 rpm.
Engine weight (dry)	–
Main bearings	7, replaceable inserts.
Valves	ohv push rods.
Fuel system	Injection pump – Bosch in-line.
Lubrication	Full flow, replaceable oil filter element.

Ford 4730 cc 6 cylinder   – Spec 21

No of cylinders	6 in-line.
Bore	3,500 in (88.9 mm).
Stroke	5.00 in (127 mm).
Displacement	4730 cc (288.7 cu in).
Gross power	–
Nett power	52.22 kW (70 bhp) at 2,200 rpm.
Nett power	–
DIN power	53.8 kW (73.15 PS) at 2,200 rpm.
Gross torque	–
Nett torque	–
DIN torque	–
Engine weight (dry)	–
Main bearings	7, replaceable inserts.
Valves	ohv push rods.
Fuel system	Injection pump – Simms in-line.
Lubrication	Full flow, replaceable oil filter element.

Cummins Vale 470 CID (170 bhp)   – Spec 22

No of cylinders	6. V formation.
Bore	4,625 in (117 mm).
Stroke	3.50 in (89 mm).
Displacement	7702 cc (470 cu in).
Compression ratio	18:1
Gross power	126.8 kW (170 bhp) at 3,000 rpm.
Nett power	120.8 kW (162 bhp) at 3,000 rpm.
DIN power	128.3 kW (167 PS) at 3,000 rpm.
Gross torque	440.3 Nm (325 lb ft) at 1,800 rpm.
Nett torque	433.6 Nm (320 lb ft) at 1,800 rpm.
DIN torque	431.5 Nm (44.08 mkg) at 1,800 rpm.
Engine weight (dry)	1210 lb (548.7 kg).
Main bearings	4, replaceable inserts.
Valves	ohv push rods.
Fuel system	Injection pump. Cummins Pt.
Lubrication	Full flow, replaceable oil filter element.

Cummins Vale 470 CID (185 bhp)   – Spec 23

No of cylinders	6. V formation.
Bore	4.625 in (117 mm).
Stroke	3.50 in (89 mm).
Displacement	7702 cc (470 cu in).
Compression ratio	18:1
Gross power	138.0 kW (185. bhp) at 3,300 rpm.

Nett power .... 131.3 kW (176 bhp) at 3,300 rpm.

DIN power .... 128.2 kW (177 PS) at 3,300 rpm.

Gross torque .... 444.4 Nm (328 lb ft) at 1,900 rpm.

Nett torque .... 437.6 Nm (323 lb ft) at 1,900 rpm.

DIN torque .... 433.2 Nm (44.25 mkg) at 1,900 rpm.

Engine weight (dry) .... 1210 lb (548.7 kg).

Main bearings .... 4, replaceable inserts.

Valves .... ohv push rods.

Fuel system .... Injection pump. Cummins Pt.

Lubrication .... Full flow, replaceable oil filter element.

DEUTZ-F6L-413-FZ (air cooled) V6.9.6 litre – Spec 24

No of cylinders .... 6. V 90°

Bore .... 4.921 in (125 mm).

Stroke .... 5.118 in (130 mm).

Displacement .... 9572 cc (583.9 cu in).

Compression ratio 17.5:1

Gross power .... 154.1 kW (206.5 bhp) at 2,500 rpm.

Nett power .... –

DIN power .... 151.8 kW (197.6 PS) at 2,500 rpm.

Gross torque .... 651.1 Nm (481.0 lb ft) at 1,500 rpm.

Nett torque .... –

DIN torque .... 639 Nm (64.8 mkg) at 1,500 rpm.

Engine weight (dry) .... 1,578 lb (716 kg).

Main bearings .... 4, replacement inserts.

Valves .... ohv push rods.

Fuel system .... Injection pump. Bosch MW type. RQ governor.

Lubrication .... Full flow, replaceable oil filter.

Perkins 640 V8 10.5 litre – Spec 25

No of cylinders .... 8. V 90°

Bore .... 4.645 in (118 mm).

Stroke .... 4.764 in (121 mm).

Displacement .... 10,480 cc (639.3 cu in).

Compression 16.25:1

Gross power .... 160.4 kW (215 bhp) at 2,600 rpm.

Nett power .... –

DIN power .... 157.4 kW (211.2 PS) at 2,600 rpm.

Gross torque .... 655.9 Nm (484 lb ft) at 1,500 rpm.

Nett torque .... –

DIN torque .... 638.6 Nm (65.3 mkg) at 1500 rpm.

Engine weight (dry) .... 1,920 lbs (871 kg).

Main bearings .... 5, replaceable inserts.

Valves .... ohv push rods.

Fuel system .... Injection pump – Bosch M. W. type. RQ governor.

Lubrication .... Full flow, replaceable oil filter.

Ford 2.4 litre – Spec 26

No of cylinders 4

Bore .... 3.69 in (93.7 mm).

Stroke .... 3.37 in (85.6 mm).

Displacement .... 2360 cc (144 cu in).

Compression ratio 21.5:1

Gross power .... 45.6 kW (61 bhp) at 3,600 rpm.

Nett power .... 42.7 kW (58 bhp) at 3,600 rpm.

DIN power .... 45.7 kW (62 PS) at 3,600 rpm.

Gross torque .... 128.8 Nm (95 lb ft) at 2,300 rpm.

Nett torque .... 124.9 Nm (92 lb ft) at 2,300 rpm.

DIN torque .... 134.4 Nm (13.7 mkg) at 2,500 rpm.

Engine weight (dry) .... 530 lb (239 kg).

Main bearings .... 5, replaceable inserts.

Valves .... ohv push rods.

Fuel system .... Injection pump – Simms in-line Bosch-rotary.

Lubrication .... Full flow, replaceable element oil filter.

Ford 3.5 litre – Spec 27

No of cylinders 6

Bore .... 3.69 in (93.7 mm).

Stroke .... 3.37 in (85.6 mm).

Displacement .... 3540 cc (216 cu in).

Compression ratio 21.5:1

Gross power .... 71.6 kW (96 bhp) at 3,600 rpm.

Nett power .... 66.4 kW (89 bhp) at 3,600 rpm.

DIN power .... 64.9 kW (87.0 PS) at 3,600 rpm.

Gross torque .... 203 Nm (149.5 lb ft) at 2,200 rpm.

Nett torque .... 200 Nm (147.5 lb ft) at 2,200 rpm.

DIN torque .... 187.5 Nm (19.1 mkg) at 2,200 rpm.

Engine weight (dry) .... 690 lbs (313 kg).

Main bearings .... 7, replaceable inserts.

Valves .... ohv, push rods.

Fuel system .... Injection pump – Simms in-line. Bosch rotary.

Lubrication .... Full flow, replaceable element oil filter.

Ford 4.2 litre (inclined version) – Spec 28

No of cylinders 4

Bore .... 4.22 in (107.2 mm).

Stroke .... 4.52 in (115.0 mm).

Displacement .... 4161 cc (254 cu in).

Compression ratio 16.1:1

Gross power .... 60.5 kW (81 bhp) at 2,600 rpm.

Nett power .... 57.5 kW (78 bhp) at 2,600 rpm.

DIN power .... 58.0 kW (79 PS) at 2,600 rpm.

Gross torque .... 258.4 Nm (190 lb ft) at 1,600 rpm.

Nett torque .... –
DIN torque .... 260 Nm (26 mkg) at 1,600 rpm.
Engine weight (dry) .... 750 lb (340 kg).
Main bearings .... 5, replaceable inserts.
Valves .... ohv, push rods.
Fuel system .... Injection pump. Bosch. Simms Minimec.
Lubrication .... Full flow, replaceable element oil filter.

Ford 6.0 litre (inclined version) – Spec 29

No of cylinders 6
Bore .... 4.125 in (104.8 mm).
Stroke .... 4.52 in (115.0 mm).
Displacement .... 5948 cc (363 cu in).
Compression ratio 16.1:1
Gross power .... 84.3 kW (113 bhp) at 2,600 rpm.
Nett power .... 80.3 kW (108 bhp) at 2,600 rpm.
DIN power .... 76.0 kW (103 P.S.) at 2,600 rpm.
Gross torque .... 337 Nm (248.5 lb ft) at 1,600 rpm.
Nett torque .... –
DIN torque .... 330 Nm (33.7 mkg) at 1,600 rpm.
Engine weight (dry) .... 975 lb (442.3 kg).
Main bearings .... 7, replaceable inserts.
Valves .... ohv push rods.
Fuel system .... Injection pump – Bosch. Simms Minimec.
Lubrication .... Full flow, replaceable element oil filter.

Ford 6.2 litre (inclined version) – Spec 30

No of cylinders 6
Bore .... 4.22 in (107.2 mm).
Stroke .... 4.52 in (115.0 mm).
Displacement .... 6224 cc (380 cu in).
Compression ratio 16.1:1
Gross power .... 91.8 kW (123 bhp) at 2,600 rpm.
Nett power .... 87.0 kW (117 bhp) at 2,600 rpm.
DIN power .... 85.0 kW (116. PS) at 2,600 rpm.
Gross torque .... 380 Nm (280 lb ft) at 1,600 rpm.
Nett torque .... –
DIN torque .... 365 Nm (37.2 mkg) at 1,600 rpm.
Engine weight (dry) .... 970 lb (440 kg).
Main bearings .... 7, replaceable inserts.
Valves .... ohv, push rods.
Fuel system .... Injection pump: Bosch Simms Minimec.
Lubrication .... Full flow, replaceable element oil filter.

Ford 6.0 litre turbo charged (inclined version) – Spec 31

No of cylinders 6
Bore .... 4.125 in (105 mm).
Stroke .... 4.524 in (115 mm).
Displacement .... 5945 cc (362.8 cu in).
Compression ratio 15.7:1

Gross power .... 111.9 kW (150 bhp) at 2,400 rpm.
Nett power .... 103.8 kW (140 bhp) at 2,400 rpm.
DIN power .... 106.0 kW (144 P.S.) at 2,400 rpm.
Gross torque .... 473.0 Nm (349 lb ft) at 1,800 rpm.
Nett torque .... –
DIN torque .... 480.0 Nm (49.0 mkg) at 1,800 rpm.
Engine weight (dry) .... 1,005 lb (456 kg).
Main bearings .... 7, replaceable inserts.
Valves .... ohv, push rods.
Fuel system .... Injection pump: Bosch. Simms Minimec.
Lubrication .... Full flow, replaceable element oil filter.
Turbo charger .... Holset, exhaust gas driven.

Cummins 8.3 litre (standard version) – Spec 32

No of cylinders .... 8 V90°
Bore .... 4.625 in (117.48 mm).
Stroke .... 3.75 in (95.25 mm).
Displacement .... 8259 cc (504 cu in).
Compression ratio 17:1
Gross power .... 146 kW (197 bhp) at 3,000 rpm.
Nett power .... 126.8 kW (170 bhp) at 3,000 rpm.
DIN power .... 126 kW (171 PS) at 3,000 rpm.
Gross torque .... 494 Nm (365 lb ft) at 1,800 rpm.
Nett torque .... –
DIN torque .... 497 Nm (51 mkg) at 1,900 rpm.
Engine weight (dry) .... 480 lbs (671 kg).
Main bearings .... 5, replaceable inserts.
Valves .... ohv, push rods.
Fuel system .... Injection pump: Cummins P.T.
Lubrication .... Full flow, replaceable element oil filter.

Ford 8.8 litre Perkins 540 – Spec 33

No of cylinders .... 8 V90°
Bore .... 4.25 in (108 mm)
Stroke .... 4.75 in (121 mm)
Displacement .... 8849 cc (539 cu in).
Compression ratio 16.5:1
Gross power .... 134.2 kW (180 bhp) at 2,600 rpm.
Nett power .... 125.2 kW (168 bhp) at 2,600 rpm.
DIN power .... 125.2 kW (169 PS) at 2,600 rpm.
Gross torque .... 555.0 Nm (410 lb ft) at 1,700 rpm.
Nett torque .... 539.7 Nm (398 lb ft) at 1,700 rpm.
DIN torque .... 534.3 Nm (54.5 m kg) at 1,650 rpm.
Engine weight (dry) .... 1,582 lb (718 kg).
Main bearings .... 5, replaceable inserts.
Valves .... ohv, push rods.

Fuel system .... Injection pump: Simms Minimec GX governor.

Lubrication .... Full flow, replaceable elements 2 oil filters.

Ford 2.5 litre D.I. (direct injection) – Spec 34

No of cylinders .... 4 in-line.
Bore .... 3.687 in (93.67 mm).
Stroke .... 3.56 in (90.54 mm).
Displacement .... 2496 cc (152.3 cu in).
Compression ratio .... 19.1 : 1.
Gross power .... 52.25 kW (70 bhp) at 4,000 rpm.
Nett power .... –
Din power .... 50.0 kW (68 PS) at 4,000 rpm.
Gross torque .... 142.1 Nm (104.8 lb ft) at 2,700 rpm.
Nett torque .... –
DIN torque .... 143 Nm (14.6 mkg) at 2,700 rpm.
Engine weight (dry) .... –
Main bearings .... 5, replaceable inserts.
Valves .... ohc.
Fuel system .... Injection pump.
Lubrication .... Full flow, replaceable oil filter.

Cummins L10 turbocharged 10 litre – Spec 35

No of cylinders .... 6 in-line.
Bore .... 4.92 in (125 mm).
Stroke .... 5.35 in (136 mm).
Displacement .... 10,000 cc (610.0 cu in).
Compression ratio .... 16.1 : 1
Gross power .... 185.7 kW (249 bhp) at 2,100 rpm.
Nett power .... –
DIN power .... 172.4 kW (238 PS) at 2,100 rpm.
Gross torque .... 1017.6 Nm (751 lb ft) at 1,300 rpm.
Nett torque .... –
DIN torque .... 991.6 Nm (101.3 mkg) at 1300 rpm.
Engine weight (dry) .... 1929 lb (875 kg)
Main bearings .... 7, replaceable inserts
Valves .... ohv pushrod. Four valves/cyl.
Fuel system .... Injection pump. Cummins PTGAFC
Lubrication .... Full flow and by-pass spin on canisters. Replaceable oil filter canister.

Cummins L10A turbocharged 10 litre – Spec 36

No of cylinders .... 6 in-line.
Bore .... 4.92 in (125 mm).
Stroke .... 5.35 in (136 mm).
Displacement .... 10,000 cc (610.0 cu in).
Compression ratio .... 16 : 1.
Gross power .... 207.38 kW (278 bhp) at 2,100 rpm.
Nett power .... –

DIN power .... 192.51 kW (265.7 PS) at 2,100 rpm.
Gross torque .... 1145 Nm (845 lb ft) at 1,300 rpm.
Nett torque .... –
DIN torque .... 1115.9 Nm (114 mkg) at 1,300 rpm.
Engine weight (dry) .... 1,92 lbf (890 kg).
Main bearings .... 7, replaceable inserts.
Valves .... ohv pushrod. Four valves/cyl.
Fuel system .... Injection pump. Cummins PTGAFC.
Lubrication .... Full flow and by-pass spin on canisters. Replaceable oil filter canisters.

Perkins 4/108 4-cylinder – Spec 37

No of cylinders .... 4 in-line.
Bore .... –
Stroke .... –
Displacement .... 1760 cc (107.4 cu in).
Compression ratio .... 22:1.
Gross power .... 38.7 kW (52 bhp) at 4,000 rpm.
Nett power .... 36.5 kW (49 bhp) at 4,000 rpm.
DIN power .... 37.7 kW (51.2 PS) at 4,000 rpm.
Gross torque .... 107.0 Nm (79 lb ft) at 2,100 rpm.
Nett torque .... 105.0 Nm (77.5 lb ft) at 2,100 rpm.
DIN torque .... 104.3 Nm (10.6 mkg) at 2,100 rpm.
Engine weight (dry) .... –
Main bearings .... 4, replaceable inserts ohv pushrods.
Valves ....
Fuel system .... Fuel pump. Mechanical.
Lubrication .... Full flow, replaceable oil filter element.

Cummins NTE 290 (255) 14 litre T.C. – Spec 38

No of cylinders .... 6 in-line.
Bore .... 5.5 in (139.7 mm).
Stroke .... 6.00 in (152.4 mm).
Displacement .... 14,000 cc (855 cu in).
Compression ratio .... 15 : 1.
Gross power .... 190 kW (255 bhp) at 1,900 rpm.
Nett power .... 179 kW (240 bhp) at 1,900 rpm.
Din power .... 179 kW (244 PS) at 1,900 rpm.
Gross torque .... 1152 Nm (850 lb ft) at 1,300 rpm.
Nett torque .... 1128 Nm (832 lb ft) at 1,300 rpm.
DIN torque .... 1140 Nm (116.0 mkg) at 1,300 rpm.
Engine weight (dry) .... –
Main bearings .... 7, replaceable inserts.
Valves .... ohv pushrods.
Fuel system .... Injection pump – Cummins PT.
Lubrication .... Full flow and by-pass spin on canister. Replaceable oil filter canister.

Cummins NTE 290 14 litre T.C.   – Spec 39

No of cylinders .... 6 in-line.
Bore .... 5.5 in (139.7 mm).
Stroke .... 6.0 in (152.4 mm).
Displacement .... 14,000 cc (855 cu in).
Compression ratio .... 15 : 1.
Gross power .... 216 kW (290 bhp) at 1,900 rpm.
Nett power .... 201 kW (270 bhp) at 1,900 rpm.
DIN power .... 201 kW (274 PS) at 1,900 rpm.
Gross torque .... 1261 Nm (930 lb ft) at 1,300 rpm.
Nett torque .... 1223 Nm (902 lb ft) at 1,300 rpm.
DIN torque .... 1230 Nm (125 mkg) at 1,300 rpm.
Engine weight (dry) .... –
Main bearings .... 7, replaceable inserts.
Valves .... ohv pushrods.
Fuel system .... Injection pump. Cummins P.T.
Lubrication .... Full flow and by-pass spin on canister. Replaceable oil filter canister.

Cummins NTE 350 (335) 14 litre T.C.   – Spec 40

No of cylinders .... 6 in-line.
Bore .... 5.50 in (139.7 mm).
Stroke .... 6.00 in (152.4 mm).
Displacement .... 14,000 cc (855 cu in).
Compression ratio .... 15 : 1.
Gross power .... 250 kW (335 bhp) at 1,900 rpm.
Nett power .... 235 kW (315 bhp) at 1,900 rpm.
Din power .... 235 kW (320 mkg) at 1,900 rpm.
Gross torque .... 1383 Nm (1020 lb ft) at 1,300 rpm.

Nett torque .... 1342 Nm (990 lb ft) at 1,300 rpm.
DIN torque .... 1342 Nm (137 mkg) at 1,300 rpm.
Engine weight (dry) .... –
Main bearings .... 7, replaceable inserts.
Valves .... ohv pushrods.
Fuel system .... Injection pump. Cummins PT.
Lubrication .... Full flow and by-pass spin on canister. Replaceable oil filter canister.

Cummins NTE 370 14 litre T.C.   – Spec 41

No of cylinders .... 6 in-line.
Bore .... 5.50 in (139.7 mm).
Stroke .... 6.00 in (152.4 mm).
Displacement .... 14,000 cc (855 cu in).
Compression ratio .... 15 : 1.
Gross power .... 276 kW (370 bhp) at 2,100 rpm.
Nett power .... 257 kW (345 bhp) at 2,100 rpm.
DIN power .... 259 kW (352 PS) at 2,100 rpm.
Gross torque .... 1383 Nm (1020 lb ft) at 1,300 rpm.
Nett torque .... 1342 Nm (990 lb ft) at 1,300 rpm.
DIN torque .... 1342 Nm (137 mkg) at 1,300 rpm.
Engine weight (dry) .... –
Main bearings .... 7, replaceable inserts.
Valves .... ohv pushrods.
Fuel system .... Injection pump. Cummins PT.
Lubrication .... Full flow and by-pass spin on canister. Replaceable oil filter canister.

Transmissions

Ford Model 'T' epicyclic transmission   – Spec 1

The typical layout consists of planetary gear clusters, three in number, the centre gear (the sun wheel) and the internal tooth gear (the annulus).

The planetary clusters are mounted on shafts fixed to the flywheel. When the flywheel revolves, the planetary cluster gears revolve with it around the centre gears (reverse, slow speed and driven gears) the planetary cluster gears revolve around the centre gear cluster.

The planetary cluster gear has three gears of different sizes fixed together, one of the three gears meshing with the transmission driven gear, one with the slow speed gear and one with the reverse gear of the centre cluster. A centre shaft is connected to the flywheel and the rear end projects through the driven gear sleeve. The inner drum of the high speed clutch is attached to this shaft.

The high speed clutch is of the multiple disc type, consisting of twenty-six alternating large and small discs that overlap one another. The inner or smaller discs are mounted on a slotted drum, teeth on the inner faces of the discs engaging in the slots of the drum. The discs, therefore, turn with the drum, but can slide along it. The outer or larger discs are similarly mounted inside a large drum. Normally the clutch is disengaged, the inner drum – with its 13 small discs – being free to revolve with the engine; while the outer drum, with the 13 larger discs inside it, remains stationary. Under these conditions, i.e. when the clutch is disengaged, each small disc revolves between two large ones without touching. However, if the discs are gradually clamped together (by spring pressure or any other similar means) the inner discs rubbing on the outer ones will gradually force the latter to turn with them, until the two sets of discs are locked together and revolve as a unit.

In the Ford vehicle, the inner disc drum of the clutch and the 13 small discs are connected with the engine and turn with it, whilst the outer drum and the larger discs are joined to, and turn with, the rear axle. The clutch discs are forced together into the high speed position by a strong clutch spring, controlled by the clutch pedal. Pressing forward on the clutch pedal removes the pressure of the spring from the clutch discs and they spring apart enough to prevent friction between the large and small discs. This is the 'neutral' position of the clutch. The clutch discs operate in oil, so that they 'take hold' gradually and smoothly when pressed together. If they were dry, they would grip suddenly and with violent jerks.

Gearbox ratios: low speed – 2.75 : 1. High speed – 1 : 1. Reverse – 3.99 : 1.

Ford three-speed synchromesh – truck transmission – Spec 2

Gear ratios:

1st	3.66 : 1
2nd	1.90 : 1
3rd	1.00 : 1
Reverse	4.15 : 1

Optional on model 'B' 12 cwt van.

1st	2.8 : 1
2nd	1.6 : 1
3rd	1.0 : 1
Reverse	3.38 : 1

Synchromesh for 2nd and 3rd gears..

Ford four-speed crash change – truck transmission – Spec 3

Gear ratios:

1st	6.32 : 1
2nd	3.09 : 1
3rd	1.69 : 1
4th	1.00 : 1
Reverse	7.44 : 1

Crash box used on trucks until 1952.

Ford 8-570-S eight-speed transmission — Spec 4

Synchromesh on all forward gears.

Gear ratios:

1st	10.71 : 1
2nd	7.04 : 1
3rd	4.93 : 1
4th	3.76 : 1
5th	2.85 : 1
6th	1.87 : 1
7th	1.31 : 1
8th	1.00 : 1
Reverse	10.66 : 1

Ouput:

DIN PS	36.05 at 1,700 rpm.
bhp	35.0 at 1,700 rpm.

Output taken at side opening power take-off point.

Torque:

kgf m	36.80 at 1,700 rpm.
lbf ft	265.0 at 1,700 rpm.

taken at side opening power take-off point.

Ford C3 automatic transmission — Spec 5

The 240 mm converter transmits engine torque to the transmission and is capable of torque multiplications at an infinitely variable rate between 2.35 : 1 and 1 : 1. Overall gear ratios are a product of this infinitely variable torque and the ratios of the transmission which are 1st 2.47 : 1, 2nd 1.47 : 1, 3rd 1.0 : 1 and reverse 2.09 : 1. Ratios are selected by the application of brake bands and clutches. The transmission is operated by a selector lever with six positions, situated on the dash board. The positions are P (park), R (reverse) N (neutral), D (drive), 2 (2nd gear lockdown), 1 (1st gear lockdown).

Ford four-speed synchromesh (Transit and Escort) — Spec 6

Gear ratios:

Gear	Escort	Transit	Transit	Transit	Transit
1st	3.656 : 1	4.412 : 1	3.163 : 1	3.96 : 1	3.65 : 1
2nd	2.185 : 1	2.353 : 1	1.950 : 1	2.28 : 1	1.97 : 1
3rd	1.425 : 1	1.505 : 1	1.412 : 1	1.41 : 1	1.37 : 1
4th	1.000 : 1	1.000 : 1	1.000 : 1	1.00 : 1	1.00 : 1
Reverse	4.235 : 1	4.667 : 1	3.346 : 1	4.24 : 1	3.66 : 1
		A	B	C	D
Code	–	M11	–	M12	M3.

Ford 4-410-S four-speed synchromesh — Spec 7

Synchromesh on all forward gears.

Gear ratios:

1st	6.49 : 1
2nd	3.21 : 1
3rd	1.67 : 1
4th	1 : 1
Reverse	7.18 : 1

Ouput:

DIN PS	36.05 at 1,700 rpm.
bhp	35.0 at 1,700 rpm.

Output taken at side opening power take-off point.

Torque:

kgf m	36.6 at 1,700 rpm.
lbf ft	259.0 at 1,700 rpm.

taken at side opening power take-off point.

Ford 6-600-S six-speed synchromesh — Spec 8

Synchromesh on all forward gears.

Gear ratios:

	Close ratio (6-600-S)	Wide ratio (6-540-SW).
1st	7.51 : 1	9.19 : 1
2nd	4.58 : 1	5.51 : 1
3rd	2.85 : 1	3.13 : 1
4th	1.87 : 1	1.87 : 1
5th	1.31 : 1	1.16 : 1
6th	1.00 : 1	1.00 : 1
Reverse	7.18 : 1	8.58 : 1

Ouput:

DIN PS	36.05 at 1,700 rpm.
bhp	35.0 at 1,700 rpm.

Output taken at side opening power take-off point.

Torque:

kgf m	36.6 at 1,700 rpm.
lbf ft	259.0 at 1,700 rpm

taken at side opening power take-off point.

Turner T4-150 four-speed synchromesh — Spec 9

Gear ratios	Wide ratio	Close ratio
1st	6.02 : 1	5.12 : 1
2nd	2.86 : 1	2.62 : 1
3rd	1.54 : 1	1.51 : 1
4th	1.00 : 1	1.00 : 1
Reverse	5.58 : 1	4.75 : 1

Ouput:

DIN PS	20.6 at 1,000 engine rpm	24.62 at 1,000 engine rpm.
bhp	20.3 at 1,000 engine rpm	24.3 at 1,000. engine rpm.

Torque:

kgf m	33.0 max	31.0 max.
lbf ft	238.0 max	223.0 max.

Power take off opening – S.A.E.6 bolt. RH side.

ZF. ZF-S5-24/3 five-speed synchromesh — Spec 10

Gear ratios:

1st	6.40 : 1
2nd	3.63 : 1
3rd	2.16 : 1
4th	1.43 : 1
5th	1.00 : 1.
Reverse	5.88 : 1

Ouput:

DIN PS	30.0 at 1,000 engine rpm
bhp	29.6 at 1,000 engine rpm

Torque:

kgf m	44.52 max.
lbf ft	322.0 max.

Power take off – S.A.E. 6 bolt – RH side.

Ford 4.310 four-speed synchromesh — Spec 11

Gear ratios	Wide ratio	Close ratio
1st	6.32 : 1	5.00 : 1
2nd	3.09 : 1	2.44 : 1
3rd	1.68 : 1	1.33 : 1
4th	1.00 : 1	1.00 : 1
Reverse	7.44 : 1	5.88 : 1

Ouput:

DIN PS	30.4 at 1,500 engine rpm	30.4 at 1,500. engine rpm.
bhp	30.0 at 1,500 engine rpm	30.0 at 1,500. engine rpm.

Torque:

kgf m	35.9 max	35.9 max.
lbf ft	260.0 max	260.0 max.

Power take off opening – S.A.E.6 bolt. RH side.

Turner T5A-3017 five-speed synchromesh — Spec 12

Gear ratios:

1st	7.49 : 1
2nd	4.38 : 1
3rd	2.40 : 1
4th	1.48 : 1
5th	1.00 : 1
Reverse	7.20 : 1

Five-speed direct.

Synchromesh on all forward gears.

Turner T5A-3018 five-speed synchromesh — Spec 13

Gear ratios:

1st	7.49 : 1
2nd	4.10 : 1
3rd	2.13 : 1
4th	1.17 : 1
5th	1.00 : 1
Reverse	7.20 : 1

Five-speed direct.

Synchromesh on all forward gears.

Used only on models with two-speed rear axles.

Turner T5C-4008 five-speed synchromesh – Spec 14

Gear ratios:

1st	7.36 : 1
2nd	4.79 : 1
3rd	2.79 : 1
4th	1.66 : 1
5th	1.00 : 1
Reverse	7.36 : 1

Synchromesh on all forward gears.
Used only on models with single speed rear axles.

Turner T5C-4007 five-speed synchromesh – Spec 15

Gear ratios:

1st	6.55 : 1
2nd	3.425 : 1
3rd	2.013 : 1
4th	1.185 : 1
5th	1.000 : 1
Reverse	6.55 : 1

Synchromesh on all forward gears.
Used only on models with two-speed rear axles.

ZF-56-70-3 six-speed synchromesh – Spec 16

Gear ratios:

1st	9.59 : 1
2nd	5.47 : 1
3rd	3.42 : 1
4th	2.19 : 1
5th	1.49 : 1
6th	1.00 : 1
Reverse	8.88 : 1

Synchromesh on all forward gears.
Used only on models with two-speed rear axles.

ZF-S6-80 + GV80 splitter, twelve-speed – Spec 17

Gear ratios:

1st	low 9.00 : 1	high 7.52 : 1
2nd	low 5.18 : 1	high 4.33 : 1
3rd	low 3.14 : 1	high 2.62 : 1
4th	low 2.08 : 1	high 1.73 : 1
5th	low 1.44 : 1	high 1.20 : 1
6th	low 1.00 : 1	high 0.83 : 1
Reverse	low 8.45 : 1	high 7.25 : 1

Splitter ratio: Low 1 : 1   High 0.836 : 1
Splitter. High and Low Overall ratios with splitter box
mounted in front of ZF-S6-80.

Ford auxiliary/transfer transmission – Spec 18

For use in the Ministry of Supply's vehicles – W.O.T.6., and W.O.T.8., during the Second World War.

Type	Two-speed.
Ratios	High 1.0 : 1.
	Low 2.42 : 1.

In addition to the normal transmission, an auxiliary/transfer transmission was fitted. Located just behind the normal transmission and connected to it by a short coupling shaft and two universal joints.

The purpose of this transmission was to enable the drive to be transmitted to the rear axle only, or to engage the front axle drive in addition to the rear axle drive. When the front axle was engaged, an overall reduction of 1.12 : 1 was made to the normal transmission ratios. There was only two positions of the change speed lever. In the forward position all the four wheels were driven, and in the rearward position the rear wheels only were driven.

ZF-S5-35/2 five-speed transmission – Spec 19

Gear ratios:

1st	6.79 : 1
2nd	3.97 : 1
3rd	2.42 : 1
4th	1.49 : 1
5th	1.00 : 1
Reverse	6.10 : 1

Synchromesh on all forward gears.

Eaton-Fuller nine-speed constant mesh. RT-6609 – Spec 20

Gear ratios:

1st	10.6 : 1
2nd	8.14 : 1
3rd	5.98 : 1
4th	4.45 : 1
5th	3.43 : 1
6th	2.37 : 1
7th	1.74 : 1
8th	1.30 : 1
9th	1.00 : 1
Reverse	9.50 : 1

Eaton-Fuller nine-speed constant mesh. RT-11609A – Spec 21

Gear ratios:

1st	12.65 : 1
2nd	8.38 : 1
3rd	6.22 : 1
4th	4.57 : 1
5th	3.40 : 1
6th	2.46 : 1
7th	1.83 : 1
8th	1.34 : 1
9th	1.00 : 1
Reverse	13.22 : 1

Eaton-Fuller nine-speed constant mesh.   – Spec 22
RT-9509C.

Gear ratios:

1st	12.49 : 1
2nd	8.34 : 1
3rd	6.11 : 1
4th	4.56 : 1
5th	3.38 : 1
6th	2.47 : 1
7th	1.81 : 1
8th	1.35 : 1
9th	1.00 : 1
Reverse	3.87 : 1 high range.
Reverse	13.07 : 1 low range.

Eaton-Fuller thirteen-speed constant mesh.   – Spec 23
RT0-9513.

Gear ratios:

1st	12.49 : 1.
2nd	8.34 : 1.
3rd	6.11 : 1.
4th	4.56 : 1.
5th	3.38 : 1.
6th	2.47 : 1.
7th	2.14 : 1.
8th	1.81 : 1.
9th	1.57 : 1.
10th	1.35 : 1.
11th	1.17 : 1.
12th	1.00 : 1.
13th	0.87 : 1.
Reverse	3.87 : 1 high range.
Reverse	13.07 : 1 low range.

Eaton two-speed axle   – Spec 1

Eaton two-speed rear axle.

Driving gear and differential assembly.

Two ratios available in each combination air change selection.

	Eaton 16620	Eaton 19220
Capacity.	2,500lbs (8850Kg) ..	22,500lbs (10200Kg)
Gear type.	Spiral bevel	Spiral bevel
Ratios.	6.14/8.53:1	4.87/6/63:1
		5.43/7.39:1
		6.16/8.40:1

Spiral bevel differential assembly

Ford single-speed rear axles type 15C, 16A & 16C. – Spec 2

Driving gear and differential assembly.

Spiral bevel driven.

	15C	16A
Capacity	16800 lb (7620 Kg) to 19500 lbs (8850 Kg).	19500 lb (8850 Kg)
Crown wheel dimeter	14.875in (380mm)	16.0in (405mm)
Ratios.	5.14:1	5.29:1
	5.57:1	5.57:1
	6.14:1	6.50:1
	6.50:1	7.20:1
	7.20:1	

	16C
Capacity	22,500 lbs (10200 Kg)
Crown wheel diameter	16.0in (405mm)
Ratios	5.29:1
	5.15:1
	6.50:1
	7.20:1

Rear Axles

Ford light commercial rear axle.   – Spec 3

Hypoid gear driven.

Used on transit & A series.

	Ford 24	Ford 27	Ford 32	Ford 34	Ford 42	Ford 52	Ford 53
Capacity	5200lb (2360Kg)	5900lb (2680Kg)	3215lb (1460Kg)	3400lb (1540Kg)	9470lb (4300Kg)	5200lb (2360Kg)	5725lb (2600Kg)
Crown wheel diameter.	8.75in (220mm)	9.76in (248mm)	7.38in (183.7mm)	7.29in (185mm)	10.5in (267mm)	8.75in (220mm)	8.75in (220mm)
Ratios.	4.62:1	4.88:1	4.63:1	4.11:1	4.88:1	4.625:1	4.63:1
	5.14:1	5.13:1	5.14:1	4.44:1	5.13:1	5.143:1	5.14:1
		5.87:1		5.143:1	5.87:1	5.833:1	5.83:1
		6.17:1			6.17:1	6.167:1	
					7.17:1		

Ford single speed rear axles — Specs 4 & 5

Types: 13A, 14B

Hypoid bevel gear driven

Driving gear and differential assemblies.

Rear axle No	4	5
	Type 13A	Type 14B
Capacity	13,000lb (5,900Kg)	15,000lb (6,800Kg) to 18,500lb (8,390Kg)
Crown wheel dia.	12.625in (320mm)	13.875in (350mm)
Ratios:	4.11:1	4.22:1
	4.71:1	4.62:1
	5.29:1	5.29:1
		6.17:1
		6.80:1
	Rear axle	Rear axle

Rockwell single speed rear axle — Specs 6, 7 & 8

Types: R170, R180 and U180

Hypoid bevel gear driven

Driving gear and differential assemblies

Rear axle	6	7
	R170	R180
Capacity	25,375.5lb (11,500Kg)	25,375.5lb (11,500Kg)
Crown wheel dia.	18.875in (479.4mm)	19.625in (498.5mm)
Ratios:	3.70:1	3.70:1
	4.11:1	4.11:1
		4.63:1

Rear axle No	8
	PU180
Capacity	28,665lb (13,000Kg)
Crown wheel dia.	19.625in (498.5mm)
Ratios:	3.70:1
	4.11:1
	4.63:1

Ford single speed rears — Specs 9, 10 & 11

Spiral bevel driven – Split type axle housing – Torque tube enclose shaft.
Rear axle assembly complete for: AA, BB, to 79 and 7V
Driving gear, Differential and axle housings for: ET6, ET and 500E range.

Rear axle No.	9	10	11
	Model AA	Model BB to 79	Model ET6, ET7, 500E
Capacity.	7,000lb (3,174Kg)	9,000lb (4,081Kg)	11,000lb (4,988Kg)
Crown wheel dia.	12.625in (321mm)	12.625in (321mm)	12.625in (321mm)
Ratios.	5.14:1	5.14:1	5.83:1
	5.17:1	5.83:1	6.67:1
	6.6:1	6.60:1	7.60:1
	7.6:1		

Tandems

Ford tandem double drive axles. six-wheelers. (ex-County Commercial Cars Ltd). — Spec 1

The double drive centre axle housing encases two crown wheels that are mounted on the differential assembly, both crown wheels are driven by two pinions.

The Foremost Rear Axle: This axle consists of two crown wheels, one fitted to the differential and the other, while attached to the differential, is allowed to rotate freely. The drive is by the input pinion driven from an enclosed drive shaft in a torque tube, driven from the transmission. This pinion is meshed with both the crown wheels. A second pinion, the output pinion, gives the through drive to the rearmost rear axle. This second pinion also meshes with the crown wheels. The action of this unit is: The input pinion, turning in a clockwise direction, causes the left-hand crown wheel to revolve also in a clockwise direction, when viewed from the right-hand side of the vehicle and, with the action of the differential, drives the half shafts and the rear hubs in a forward direction. The action of the input pinion also meshing with the right-hand crown wheel causes this second crown wheel to revolve in an anti-clockwise direction, revolving free of the differential. With both crown wheels revolving in their respective direction the output pinion revolves in an anti-clockwise direction and completes the through drive.

The Rearmost Rear Axle: This axle is similar to that of the same type used on the four-wheeled vehicles, but for one difference the crown wheel is located on the opposite side of the differential in this location and meshing with the output pinion rotating in an anti-clockwise direction, the crown wheel rotates in a clockwise direction, giving a forward motion.

The rear hubs and brakes are the same design as those used on the four-wheeled vehicles.

The specification for the rear axles relative to the bearings and gears is identical with the standard fully floating Ford rear axle.

Eaton Tandem Axles 38DT/18220 (Bogie type 410). Six-wheelers. ('D' series and Cargo) — Spec 2

A two-speed tandem drive axle of through drive design which eliminates excessive gearing. Synchronisation of the gear change in each rear axle is ensured by a common air operated shift.

An inter-axle differential mounted on the input shaft distributes power equally between the foremost and the rearmost rear axles, and permits all four wheels to travel at different speeds due to road conditions, eliminating tyre scrub. A lockout device permits drive to both rear axles giving maximum traction for the off-highway conditions.

Foremost axle through drive is created by a set of spur gears driving the foremost drive pinion and a through shaft to the inter-axle propeller shaft.

The rearmost axle is a standard two-speed rear axle used on four-wheeled vehicles.

	Foremost 38DT.	Rearmost 18220.
Capacity	41,000 lb (18,595 kg)	41,000 lb (18,595 kg).
Differential gears	Spiral bevels	Spiral bevels.
Ratios	4.87/6.65 : 1	4.87/6.65 : 1
	5.57/7.6 : 1	5.57/7.6 : 1
	6.14/8.38:1	6.14/8.38:1
	6.50/8.87:1	6.50/8.87:1

Eaton tandem axles 30DS/Ford 15C and Eaton 38DS/Ford 16C (Bogie type 300/358, 410).   – Spec 3

A single-speed tandem driver axle version, operates the through drive from foremost to rearmost rear axles in the same way as the two-speed version. A third-inter-axle differential and lockout are provided.

	Foremost 30DS.	Foremost 38DS.
Capacity	30,000 lb (13,610 kg)	41,000 lb (18,595 kg).
	16,260 lb (35,840 kg)	
Differential gears	Spiral bevels	Spiral bevels.
Ratios	6.14 : 1	5.29 : 1
	6.50 : 1	5.57 : 1
	7.20 : 1	6.50 : 1
		7.20 : 1
	Rearmost Ford 15C	**Rearmost Ford 16C**

Ford front wheel drive axle assembly. WOT6 & 8 3 ton and 30CWT 4 x 4 trucks.   – Spec 1

It is a spiral bevel gear driven axle with a vertically split axle housing. The drive gears and the differential were identical to those used in the rear axle drive, but with special tubular axle arms on the end of which was a flange. A spherical housing was bolted to each of the ends of the axle arms. These housings accommodated a steering joint and a constant velocity universal joint. An outer spherical split type casing enveloped the spherical housing and were bolted together and fitted with sealing gaskets. The steering was achieved by the fore and aft movement or rotation of the outer spherical casing on the spherical inner housing. The whole assembly was filled with lubricant to enable the frictionless constant velocity joint to work smoothly. Each end of the constant velocity joint was attached to the axle half shafts. One half shaft from the joint to the differential and one half shaft to the other end of the joint to the front hub driving flange. The whole front axle drive was driven from an open drive shaft from the auxiliary/transfer gearbox.

Type	Spiral bevel.
Differential	Bevel gear type. Four pinions.
Steering pivots	Two adjustable taper roller bearings.
Ratios	WOT 6 – 7.2 : 1. WOT 8 – 6.66 : 1.

Vehicle Specifications

Model	Engine	Transmission	Tyre size & wheel type	Brake size & system	Electrical	Front axle & track	Rear axle	Suspension	Wheelbase
T Van Van	No 1 Spec.	No 1 Spec.	30" x 3" - F 30" x 3.5" R wooden spoke wheels.	Mechanically operated	6 volt	'T' beam Front Track 56.0 in (1.42 m)	Spiral bevel gear driven semi-floating	Transverse Front and rear springs	100.0 in (2.54 m)
'TT' 1 ton						'T' Beam Front Track	Worm gear driven three-quarter floating.		
'A' 10 cwt Van	14.9 hp four cyl. petrol	3-speed crash change	4.50 21F & R Wire spoke wheels	Mechanically operated	6 volt	'T' beam Front Track	Spiral bevel gear driven three-quarter	Transverse Front and rear springs	103.5 in. (2.63 m)

Model	Engine	Transmission	Tyre size & wheel type	Brake size & system	Electrical	Front axle & track	Rear axle	Suspension	Wheelbase
'AA' 1 ton	No 6 Spec.	3 speed crash change.	20 x 6 F 30 x 5 R wire wheels later disc wheels.			'I' Beam Front Track	No 9 Spec. Three quarter floating.	Transverse Front cantilever semi-elliptic R	131.5 in (3.34 m)
30 cwt			30" x 5" F 32 x 6 R wire spoke wheels later change to disc type wheels	11.0" Dia. Mechanically operted.	6 volt 80 amp battery	'I' Beam Front Track	Worm gear driven change to spiral bevel driven. three quarter floating	Transverse Front cantilever semi-elliptic rears.	131.5 in (3.34 m)
B 12 cwt	No 7 Spec.	No 2 Spec.	5.25 x 18F 6.00 x 18R Wire spoke wheels	12.0" Dia. Mechanically operated.	6 volt 80 amp battery	'I' Beam Front Track	Spiral bevel three-quarter floating	Transverse F & R springs	106.0 in (3.69 m).
'BB' 30 cwt	No 7 Spec.	No 3 Spec.	20 x 6 LP F 32 x 6 HP R Single rears	14" Dia. Mechanically operated.		'I' Beam Front Track	No 10 Spec. Fully floating	Transverse-Fronts spring. semi-elliptic longitudinal springs – rear.	131.5 in (3.34 m)
2 ton			20 x 6 LP.F 32 x 6 HP rear Dual rears.						157.0 in (3.98 m) long W/B 131.0 in (3.32 m) Short W/B.
1935 2 ton & 30 cwt 6 wheelr single drive, double drive	No 2 Spec. No 7 Spec.	No 3 Spec.	32 x 6 F & R Dual rear Disc wheels	14" Dia Mechanically operated	6 volt 80 amp battery	'I' Beam Front Track	No. 10 Spec. fully floating No 1. Spec. Tandem axles.	Transverse Front spring. Semi-elliptic longitudinal rear springs	131.0 in 3.32 in) Short W/B 157.0 in (3.98 in) long W/B plus 42.125 in extension
1935 6 whlrs	No 2 Spec.								
BBE 2 ton Van F/C 2 ton Truck	No 2 Spec.	No 3 Spec.	6.00 x 20F 32 x 7 R Single rears. disc wheels			'I' Beam Front track 63.5 in (1.61 m)		longitudinal semi-elliptic springs F & R	118.01 in (2.997 m)
1935 6 whlrs single drive F/C	No 2 Spec.						No 10 Spec. Fully Floating		118.0 in (2.997in)
51 2 ton N/C	No 2 Spec.	No 3 Spec.	6.00 x 20 Dual rears	14" Dia Mechanically operated	6 volt 80 amp battery	'I' Beam Front Track 55.0 in (1.397 m)	No 10 Spec. Fully Floating	Transverse Front spring. longitudinal semi-elliptic elliptic rear springs	131.5 in (3.34 m) Short W/B 157.0 in (3.98 m) Long W/B

Model	Engine	Transmission	Tyre size & wheel type	Brake size & system	Electrical	Front axle & track	Rear axle	Suspension	Wheelbase
3 ton N/C			6.50 x 20 F 32 x 6 HDR Dual rears						
6 wheelr Single drive double drive			6.00 x 20 F & R Dual rears.				No. 10 Spec. Tandem fully floating No 1 Tandem fully floating		13.15 in (3.34 m) Short W/B 157.0 in (3.98 m) Long W/B plus 42.125 ins. Extension
61 25 cwt Van & Truck	No 2A Spec.	No 2 Spec.	6.00 x 20F 30 x 5R Single rears	12" Dia F 14" Dia R Mechanically operated	6 volt 95 amp battery	'I' Beam Front Track 55.0 in (1.397 m)	No 10 Spec.	Transverse F & R springs.	106.0 in (2.69 m)
67 15 cwt Van	No 2 Spec.	No 2	6.00 x 16F 6.50 x 16R wire spoke wheels	12" Dia F & R Mechanically operated	6 volt 95 amp battery	'I' Beam Front Track 55.0 in (1.397 m)	Spiral bevel Three-quarter floating	Transverse F & R springs	112.0 in (2.84 m)
TUG 3 wheelr Artic	No 4 Spec.	3 speed synchromesh	18 x 7-F 23 x 5.R single rear tyres 1-single Front Disc wheels	12" Dia Rear only	6 volt 60 amp battery	Single wheel and fork	Spiral bevel gear driven Three-quarter floating	Transverse Rear Spring Coil Front spring	88.5 in (2.24 m)
73 15 cwt Van	No 2 Spec.	No 2 Spec.	6.00 x 16F 6.50 x 16R Single rears wire spoke wheels	12" Dia F & R mechanically operated	6 volt 95 amp battery	'I' Beam Front Track 55.0 in (1.397 m)	Spiral bevel Three-quarter floating	Transverse F & R springs	112.0 in (2.84 m)
77 15 cwt									
79 3 ton	No 2 Spec.	No 3 Spec.	32 x 6TT.F 32 x 6 HO.R Disc wheels	14" Dia. F 15" Dia. R Hydraulic	6 volt 95 amp battery	'I' Beam Front Track 57.0 in (1.44 m)	No 10 Spec. fully floating	Transverse Front spring. longitudinal semi-elliptic rear springs	131.0 in. (3.32 m) Short W/B 157.0 in (3.98 m) Long W/B
2 ton			32 x 6 F&R						131.0 in (3.32 m)
6 Wheelr single drive Double drive			32 x 6 HD F & R	14" Dia F 16" Dia R Mechanically operated			No 1 Tandem axles Fully Floating No 1 Tandem axles Fully Floating		131.0 in (3.32 m) Short W/B 157.0 in Long W/B Plus 42.44" extension
7V 2 ton F/C	No 2 Spec.	No 3 Spec	6.00 x 20 F & R	14" Dia F & R Mechanically operated	6 volt 96 amp battery	'I' Beam Front Track 64.0 in (1.625 m)	No 11 Fully Floating	Longitudinal semi-elliptic Frant & Rear springs	118.0 in (2.99 m)
3 Ton F/C continued			32 x 6 HD F & R						118.0 in (2.99 m) Short W/B

Model	Engine	Transmission	Tyre size & wheel type	Brake size & system	Electrical	Front axle & track	Rear axle	Suspension	Wheelbase
7V 2 ton F/C Van	No 2 Spec.	No 3 Spec.	32 x 6TT.F 34 x 7HD.R Single rears	14" Dia F 16" Dia R Mechanically operated	6 volt 96 amp battery	'I' Beam Front Track 64.0 in (1.62 m)	No 11 Spec. fully floating	Semi-elliptic longitudinal Front & Rear springs	118.0 in (2.997 m) Short W/B
Artic F/C			32 x 6 HD.F 34 x 7 HD. R Dual rears	16" Dia F & R Mechanically operated		'I' Beam Front Track 63.5 in (1.61 m)			
6 whlrs F/C double drive			32 x 6HD F & R Dual rears				No 1 Tandem axle Spec. Fully floating		118.0 in (2.997 m) Short W/B 143.5 in (3.645 m) Long W/B Plus 42.44" extension
E88W F/C 25 cwt Van Truck	No 7 Spec.	No 2 Spec.	30 x 5F 32 x 6TTR Single rear	12" Dia F 14" Dia R Mechanically operated	6 volt 96 amp battery	'I' Beam Front Track 55.0 in (1.397 m)	No 10	Transverse F & R springs	106.0 in (2.69 m)
E83W Semi F/C Van	No 5 Spec.	3 speed Synchromesh		11" Dia F & R Mechanically operated	6 volt 63 amp battery	'I' Beam Front Track 50.5 in (1.282 m)	Spiral bevel gear driven Three-quarter floating	Transverse F & R springs	90.0 in (2.28 m)
81T N/C 2 ton	No 2 Spec.	No 3 Spec.	32 x 6 TT F & R	14" Dia F & R Hydraulic	6 volt 96 amp battery	'I' Beam Front Track 57.0 in (1.447 m)	No. 10 fully floating	Transverse Front spring, longitudinal semi-elliptic rear springs	134.0 in (3.4 m)
817T 2 ton N/C									157.0 in (3.98 m)
E88T N/C 2 ton	No 7 Spec.								134.0 in (3.4 m)
E887T N/C 2 ton									157.0 in (3.98 m)
81C 15 cwt Van	No 2 Spec.	No 2 Spec.	6.50 c 16 F & R Single rears wire spoke wheels	12" Dia F & R Mechanically operated	6 volt 96 amp battery	'I' Beam Front Track 55.5 in (1.41 m)		Transverse F & R springs	112.0 in (2.84 m)
82C 15 cwt Van	No 2A Spec.								
E88C 15 cwt Van	No 7 Spec.								
91C 15 cwt Van	No 2 Spec.								
92C 15 cwt Van	No 2A Spec.								

Model	Engine	Transmission	Tyre size & wheel type	Brake size & system	Electrical	Front axle & track	Rear axle	Suspension	Wheelbase
98C 15 cwt Van	No 7 Spec.								
ET6 2 Ton	No 2 Spec.	No 3 Spec.	6.50 x 20 F & R Dual rears	14" Dia F & R Hydraulic	6 volt 96 amp battery	'I' Beam Front track 68.5 in (1.74 m)	No 11 Spec. Fully floating	Semi-elliptic longitudinal	128.0 in (3.25 m)
ET7 2 Ton	No 20 Spec.								
ET6 3 Ton	No 2 Spec.		32 x 6-8 ply F & R Dual rear						
ET7 3 Ton	No 20 Spec.								
ET6 2 Ton Van	No 2 Spec.								
ET7 2 Ton Van	No 20 Spec.								
ET6 4 Ton	No 2 Spec.		32 x 6-10 ply F & R Dual rears	16" Dia F & R Hydraulic		'I' Beam Front Track 67.6 in (1.72 in)			128.0 in (3.25 m) Short W/B 157.0 in (3.98 m) Long W/B
ET7 4 Ton	No 20 Spec.								
ET6 5 Ton	No 2 Spec.	No 3 Spec.	34 x 7-10 ply F & R Dual rears	16" Dia F & R Hydraulic	6 volt 96 amp battery	'I' Beam Front Track 70.6 in (1.79 m)		Semi elliptic longitudinal Front & R springs	128.0 in (3.25 m) Short W/B 157.0 in (3.98 m) long W/B
ET7 5 ton	No 20 Spec.								
ET6 5 ton (4 cubic yard) tipper	No 2 Spec.								122.0 in (3.09 m)
ET7 5 ton (4 cubic yard) tipper	No 20 Spec.								
ET6 artic	No 2 Spec.								
ET7 artic	No 20 Spec.								
ET6 6 Wheelr. double drive	No 2 Spec.		32 x 6-10 ply F & R Dual rears			'I' Beam Front Track 67.6 in (1.72 m)	No 1 Spec. Tandem axle fully floating		128.0 in (3.25 m) Short W/B 157.0 in (3.98 m) Long W/B Plus 42.49 extension

Model	Engine	Transmission	Tyre size & wheel type	Brake size & system	Electrical	Front axle & track	Rear axle	Suspension	Wheelbase
500E Series 2 ton	No 8 Spec.	No 3 Spec.	6.50 x 20 F & R Dual rears	14" Dia F & R Hydraulic	6 volt 96 amp battery	'I' beam Front Track 68.5 in (1.74 m)	No 11 Spec. fully floating	Semi elliptic longitudinal front & rear springs	128.0 in (3.25 m)
2 ton	No 19 Spec.								
3 ton	No 8 Spec.		32 x 6-8 ply F & R Dual rears						
3 ton	No 19 Spec.								
4 ton	No 8 Spec.	No 3 Spec.	32 x 6-10 ply F & R Dual rears	16" Dia F & R Hydraulic	6 volt 96 amp battery	'I' Beam Front Track 67.6 in (1.72 m)		Semi-elliptic longitudinal Front & Rear springs	128.0 in (3.25 m) Short W/B 157.0 in (3.98 m) Long W/B
4 ton	No 19 Spec.								
Trader forward control 30 cwt	No 8 Spec.	No 11 Spec.	6.50 x 20 F & R Single rear	14" Dia F & R Hydraulic	12 volt	'I' Beam Front Track	No 5 Spec. fully floating	Semi-elliptic longitudinal Front & Rear Springs	118.0 in (2.997 m)
30 cwt	No 19 Spec.								
2 ton	No 8 Spec.		7.00 x 20.8p F & R Dual rears						
2 ton	No 19 Spec.								
3 ton	No 8 Spec.		7.00 x 20.10p F & R Dual rear						118.0 in (2.997 m) Short W/B 138.0 in (3.50 m) Long W/B
3 ton	No 19 Spec.								
4 ton	No 8 Spec.			16" Dia F & R Hydraulic					138.0 in (3.50 m) Short W/B 152.0 in (3.86 m) Long W/B
4 ton	No 19 Spec.								
5 ton	No 8 Spec.		7.50 x 20 F & R Dual Rear						
5 ton	No 19 Spec.								
5 ton	No 9 Spec.								
5 ton	No 21 Spec.								

Model	Engine	Transmission	Tyre size & wheel type	Brake size & system	Electrical	Front axle & track	Rear axle	Suspension	Wheelbase
5 cubic yard Tipper	No 9 Spec.	No 11 Spec.	7.50 x 20.10 ply F & R Dual rears	16" Dia F & R Hydraulic Servo assisted	12 volt	'I' Beam Front Track			108.0 in (2.743 m)
5 cubic yard Tipper	No 21 Spec.								
7 ton	No 9 Spec.		8.25 x 20 F & R Dual Rears	16" Dia F & R Hydraulic Servo assisted	12 volt	'I' Beam Front Track			138.0 in (3.50 m) Short W/B 160.0 in (4.064 m) Long W/B
7 ton	No 21 Spec.								
6 cubic yard Tipper	No 9 Spec.		8.25 x 20 F & R Dual rears	16" Dia F & R Hydraulic Servo assisted					108.0 in (2.743 m)
6 cubic yard Tipper	No 21 Spec.								
6 wheelr 4 spring	No 9 Spec.						Tandem axles Hypoid bevel gear driven double drive		108.0 in (2.743 m) Short W/B 138.0 in (3.50 m) Medium W/B 160.0 in (4.064 m) Long W/B
6 wheelr 4 spring	No 21 Spec.								
6 wheelr 2 spring	No 21 Spec.								
4 x 4 chassis	No 21 Spec.		9.00 x 20 F & R Dual rears			Front drive axle	Hypoid bevel driven Front and rear axles		
Trader normal control									
30 cwt	No 8 Spec.	No 11 Spec.	7.00 x 16 6 ply-F 7.50 x 16 R.S.C.R. Single rears	13" Dia F & R Hydraulic Servo assisted	12 volt 57 amp battery	'I' Beam Front Track 71.5 in (1.816 m)	No 5 Fully Floating	Semi- elliptic longitudinal front & rear springs	132.0 in (3.35 m)
30 cwt	No 19				12 volt 129 amp battery				
2 ton	No 8 Spec.		6.50 x 16 8 ply F & R Dual rears		12 volt 57 amp battery				132.0 in (3.35 m) Short W/B 146.0 in (3.71 m) Long W/B
2 ton	No 19 Spec.				12 volt 129 amp battery				
3 ton	No 8 Spec.		7.50 x 16 8 ply F & R Dual rears		12 volt 57 amp battery				146.0 in (3.71 m) Short W/B 166.0 in (4.216 m) Long W/B
3 ton	No 19 Spec.				12 volt 129 amp battery				
4 ton	No 8 Spec.		7.50 x 16 R.S.C. F & R Dual rears		12 volt 57 amp battery				
4 ton	No 19 Spec.								

Model	Engine	Transmission	Tyre size & wheel type	Brake size & system	Electrical	Front axle & track	Rear axle	Suspension	Wheelbase
5 ton	No 8 Spec.		7.50 x 20 12 ply F & R Dual rears	14" Dia F. 15.25" Dia R. Hydraulic Servo assisted.	12 volt 57 amp battery				
5 ton	No 19 Spec.				12 volt 129 amp battery				
K150	No 28 (vertical version) Spec.		7.00 x 16 6 ply-F 7.50 x 16 RSC-R Single rears	13" Dia F & R Hydraulic Servo assisted.	12 volt 129 amp battery				132.0 in (3.35 m)
K200	No 28 (vertical version) Spec.		6.50 x 16 8 ply F & R Dual rears						132.0 in (3.35 m) Short W/B 146.0 in (3.71 m) Long W/B
K300			7.50 x 16 8 ply F & R Dual rears						146.0 in (3.71 m) Short W/B 166.0 in (4.216 m) Long W/B
K400	No 28 (vertical version) Spec.		7.50 x 16 F & R R.S.C. Dual rears						
K500 Drop frame	No 28 (vertical version) Spec.		7.50 x 20 12 ply F & R Dual rears	14" Dia F 15.25 Dia R Hydraulic Servo assisted.					
K500 Straight frame	No 29 (vertical version) Spec.		7.50 x 20 12 ply F & R Dual rears						170.0 in (4.318 m) Short W/B 184.0 in (4.674 m) Long W/B
K600	No 29 (vertical version) Spec.		8.25 x 20 12 ply F & R Dual rears	15.25" Dia F & R Hydraulic Air assisted	12 volt 185 amp battery	'I' Beam Front Track			
K700	No 29 (vertical version)		9.00 x 20 F & R Dual rears						
K700 Tipper	No 30 (vertical version)								151.0 in (3.83 m)
400E Series 10 cwt 12 cwt	1703 cc ohv Petrol 4 cylinder	3 speed Synchromesh steering column change	590 x 15 F & R single rears	9" Dia F & R Hydraulic serv assisted	12 volt	Independent suspension front Front Track	Hypoid bevel gear driven Three-quarter floating.	Coil springs Front independent suspension longitudinal Semi-elliptic rear springs	84.0 in (2.133 m)
15 cwt			640 x 15 F & R Single rear						

Model	Engine	Transmission	Tyre size & wheel type	Brake size & system	Electrical	Front axle & track	Rear axle	Suspension	Wheelbase
10 cwt 12 cwt 15 cwt	Perkins 4/99 4 cylinder diesel		590 x 15 F & R Single rear 540 x 15 F & R Single rear						
'D' series D0607	No 28 Spec.	No 11 Spec.	7.00 x 16 Radial F & R Dual rears	13'' Dia. F 12.12''Dia R Dual line Air/Hydraulic	12 volt	'I' Beam Front Track 71.5 in (1.81 m)	No 4 fully floating	Semi- elliptic longitudinal Front & Rear springs	120.0 in (3.05 m) Short W/B 134.0 in (3.40 m) long W/B
D0610	No 29 Spec.	No 7 Spec.							
D0707	No 28 Spec.	No 11 Spec.	7.50 x 16 Radial F & R Dual rears						
D0710	No 29 Spec.	No 7 Spec.							
D0807	No 28 Spec.	No 11 Spec.		13'' Dia F & R Dual line Air/Hydraulic		'I' Beam Front Track 73.6 in (1.87 m)			
D0810	No 29 Spec.	No 7 Spec.					No 5 Spec. fully floating		
D0907	No 28 Spec.	No 11 Spec.	8.25 x 16 Radial F & R Dual rears			'I' Beam Front Track 75.2 in (1.910 m)	No 4 Spec. fully floating		120.0 in (3.05 m) Short W/B 134.0 in (3.40 m) Medium W/B 156.0 in (3.96 m) Long W.B
D0910	No 29 Spec.	No 7 Spec.					No 5 fully floating		
D0911	No 30 Spec.	No 8 Spec.							
D1010	No 29 Spec.	No 7 Spec.	8.25 x 17 Radial F & R Dual rears						
D1110	No 29 Spec.	No 7 Spec.	10 x 22.5 Radial tubeless Dual rears F & R	15.25 Dia F 15.50 Dia R Dual line Air/ Hydraulic					
D111	No 30 Spec.	No 8 Spec.					No 2/15C fully floating		
D1114	No 31 Spec.	No 8 Spec.	10 x 22.5 Radial tubeless Dual rears F & R	15.5'' Dia F & R Dual line Air/ Hydraulic		'I' Beam Front Track 74.5 in (1.89 m)	No.2/16A fully floating		120.0 in (3.050 m) 134.0 in (3.40 m) 156.0 in (3.90 m) 182 in (4.62 m) 206 in (5.23 m)

Model	Engine	Transmission	Tyre size & wheel type	Brake size & system	Electrical	Front axle & track	Rear axle	Suspension	Wheelbase
D1210	No 29 Spec			15.25'' F 15.5'' R Dual rears Dual line Air/ Hydraulics			No 5 fully floating		
D1211	No 30 Spec.						No 2/15C fully floating		
D1311				15.5'' F & R Dual rears Dual line Air/ Hydraulic					
D1314	No 31 Spec.						No 2/16A fully floating		
D1411	No 30 Spec.		11 x 22.5 Radial tubeless F & R Dual rears			'I' Beam Front Track 78.0 in (1.980 m)	No 2/16C fully floating		
D1414	No 31 Spec.								
D1614									159.0 in (4.04 m) 179.0 in (4.55 m) 206.0 in (5.23 m) 226.0 in (5.740 m)
D1617	No 33 Spec.								
D1618	No 32 Spec.								
D1610 artic	No 29 Spec.	No 7 Spec.	7.50 x 20 Radial F & R Dual rears	15.25'' Dia F & R Dual line Air/ Hydraulic	12 volt	I Beam Front Track 75.2 in (1.91 m)	No 5 fully floating	Semi elliptic longitudinal Front and rear springs	94.0 in (2.39 m)
D1710 artic	No 29 Spec.	No 8	8.25 x 20 Radial F & R Dual rears	15.25 Dia F 15-50 Dia R. Dual line Air/ Hydraulic			No 2/15C fully floating		
D1911 artic	No 30 Spec.					'I' Beam Front Track 75.2 in (1.91 m) 73.7 in (1.87 m) narrow track	No 2/16A fully floating		
D2014 artic	No 31 Spec.		10 x 22.5 Radial tubeless F & R Dual rears			'I' Beam Front Track 73.7 in (1.87 m)			

Model	Engine	Transmission	Tyre size & wheel type	Brake size & system	Electrical	Front Axle & track	Rear axle	Suspension	Wheelbase
D2114 artic									
D2417 artic	No 33 Spec.			15.50" Dia F & R Dual line Full air		'I' Beam Front Track 74.6 in (1.90 m)	No 2/16C fully floating		114.0 in (2.90 m)
D2418 artic	No 32 Spec.								
D2817 artic	No 33 Spec.	No 4 Spec.	11 x 22.5 Radial tubeless F & R Dual rears			'I' Beam Front Track 78.7 in (1.98 m)	Eaton single speed fully floating		
D2818 artic	No 32 Spec.								
D1210 Tipper	No 29 Spec.	No 8 Spec.	10 x 22.5 Radial tubeless F & R Dual rears	15.25" Dia F 15.5" Dia R Dual line Air/ Hydraulic		'I' Beam Front Track 74.6 in (1.895 m)	No 5 fully floating		108.0 in (2.740 m) 120 in (3.05 m) 134.0 in (3.40 m)
D1211 Tipper	No 30 Spec.						No 2/15C fully floating		
D1311 Tipper							No 2/16A fully floating		
D1314 Tipper	No 31 Spec.								
D1411 Tipper	No 29 Spec.		11 x 22.5 Radial tubeless F & R Dual rears	15.5" Dia F & R Dual line Air/ Hydraulic		'I' Beam Front Track 78.0 in (1.980 m)	No 2/16C Fully floating		
D1414 Tipper	No 31 Spec.								
D1614 Tipper									128.0 in (3.25 m) 147.0 in (3.73 m)
D1617 Tipper	No 39 Spec.								
D1618 Tipper	No 32 Spec.								
D2414 Tandem 4 Spring and Twin Spring versions	No. 31 Spec.	No 4 Spec.				'I' Beam Front Track 78.7 in (2.00 m)	Tandem axle No 2 Spec.		147.0 in (3.73 m) 169.0 in (4.29 m) 195.0 in (4.950 m) 237.0 in (6.02 m)
D1711 Tandem 4 Spring	No 30 Spec.		9.00 x 20 Radial F 8.25 x 20 Radial R			'I' Beam Front Track 74.6 in (1.895 m)			138.0 in (3.510 m) 154.0 in (3.910 m) 178.0 in (4.52 m) 190.0 in (4.830 m)
D2014 Tandem 4 Spring	No 31 Spec.		11 x 22.5 Radial tubeless F 10 x 22.5 Radial Tubeless R Dual rears			'I' Beam Front Track 78.7 in (2.00 m)			

Model	Engine	Transmission	Tyre size & wheel type	Brake size & system	Electrical	Front axle & track	Rear axle	Suspension	Wheelbase
D2414 4 Spring and Twin Spring versions									
D2417 4 spring and twin spring versions	No 33 Spec.	No 8 Spec.							147.0 in (3.370 m) 169.0 in (4.29 m) 195.0 in (4.950 m) 237.0 in (6.020 m)
D2418 4 spring and twin spring versions	No 32 Spec.								
'A' series A0406	No 26 Spec.	No 11 Spec.	7.50 x 14 F & R Dual rears	10.0" Dia F & R Dual circuit hydraulic/ vacuum booster	12 volt 68 amp battery	'I' Beam Front Track 69.9 in (1.775 m)	No 3/24 fully floating	Semi-elliptic longitudinal front & rear springs	120.0 in (3.050 m) short W/B 145.0 in (3.680 m) long W/B
A0409	No 27 Spec.	No 11 Spec.	7.50 x 16 Radial F & R Dual rears	12.5" Dia F 10.0" Dia R Dual circuit hydraulic/ vacuum booster	12 volt 242 amp battery		No 3/27 fully floating		130.0 in (3.30 m) short W/B 156.0 in (3.96 m) long W/B
A0410	No 17 Spec.	No 11 Spec.			12 volt 55 amp battery				
A0506	No 26 Spec.	No 11 Spec.	6.5Q x 16 10 Ply F & R Dual rears	12.5" Dia F 12.0" Dia R Dual circuit hydraulic/ vacuum booster	12 volt 68 amp battery	'I' Beam Front Track 71.5 in (1.815 m)	No 3/42 fully floating		130.0 in (3.30 m) 145.0 in (3.680 m) 156.0 in (3.96 m)
A0509	No 27 Spec.	No 11 Spec.			12 volt 242 amp battery				
A0510	No 17 Spec.			2.5" Dia F & R Dual circuit hydraulic/ vacuum booster	12 volt 55 amp battery				
A0609	No 27 Spec.		7.00 x 16 12 ply F & R Dual rears		12 volt 242 amp battery	'I' Beam Front Track 69.9 in (1.775 m)			
A0610	No 17 Spec.								
A0609 Tipper	No 27 Spec.				12 volt 120 amp battery				120.0 in (3.050 m)

Model	Engine	Transmission	Tyre size & wheel type	Brake size & system	Electrical	Front Axle & track	Rear axle	Suspension	Wheelbase
A0610 Tipper	No 17 Spec.				12 volt 55 amp battery				

Transit to 1986

Model	Engine	Transmission	Tyre size & wheel type	Brake size & system	Electrical	Front Axle & track	Rear axle	Suspension	Wheelbase
80 Van & Kombi	No 15 Spec.	No 6/C Spec.	185 x 14 Radial F & R single rears	10.6'' Dia Disc - F 9.0'' Dia Drum R	12 volt 38 amp battery	'I' Beam Front Track 64.5 in (1.640 m)	No 3/32 Spec. fully floating	Semi-elliptic longitudinal front and rear springs	106.0 in (2.690 m)
100 Kombi			195 x 14 R.C. F & R Single rears	Dual circuit hydraulic/ vacuum booster					
120 Van & Kombi		No 6/A Spec.	205 x 14 R.C. F & R Single rear	10.6'' Dia Disc - F 10.0'' Dia Drum -R Dual circuit hydraulic/ vacuum booster			No 3/34 Spec. fully floating		
130 Van	No 16 Spec.	No 6/A Spec.	185 x 14 SR F & R Dual rears				No 3/52 Spec. fully floating		118.0 in (3.00 m)
160 Van									
175 Van	No 26 Spec.	No 6/A Spec.			12 volt 68 amp battery				
190 Van	No 16 Spec.		195 x 14 RC F & R Dual rears		12 volt 38 amp battery		No 3/53 Spec. fully floating		
100 Van Long W/B	No 16 Spec.	No 6/D Spec.		10.6'' Dia Disc - F 9.0'' Dia Drum - R Dual circuit hydraulic/ vacuum booster			No 3/34 Spec. fully floating		118.0 in (3.00 m)
100 Parcel Van			205 x 14 RS F & R Single rears						106.0 in (2.69 m)
160 Parcel Van			185 x 14 SR F & R Dual rears	10.6'' Dia Disc - F 10.0'' Dia Drum - R Dual circuit hydraulic/ vacuum booster			No 3/52 Spec. fully floating		118.0 in (3.00 m)
12 str Bus	No 15 Spec.	No 6/C Spec.	195 x 14 RC F & R Single rears	10.6'' Dia Disc - F 9.0'' Dia Drum - R Dual circuit hydraulic/ vacuum booster			No 3/32 Spec. fully floating		106.0 in (2.69 m)

Model	Engine	Transmission	Tyre size & wheel type	Brake size & system	Electrical	Front Axle & track	Rear axle	Suspension	Wheelbase
13 STR Crew Bus	No 15 Spec.	No 6/A Spec.	205 x 14 RC F & R Single rear	10.6'' Dia Disc - F 10.0'' Dia Drum - R Dual circuit hydraulic/ vacuum booster			No 3/52 Spec. fully floating		
15 STR Bus	No 16		185 x 14 SR F & R Dual rears						118.0 in (3.00 m)
17 STR Crew Bus									

New transit 1986 –

Model	Engine	Transmission	Tyre size & wheel type	Brake size & system	Electrical	Front Axle & track	Rear axle	Suspension	Wheelbase
80 Van	No 15 Spec.	No 6/C Spec.	185 x 14 SR F & R Single rear	10.6'' Dia Disc - F 9.0'' Dia Drum - R Dual circuit hydraulic/ vacuum booster	12 volt 360CCA battery	Independent suspension Front Track 64.8 in (1.648 m)	No 3/32 Spec. fully floating	Independent coil spring Front semi- elliptic longitudinal Rear springs	110.8 in (2.815 m)
100 Van			185 x 14 R.6PR Single rears						
120 Van	No 16 Spec.	No 6/A Spec.	195 x 14 R.6PR Single rear	10.6'' Dia Disc - F 10.0'' Dia Drum - R Dual circuit hydraulic/ vacuum booster			No 3/34 Spec. fully floating		
100 LWB Van		5 speed	195 x 14 R. 8PR Single rear	10.6'' Dia Disc - F 9.0'' Dia Drum - R Dual circuit hydraulic/ vacuum booster		'I' Beam Front Track 65.2 in (1.658 m)		Semi elliptic longitudinal Front and Rear springs	118.9 in (3.020 m)
130 Van			185 x 14 SR F & R Dual rears	10.6'' Dia Disc - F 10.0'' Drum - R Dual circuit hydraulic/ vacuum booster			No 3/52 Spec. fully floating		
160 Van									
190 Van			185 x 14 R. 6PR F & R Dual rears				No 3/53 Spec. fully floating		
12 STR Bus		No 6/A	195 x 14 F & R Single rear	10.6'' Dia Disc - F 9.0'' Dia Drum - R Dual circuit hydraulic/ vacuum booster		Independent suspension Front Track 64.8 in (1.648 m)	No 3/32 Spec. fully floating	Independent front coil suspension Semi- elliptic longitudinal rear springs	110.8 in (2.81 m)

Model	Engine	Transmission	Tyre size & wheel type	Brake size & system	Electrical	Front Axle & track	Rear axle	Suspension	Wheelbase
15 STR Bus			185 x 14 SR. F & R Dual rears	10.6" Dia Disc-F 10.0" Dia Drum - R Dual circuit hydraulic/ vacuum booster		'I' Beam Front Track 65.2 in (1.658 m)	No 3.52 Spec. fully floating	Semi elliptic longitudinal Front & Rear springs	118.9 in (3.020 m)

Cargo range – selected models:-

Model	Engine	Transmission	Tyre size & wheel type	Brake size & system	Electrical	Front Axle & track	Rear axle	Suspension	Wheelbase
0609	No 28 Spec.	No 11 Spec.				'I' Beam Front Track 74.88 in (1.902 m)	No 4 Spec. fully floating	Semi- elliptic longitudinal front & rear springs	126.0 in (3.20 m) 147.0 in (3.725 m) 172.2 in (4.375 m) 196.0 in (4.975 m)
0811	No 29 Spec.	No 11 Spec.							

Example of sleeper cab version:-

Model	Engine	Transmission	Tyre size & wheel type	Brake size & system	Electrical	Front Axle & track	Rear axle	Suspension	Wheelbase
0811	No 29 Spec.	No 7 Spec.				'I' Beam Front Track 82.9 in (2.106 m)	No 5 Spec. fully floating		141.7 in (3.60 m) 167.3 in (4.25 m) 191.0 in (4.850 m)
0915	No 31 Spec.	No 8 Spec.					No 2/16A fully floating		121.0 in (3.075 m) 141.7 in (3.60 m) 167.3 in (4.25 m) 191.0 in (4.850 m)
1613	No 30 Spec.	No 8 Spec.				'I' Beam 81.85 in (2.079 m)	No 2/16C fully floating		141.7 in (3.600 m) 167.3 in (4.25 m) 197.0 in (5.00 m)
0809 Tipper	No 28 Spec.	No 7 Spec.				'I' Beam Front Track 74.88 in (1.902 m)	No 5 Spec. fully floating		126.0 in (3.20 m)
1311 Tipper	No 29 Spec.	No 8 Spec.				'I' Beam Front Track 83.62 in (2.124 m)	No 2/15C fully floating		121.0 in (3.075 m) 141.7 in (3.600 m)
1620 Tipper	No 24 Spec.	No 17 Spec.				'I' Beam Front Track 81.73 in (2.076 m)	Eaton 23120 spiral bevel fully floating		138.5 in (3.520 m) 151.5 in (3.850 m)
2417 Tandem 4 spring 6 x 2, 2-spring 6 x 4	No 33 Spec.	No 8 Spec.					Tandem No 3 Spec.		149.0 in (3.784 m) 168 in (4.260 m) 194.3 in (4.936 m) 216.5 in (5.500 m)

Model	Engine	Transmission	Tyre size & wheel type	Brake size & system	Electrical	Front Axle & track	Rear axle	Suspension	Wheelbase
2417 Tipper Tandem 4 spring 6 x 2 2 spring 6 x 4							Tandem No 3 Spec.		149.0 in (3.784 m) 167.7 in (4.260 m) 194.3 in (4.936 m)
2820 artic	No 24 Spec.	No 17 Spec.					Eaton 23120 Spiral bevel fully floating		118.1 in (3.00 m)
2824 artic	No 35 Spec.	No 21 Spec.							130.0 in (3.30 m) (138.5 in (3.520 m)
Transcontinental 'H' series:-									
H3824 4 x 2	No 38 Spec.	No 23 Spec.	12-22.5 Radial tubeless 16P.R F & R XZA tread Front	15.5'' Dia F & R Dual line Air.	24 volt 242 amp (4-6 volt) batteries	'I' Beam Front Track	No 7 Spec. fully floating	Semi-elliptic longitudinal front & rear springs	155.0 in (3.937 m) 177.0 in (4.496 m)
H4427 4 x 2	No 39 Spec.								
H4432 4 x 2	No 40 Spec.								
H4435 4 x 2 (16000)	No 41. Spec.								
H3424 4 x 2	No 38 Spec.						No 6 Spec.		177.0 in (4.496 m)
H4428	No 39 Spec.						No 7 Spec.		
H4435 (19000)	No 41 Spec.		12 - 22.5 Radial 18 PR F & R Tubeless				No 8 Spec. fully floating		
HA3824 4 x 2 artic	No 38 Spec.	No 22 Spec.	12-22.5 Radial tubeless F & R Dual rears XZA tread Front	15.50'' Dia F & R Dual line Air	24 volt 242 amps (4-6 volt) batteries	'I' Beam Front Track	No 7 Spec. fully floating	Semi-elliptic longitudinal front & rear springs	121.0 in (3.073 m) 138.0 in (3.505 m)
HA4427	No 39 Spec.								
HA4432	No 40 Spec.								
HA4435	No 41 Spec.								
HT4427 Tandem 6 x 4 4-spring	No 39 Spec.						Similar to No 3 Tandem Spec.		191.0 in (4.851 m) 209.0 in (5.309 m)
HT4432 Tandem 6 x 4 4 spring	No 40 Spec.								

Model	Engine	Transmission	Tyre size & wheel type	Brake size & system	Electrical	Front Axle & track	Rear axle	Suspension	Wheelbase
HT 4435 Tandem 6 x 4 4 spring	No 41 Spec.								
HA4428 artic Tandem 6 x 4 4 spring	No 39 Spec.								132.0 in (3.353 m)
HA4432 artic Tandem 6 x 4 4 spring	No 40 Spec.								
HA4435 artic Tandem 6 x 4 4 spring	No 41 Spec.								
P.S.V.									
A coach	14.9 4 cyl	3 speed	30 x 4.50 F & R Single rear	11.0'' Dia F & R Mechanically operated	6 volt 80 amp battery	'I' Beam Front Track 55.75 in (1.416 m)	Spiral bevel gear driven. 3/4 floating	Transverse springs Front & rear	103.5 in (2.63 m)
AA Coach	No 6 Spec.	No 2 Spec.	30 x 5-F 32 x 6-R Single rear			'I' Beam Front Track 56.0 in (1.422 m)	No 9 Spec Three quarter floating	Transverse Front springs cantilever rear springs	131.0 in (3.32 m)
BB Coach	No 7 Spec.	No 3 Spec.	20 x 6'' F & R Dual rears	14.0'' Dia F & R Mechanically operated	6 volt 80 amp battery	'I' Beam Front Track 56.0 in (1.422 m)	No 10 Spec. fully floating	Transverse Front semi-elliptic rears	157.0 in (3.98 m)
568E	No 9 Spec.	No 11 Spec.	8.25 x 20 F & R Dual rears	16.0'' Dia F & R Hydraulic Serv assisted	24 volt 120 amp battery	'I' Beam Front Track 75.0 in (1.905 m)	No 5 Spec. fully floating	Semi-elliptic longitudinal F & R springs	212.0 in (5.38 m)
570E	No 21 Spec.				24 volt 129 amp battery				
674E	No 18		9.00 x 20 F & R Dual rears	15.25'' Dia F 15.50'' Dia R Hydraulic Air booster	24 volt 120 amp battery	'I' Beam Front Track 80.6 in (2.047 m)			226.0 in (5.74 m)
676E	No 30 Spec. vertical version				24 volt 129 amp battery				
R1011	No 30 Spec. inclined version	No 8 Spec.	10-22.5 Radial tubeless	15.50'' Dia F & R Hydraulic Air booster			No 2/15C Spec. fully floating		192.0 in (4.88 m)
R1014	No 31 Spec. inclined version						Eaton 17100 Spiral bevel		

190

Model	Engine	Transmission	Tyre size & wheel type	Brake size & system	Electrical	Front Axle & track	Rear axle	Suspension	Wheelbase
R1114	No 31 Spec.	No 8 Spec.	10-22.5 Radial tubeless F & R Dual rears	15.50" Dia F & R Hydraulic Air booster	24 volt 129 amp battery	'I' Beam Front Track 80.6 in (2.047 m)	fully floating	Semi-elliptic longitudinal front & rear springs	226.0 in (5.740 m)

Military

Model	Engine	Transmission	Tyre size & wheel type	Brake size & system	Electrical	Front Axle & track	Rear axle	Suspension	Wheelbase
W0T1 3 ton Tandem	No 2 Spec.	No 3 Spec.	9.00 - 16 Cross Country Single rears	14.0" Dia F & R Mechanically operated	6 volt 110 amp battery	'I' Beam Front Track 66.7 in (1.694 m)	No. 11 fully floating	Semi-elliptic longitudinal Front & rear springs	143.5 in (3.64 m) plus 42.44 in extension
W0T2 15 cwt Truck						'I' Beam Front Track 58.6 in (1.488 m)			106.0 in (2.692 m)
W0T3 1 Ton/ 30 cwt Truck						'I' Beam Front Track 64.88 in (1.647 m)			143.5 in (3.64 m)
W0C1 15 cwt Truck	No 3 Spec.	No 3 Spec.	9.00 - 13 Cross Country Single rear	11.0" Dia F & R Hydraulic operated	6 volt 120 amp battery	'I' Beam Front Track 60.12 in (1.527 in)	Spiral bevel gear driven semi floating	Transverse Front & Rear springs	112.0 in (2.844 m)
W0T6 3 ton 4 x 4	No 2 Spec.		10.0 x 20 Cross Country Single rear	14" Dia F & R mechanically operated.	12 volt 75 amp battery	Front wheel drive Spiral bevel Fully floating Front Track 70.0 in (1.778 m) Spec. No 1	No 11 Spec. fully floating	Semi-elliptic longitudinal front & rear springs	143.5 in (3.64 m)
W0T8 30 cwt 4 x 4			10.50 x 16 Cross Country Single rear						118.0 in (2.997 m)
R01T Ambulance	No 3 Spec.	No 11 Spec.	6.0 x 20 F & R Dual rears		6 volt 57 amp battery	'I' Beam Front Track 63.5 in (1.613 m)		Transverse Front spring semi-elliptic longitudinal rear springs	134.0 in (3.404 m)
E018T Truck	No 3 Spec.	No 11 Spec.	32 x 6 HD F & R Dual rears	– Hydraulic	6 volt	'I' beam Front Track 57.8 in (1.468 m)	No 11 Spec. fully floating		158.0 in (4.013 m)
E01T Truck			32 x 6 HO F & R Single rear	– Hydraulic		'I' Beam Front Track 56.0 in (1.422 m)	Spiral bevel gear Three-quarter floating		134.0 in (3.40 m)
E01Y Van		No 3 Spec.	32 x 6-TT F & R single rear	– Hydraulic					122.0 in (3.099 m)
EC098T Truck		No 11 Spec.	10.50 x 16 F & R Single rear	– Hydraulic	6 volt 120 amp battery	'I' Beam Front Track –		Semi-elliptic front & rear springs longitudinal	158.0 in (4.013 m)

Model	Engine	Transmission	Tyre size & wheel type	Brake size & system	Electrical	Front Axle & track	Rear axle	Suspension	Wheelbase
E917T Tandem Truck	No 2 Spec.	No 3 Spec.	9.00 x 20 F & R Single rear	– Hydraulic	6 volt 100 amp battery	'I' Beam Front Track 55.0 in (1.397 m)	Tandem No 1 Spec.		178.0 in (4.571 m)
EC011Q reactor 4 x 4	No 3 Spec.	No 3 Spec.	10.50 x 20 F & R Single rear	– Hydraulic	6 volt 90 amp battery	Front wheel drive Spec. No 1 Front Track 68.25 in (1.733 m)	Spiral bevel gear driven fully floating		101.0 in (2.565 m)
EC018Q Chassis Cab 4 x 4									158.0 in (4.013 m)
EC098U Dump Truck				– Hydraulic		'I' Beam Front Track –	Spiral bevel gear driven Two speed axle fully floating		
EC196T Chassis Cab			7.50 x 20 F & R Dual rears						176.0 in (4.470 m)
EC011DF			9.00 x 13 F & R Single rear	– Hydraulic	6 volt 90 amp battery	'I' Beam Front Track 59.25 in (1.511 m)	Spiral bevel gear driven fully floating		101.0 in (2.565 m)